STATISTICAL ANALYSIS ON KEY ECONOMIC AREAS OF China

STATISTICAL ANALYSIS ON KEY ECONOMIC AREAS OF China

Editor-in-chief: **Xianchun Xu**
Tsinghua University, China

Editors

Zhongwen Zhang
Tsinghua University, China

**Youjuan Wang · Yuan Jiang · Faqi Shi
Xiongfei Xu · Zhan Zhang**
National Bureau of Statistics, China

NEW JERSEY · LONDON · SINGAPORE · BEIJING · SHANGHAI · HONG KONG · TAIPEI · CHENNAI · TOKYO

Published by

World Scientific Publishing Co. Pte. Ltd.

5 Toh Tuck Link, Singapore 596224

USA office: 27 Warren Street, Suite 401-402, Hackensack, NJ 07601

UK office: 57 Shelton Street, Covent Garden, London WC2H 9HE

Library of Congress Cataloging-in-Publication Data
Names: Xu, Xianchun, editor.
Title: Statistical analysis on key economic areas of China /
    editor-in-chief, Xianchun Xu, Tsinghua University, China ;
    editors, Zhongwen Zhang, Tsinghua University, China, [and five others].
Other titles: Zhongguo Zhong dian jing ji ling yu tong ji fen xi. English
Description: New Jersey : World Scientific, [2021] | Includes bibliographical references and index.
Identifiers: LCCN 2020042508 | ISBN 9789811229060 (hardcover) |
    ISBN 9789811229077 (ebook) | ISBN 9789811229084 (ebook other)
Subjects: LCSH: China--Economic conditions--2000- | China--Statistics. |
    Economic development--China--Statistical methods. | Economic indicators--China.
Classification: LCC HC427.95 .Z4628313 2021 | DDC 330.951--dc23
LC record available at https://lccn.loc.gov/2020042508

British Library Cataloguing-in-Publication Data
A catalogue record for this book is available from the British Library.

中国重点经济领域统计分析
Originally published in Chinese by Peking University Press
Copyright © Peking University Press 2018

For any available supplementary material, please visit
https://www.worldscientific.com/worldscibooks/10.1142/12065#t=suppl

Translator: Huayu Li
Desk Editor: Tan Boon Hui

Printed in Singapore

Editorial Board

Members of the Academic Steering Committee, Tsinghua China Data Center

Ning Jizhe, Deputy Chairman of the National Development and Reform Commission, Commissioner and Secretary of the Party Leadership Group of the National Bureau of Statistics, and Co-chair of the Center

Qiu Yong, President, Tsinghua University and Co-chair of the Center

Sheng Laiyun, Deputy Commissioner and Member of the Party Leadership Group of the National Bureau of Statistics

Xiang Botao, Deputy Secretary of the CPC Committee, Tsinghua University

Peng Gang, Vice President, Tsinghua University

Xu Xianchun, Director, Tsinghua China Data Center

Xu Ronghua, Director-General, Department of Statistical Design and Management, National Bureau of Statistics

Liu Aihua, Director-General, Department of Comprehensive Statistics, National Bureau of Statistics

Cheng Zilin, Inspector, Department of Comprehensive Statistics, National Bureau of Statistics

Zhao Tonglu, Director-General, Department of National Accounts, National Bureau of Statistics

Lu Shan, Director-General, Department of Industrial Statistics, National Bureau of Statistics

Liu Wenhua, Director-General, Department of Energy Statistics, National Bureau of Statistics

Zhai Shanqing, Director-General, Department of Trade and External Economic Relations Statistics, National Bureau of Statistics

Dong Lihua, Director-General, Department of Trade and Economics, National Bureau of Statistics

Zhang Yi, Director-General, Department of Population and Employment Statistics, National Bureau of Statistics

Wan Donghua, Director-General, Department of Social, Science and Technology and Cultural Statistics, National Bureau of Statistics

Li Suoqiang, Director-General, Department of Rural Surveys, National Bureau of Statistics

Fang Xiaodan, Director, Department of Household Surveys, National Bureau of Statistics

Du Xishuang, Director-General, Department of Service Statistics, National Bureau of Statistics

Hu Hanzhou, Director, Census Center, National Bureau of Statistics

Zhao Jianhua, Director, Data Management Center, National Bureau of Statistics

Yu Fangdong, Director, Statistical Education and Training Center, National Bureau of Statistics

Lyu Haiqi, Director, Research Institute of Statistical Sciences, National Bureau of Statistics

Zhong Shouyang, Director-General, Statistical Information Management Center, National Bureau of Statistics

Bai Chong'en, Dean, School of Economics and Management, Tsinghua University

Qian Yingyi, Professor, School of Economics and Management, Tsinghua University

Zhong Xiaohan, Deputy Secretary of the CPC Committee, Vice Dean, School of Economics and Management, Tsinghua University

Liu Taoxiong, Secretary of the CPC Committee, School of Social Sciences, Tsinghua University

Li Qiang, Professor, School of Social Sciences, Tsinghua University

Xue Lan, Dean, Schwarzman College, Tsinghua University

Qian Yi, Professor, School of Environment, Tsinghua University, Academician of the Chinese Academy of Engineering

Jiang Yi, Director, Building Energy Conservation Research Center, Tsinghua University, Academician of Chinese Academy of Engineering

Mao Qizhi, Professor, School of Architecture, Tsinghua University

Liu Hongyu, Professor, School of Civil Engineering, Tsinghua University

Li Zheng, Director, Laboratory of Low Carbon Energy, Executive Vice-Dean, Institute of Climate Change and Sustainable Development, Tsinghua University

Cui Baoguo, Professor, School of Journalism and Communication, Director, Media operation and management Center, Tsinghua University

Shi Jinghuan, Executive Vice-Dean, Institute of Education, Tsinghua University

Su Jun, Director, Think Tank Research Center, Tsinghua University

Yang Yongheng, Director, Liberal Arts Division, Tsinghua University

Yuan Wei, Secretary-General, Tsinghua University Education Foundation

Members of the Executive Committee, Tsinghua China Data Center

Bai Chong'en, Director of Executive Committee, and Dean, School of Economics and Management, Tsinghua University

Liu Taoxiong, Deputy Director of Executive Committee, and Secretary of the CPC Committee, School of Social Sciences, Tsinghua University

Zhong Xiaohan, Deputy Director of Executive Committee, and Deputy Secretary of the CPC Committee, Vice Dean, School of Economics and Management, Tsinghua University

Xu Xianchun, Member of Executive Committee, and Director, Tsinghua China Data Center

Liu Aihua, Member of Executive Committee, and Director-General, Department of Comprehensive Statistics, National Bureau of Statistics

Zhao Tonglu, Member of Executive Committee, and Director-General, Department of National Accounts, National Bureau of Statistics

Su Jun, Member of Executive Committee, and Director, Think Tank Research Center, Tsinghua University

Yang Yongheng, Member of Executive Committee, and Director, Liberal Arts Division, Tsinghua University

Director:

Xu Xianchun, Professor, School of Economics and Management, Tsinghua University

Deputy Director:

Lu Yi, Professor, School of Economics and Management, Tsinghua University

Liu Jingming, Professor, School of Social Sciences, Tsinghua University

Preface

The reform and opening-up has contributed to China's long-term and rapid economic development, a much stronger economic strength, and a much better life for its people. Meanwhile, the deepening economic integration between China and the world has resulted in an increasingly complex environment, growing influencing factors, and severe challenges to China's economic development. Under the "new normal" of Chinese economy, accurate analysis of the economic situation is essential for scientific decision-making and sustained and healthy economic development and to build a moderately prosperous society in all respects. By applying statistical and national economic accounting methods, and based on detailed statistics and national economic accounting data, this book presents an in-depth analysis of the key economic fields, such as real estate economy, automotive industry, high-tech industry, investment, opening-up, income distribution of residents, economic structure, balance of payments structure, and financial operation, since the reform and opening-up, especially in recent years. It aims to depict the performance and characteristics of these key economic fields and their roles in the development of the national economy, thus providing useful suggestions for economic decision-making, and facilitating the sustained and healthy development of the economy and the realization of the goal of building a moderately prosperous society in all respects. This book consists of nine research chapters.

The first chapter is about the role of real estate economy in China's national economic growth. Based on the theory and method of statistics and national economic accounting, this chapter scientifically defines the scope and connotation of real estate economy. On this basis, it presented systematical, complete, and quantitative analyses on the important role of real estate economy in China's national economic growth from three aspects: investment in real estate, production of real estate industry, and consumption in real estate, and puts forward some suggestions on how to maintain the reasonable growth of the real estate economy.

The second chapter is about the important role of the automotive industry in economic development, transformation, and upgrading and in the implementation strategy of building a manufacturer of quality. This chapter adopts the theory and method of statistics and national economic accounting to analyze the impact of the automotive industry on China's national economic growth from the perspective of production and demand, reveals the important role of the automotive industry in the strategy of transformation from an economic power to a manufacturer of quality, and proposes the development path of China's automotive industry under the strategy of building a manufacturer of quality.

The third chapter illustrates the role of the development of high-tech industry in economic growth and employment promotion. This chapter systematically and completely analyzes the impact of the development of high-tech industry on China's national economic development from the perspectives of investment, production, and employment by using the theory and method of statistics and national economic accounting and reveals the importance of promoting the rapid development of high-tech industry in coping with the downturn of the economy and changing the development mode.

The fourth chapter presented a research on China's investment growth and its relationship with the fiscal policy. This chapter differentiates and analyzes the total investment in fixed assets and gross fixed capital formation (GFCF), which are the two major indicators that reflect the development and changes of investment in fixed assets. On this basis, it analyzes the growth performance of investment in fixed assets and its contribution to the economic growth since the reform and opening-up, explains and analyzes the impact of the fiscal policy on the growth of investment in fixed assets in China, and suggests fully leveraging the fiscal policy to stabilize investment growth.

The fifth chapter deals with the measurement and analysis of the contribution of opening-up to China's economic growth. By using the theory and method of statistics and national economic accounting, this chapter reviews the tremendous changes in China's opening-up areas since China's accession to the World Trade Organization and systematically analyzes the contribution of opening-up to China's economic growth from the perspectives of foreign trade, actual utilization of foreign capital, and factor income from abroad. It also proposes suggestion on how to better play the role of opening-up and promote China's economic growth.

The sixth chapter is about the income distribution of Chinese households. It systematically expounds the status of household income distribution in China since the 12th Five-Year Plan, reviews the growth of household income and the changes in its proportion to total disposable national income, analyzes the changes in the composition of household income, reveals the multi-dimensional evolution of household income gap, and examines the Gini coefficient of Chinese household income in the world perspective.

The seventh chapter presents changes in China's economic structure and the challenges it faces. This chapter systematically analyzes the changes in China's industrial structure, demand structure, regional structure, income distribution structure, foreign trade structure and other important economic structures in recent years; reveals the challenges that China's economic structure still faces in various fields; and puts forward some suggestions on China's economic restructuring.

The eighth chapter demonstrates changes in China's balance of payments structure. It systematically expounds the changes in China's balance of payments structure from 2003 to 2015, reviews the changes in the operating environment of the balance of payments, analyzes the phased characteristics of the overall balance of payments, and reveals the specific changes in major items of balance of payments from the aspects of trade in goods and services, primary and secondary distribution of income, direct investment, portfolio investment, and other investments.

The ninth chapter delivers researches on the characteristics, challenges, and development trends of China's financial performance. It reviews the major reforms in China's financial sector in 2015, analyzes the characteristics of the main financial indicators such as money supply, social financing scale, and loan and market rates from both overall and structural aspects; reveals the prominent issues faced in financial performance; and provides a blueprint for its future development.

Xu Xianchun
January 2021

Contents

3. **Research on the Role of Development of the
    High-tech Industry in Economic Growth
    and Employment Promotion**   **87**

    *Zhang Zhongwen, Ye Yindan, Xu Xianchun,
    and Zhao Yanpeng*

Chapter 1

Research on the Role of Real Estate Economy in China's National Economic Growth*

Xu Xianchun, Jia Hai, Li Jiao, and Li Junbo[†]

Abstract

This paper scientifically defines the scope and connotation of real estate economy by using the theory and method of statistics and national accounting. On this basis, it systematically and quantitatively analyzes the important role of the real estate economy in China's economic growth from three aspects: investment, production, and consumption in the real estate industry. The results show that healthy development of the economy is of great significance, but at the same time, too fast or too slow growth of the real estate economy will adversely affect the stable growth of the economy. A reasonable growth of the real estate economy is essential to the healthy and stable growth of the economy.

Since the reform and opening-up, especially since the 1990s, the rapid urbanization and deepening reform of the urban housing system have highlighted the important role of real estate in the development of the economy and improvement of people's living standards. Hence, the research on the relationship between real estate and economy has become an important area of economics research. Some scholars study the driving

---

*This paper was previously published in *Social Sciences in China*, Issue 1, 2015.
[†]Xu Xianchun is a Senior Statistician at the National Bureau of Statistics; Jia Hai is a Senior Statistician at the Department of Investment and Construction Statistics, National Bureau of Statistics; Li Jiao is a Senior Statistician at the Department of Investment and Construction Statistics, National Bureau of Statistics; Li Junbo is a Statistician at the Department of Investment and Construction Statistics, National Bureau of Statistics.

effect of real estate as an industry on other industries of the economy.[1] Some scholars study the role of real estate in the economic growth of China based on the proportion of value added of the real estate industry to GDP and the contribution of the growth of real estate investment to the growth of total investment in fixed assets.[2] Some scholars study the impact of real estate on the household consumption and economic growth of China based on housing price changes.[3] Some scholars study the impact of real estate on China's economic growth by analyzing the relationship between real estate investment and GDP.[4] However, all researches on the role of real estate in China's economic growth lack systematic and comprehensive analysis. Based on the theory and method of statistics and national accounts, this report clearly defines three areas, i.e. investment, production, and consumption in the real estate, as the real estate economy. On this basis, from these three closely related areas, this report systematically and completely studies the role of real estate economy in China's economic growth and explores the significance of reasonable growth of real estate economy to the sustained and healthy development of China's economy. In the field of real estate investment, it quantitatively estimates the contribution of real estate investment to the economic growth according to the relationship between real estate investment and total investment in fixed assets in investment statistics, and the relationship between total investment in fixed assets and gross fixed capital formation (GFCF) in the accounting of GDP by the expenditure approach. In the field of real estate production, it quantitatively estimates not only the contribution of the real estate as an industry to the economic growth but also the contribution of real estate investment to economic growth through driving growth of related industries such as construction, manufacturing, transportation,

---

[1]Wang, G., & Shuixing, L. (2004). The driving effects on real estate to related industries, *Economic Research Journal*, Issue 8; Li, Y., & Wang Qingshi (2011). Research on driving effects of real estate industry on related industries of the national economy in China, *Journal of Shandong University of Finance and Economics*, Issue 1; Yan, Y., Feng, C., & Song, Z. (2007). Driving effect of real estate industry to national economy. *Journal of Construction Economy*, Issue 6.

[2]Li, Q. (2002). The relationship between real estate and national economy in China. *China Real Estate*, Issue 6.

[3]Zhao, Y., Zhang, Y., & Zhao, W. (2011). Research on the relationship between real estate market and resident consumption and economic growth: An empirical analysis based on wealth effect of real estate market from 1994 to 2011. *Economic Science*, Issue 6.

[4]Shen, Y. & Liu, H. (2004). Relationship between real estate development investment and GDP in China. *Journal of Tsinghua University (Science and Technology)*, Issue 9.

wholesale, and retail by using the input-output model. In the field of real estate consumption, it quantitatively estimates the contribution of housing-related expenditures such as rent expenditure, housing maintenance and management fees, utilities cost, and virtual expenditure of services for self-owned housing to economic growth. This report offers a valuable reference for comprehensive and objective understanding of the role of the real estate economy and for the formulation of scientific and rational policies on the real estate economy.

1.1. Definition of Real Estate Economy

The real estate economy in this report includes activities concerning investment, production, and consumption in the real estate sector.

Investment activities in real estate refer to economic activities such as the unified development of buildings, affiliated facilities, land development, and acquisition by real estate developers. In the cycle of the real estate economy, real estate investment activities, as the starting point, result in the completion of buildings, such as residential buildings, which then enter the production and consumption phases to effectively sustain the cycle.

Production activities in real estate refer to the production activities of the real estate industry itself and real-estate–related industries. Real estate production activities include real estate development and operations, property management, real estate intermediary services, self-owned real estate operations, and other real estate production activities. The production activities of real-estate–related industries include those concerning buildings, building materials, logistics, finance, and other industries closely related to real estate. Real estate production activities, which spur the development of the real estate industry and real-estate–related industries, constitute an important step in the cycle of the real estate economy.

Real estate consumption activities refer to consumption of residential housing and related services, including rent, maintenance, property management, intermediary services, utilities, services for self-owned housing, and other activities. Real estate consumption activities, which refer to the use of real estate investment and production services, are the ultimate goal of real estate investment and production activities.

China's real estate economy is studied herein from investment, production, and consumption perspectives because the role of the real estate economy in economic growth is reflected in these three different yet closely linked areas. In the investment area, the contribution of the real estate economy to economic growth is made by real estate investment;

in the production area, it is made by the real estate industry and related industries; while in the consumption perspective, it is made by the consumption of housing services and related services. Real estate investment enables real estate production, real estate production serves real estate consumption, while the upgrading of real estate consumption spurs new real estate investment.

1.2. Contribution of Real Estate Investment to Economic Growth

1.2.1. *Concept and statistical method of real estate investment*

Real estate investment refers to all investment in housing buildings, affiliated facilities developed in a unified way by real estate development corporations (hereinafter referred to as "real estate developers"), as well as their land development projects and land acquisitions. Among them, buildings include residential buildings, factory buildings, warehouses, restaurants, hotels, resorts, and office buildings; affiliated facilities include roads within residential areas built as part of the overall plan of a real estate project, as well as green space and other necessary facilities built to improve the quality of commercial housing; land development projects refer to pre-construction projects, including infrastructure projects such as electricity, roads, heating, fuel, water supply, drainage, communication, and leveling site; land acquisition investment refers to the fees paid by real estate developers in order to acquire land-use rights through various means (e.g. "bidding, auction and listing," transfer, allocation, etc.).

Real estate investment comprises the cost of construction projects, installation projects, the purchase of equipment and instruments, and other expenses. The construction projects refer to the construction of various houses and buildings; the installation projects refer to the installation of various equipment and devices, excluding the value of the installed equipment; the purchase of equipment and instruments refers to the value of the equipment, tools, and instruments that are purchased or manufactured, which meet the fixed assets standards; other expenses refer to the expenses incurred during the construction and purchase of fixed assets other than the above-mentioned components, including land acquisition expenses.

Real estate investment is calculated through a comprehensive statistical survey, which is a full-count statistical survey of investments involved in all real estate development projects made by real estate developers.

1.2.2. *Historical changes of real estate investment*

The commencement and development of real estate investment in China is closely related to the housing system reform and its deepening.

Before 1980, the housing of urban households in China was constructed, distributed, and managed by the state, thus forming a public housing allocation system featured with "unified management, unified allocation and buy-to-let housing." In April 1980, Deng Xiaoping delivered an important speech on the housing issue. In June of that year, the CPC Central Committee and the State Council officially approved housing commercialization, ushering in the reform of China's urban housing system. Shenzhen Special Economic Zone Real Estate Company, established in Shenzhen on January 8, 1980, was considered to be the first commercial housing development enterprise in the People's Republic of China. The Company cooperated with a Hong Kong-based company to build Donghu Liyuan, the first commercial housing project constructed in line with the principle of "compensation trade" (the Shenzhen company provided a piece of land; the Hong Kong company provided the fund; they cooperated on the construction and shared the profit). However, due to the obscure way of land transaction at that time, Donghu Liyuan was not a commercial housing project in the real sense. In January 1988, the first National Conference on Housing System Reform was held in Beijing, which officially announced to include the housing system reform in the reform programs of the central and the local governments starting that year and carry out the reform in phases and step by step throughout the country. In this reform aiming at housing commercialization as the end, the basic idea was to increase both the housing rent and the salary, thus encouraging employees to buy housing apartments. It was in that year that Dongxiao Garden in Shenzhen, the first commercial housing estate of the People's Republic of China, was completed, where the land-use right was acquired through auction and apartments were sold based on mortgage loans. From then on, real estate developers took root, flourished, and thrived. The number of real estate developers in China grew from 1,991 in 1986 to 24,378 in 1998.[5] Also in 1998, *Notice on Further Deepening the Reform of Urban Housing System and Accelerating Housing Construction*, issued by the State Council, clearly pointed out that starting from the second half of 1998, the allocation

---

[5]The National Bureau of Statistics of the People's Republic of China (1998). *The Statistical Annual Report on Real Estate Development in China.*

of housing units in kind would be stopped, with monetization of housing allocation and commercialization of housing supply system gradually in place, which marked a fundamental change in the housing supply and allocation mechanism in China and the housing system reform in full swing.

With the reform and development of the housing system, real estate investment activities in China have been developing from scratch and growing stronger. In order to carry out timely statistical monitoring, in 1986, the National Bureau of Statistics, the former State Development Planning Commission, and the former Ministry of Construction jointly issued a document requesting the expansion of commercial residential building statistics to commercial housing statistics. The former Ministry of Construction formally established a statistical system for commercial housing construction, marking initial shape of statistics on real estate investment. Real estate investment statistics by governmental comprehensive statistics departments officially started in 1990 and were included into the investment in fixed assets statistics system alongside capital construction, renovation, and transformation. In 2005, the real estate investment statistics system was listed separately from the investment in fixed assets statistics system and became an independent statistical system in the national statistical survey system.

Therefore, the earliest data on real estate investment in China were generated in 1986, with only an amount of 10.1 billion yuan. After nearly 30 years of development, real estate investment reached 8,601.3 billion yuan in 2013,[6] or 852 times of that in 1986, with an average annual growth of 28.4%.

The year 2000 is a line of demarcation for the evolution of real estate investment. Before 2000, real estate investment grew at a rapid yet unstable pace. From 1987 to 1999, the average annual growth rate was 33%, of which the growth was 117.5% in 1992, and 165% in 1993, reaching an all-time high. Meanwhile, there were also historical lows of −7.1% in 1990 and −1.2% in 1997. After 2000, real estate investment grew steadily, with an average annual growth rate of 24.3% from 2000 to 2013. The difference between the highest growth rate in 2010 and the lowest in 2009 was 17.1 percentage points, and the growth rate in most years ranged from 20%–30% (see Figure 1.1).

The housing system reform has promoted the sustainable development of real estate investment, and a large number of commercial buildings

---

[6] *China Statistical Yearbook 2014*, p. 279.

Figure 1.1. Real estate investment and growth rate during 1987–2013

Source: Data on real estate investment is from *China Statistical Yearbook 2014*, p. 279. Unless otherwise specified, data in this report are all from the *Yearbook*.

to meet different needs were marketed, greatly alleviating the serious urban housing shortage lasting from the founding of the People's Republic of China to the 1990s. The per capita housing construction area of urban residents increased significantly from 6.7 square meters in 1978 to 32.9 square meters in 2012.[7] The housing conditions have fundamentally improved, thanks to the growing real estate investment.

1.2.3. *Contribution of real estate investment to the growth of total investment in fixed assets*

Total investment in fixed assets refers to the workload of fixed assets constructed and purchased and the related expenses in a certain period of time by the whole society expressed in currency.[8] Total investment in fixed assets includes investment in construction project of 5 million yuan or more,[9] real estate investment, and investment in the fixed assets by rural

---

[7]Due to the adjustment of statistical coverage, the calculation of per capita housing area in urban and rural areas has been discontinued since 2013. Data related to the fourth part of this report, "Contribution of Real Estate Consumption to National Economic Growth" was also as of 2012.

[8]The National Bureau of Statistics (2013). *National Statistical Survey Program (2013) (II)*, p. 1,209

[9]With the rapid development of China's economy, the number of construction projects rose rapidly. The threshold of investment statistics for construction projects was raised from 20,000 yuan to 50,000 yuan in 1983, from 50,000 yuan to 500,000 yuan in 1997, and from 500,000 yuan to 5 million yuan in 2011.

households. The real estate investment plays an important part in the total investment in fixed assets.

Looking at the share in the total investment in fixed assets, the proportion of real estate investment showed a significant growth from 3.2% in 1986 to 15.7% in 1995, with an average annual proportion of 8.5%. It was a period of adjustment from 1996 to 2000, during which the share first fell and then rose, reaching 12%–15%, with an average annual proportion of 13.7%. The share was basically stable from 2001 to 2013, rising slightly from 17.0% in 2001 to 19.2% in 2013. The average annual proportion in this period rose further to 18.3%, which was only lower than the investment in the manufacturing industry, making real estate as the second key area of total investment in fixed assets (see Figure 1.2).

Looking at the contribution rate of the growth of real estate investment to the growth of total investment in fixed assets, it fluctuated dramatically from 1987 to 1998, averaging at 7.7%. The contribution rate in 1989, 1990, and 1997 was negative, while that for 1993 was as high as 24.2%. The contribution rate for 1999–2004 remained at a high level of 26.2% on the average. Except for 2003, the contribution rate in other years was more than 20%, and that in 1999 was 33.8%, a historical high. The contribution rate from 2005 to 2013 was relatively stable, averaging at 17.8%, and that for 2009 in particular was only 9.7% due to the impact of the international financial crisis. From 1987 to 2013, the contribution rate of investment growth in real estate to the growth of total investment in fixed assets averaged at 15.1% (see Table 1.1).

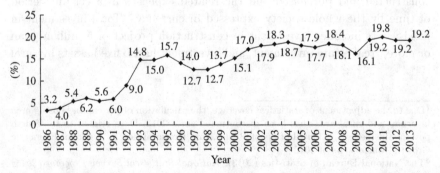

Figure 1.2. Proportion of real estate investment to total investment in fixed assets from 1986 to 2013

Source: Data on total investment in fixed assets and real estate investment are from *China Statistical Yearbook 2014*, p. 279.

Table 1.1. Contribution of real estate investment to the growth of total investment in fixed assets

Year	Real estate investment (100 million yuan)	Proportion to total investment in fixed assets (%)	Contribution to the growth of total investment in fixed assets (%)
1987	149.88	4.0	7.3
1988	257.23	5.4	11.2
1989	272.65	6.2	−4.5
1990	253.25	5.6	−18.2
1991	336.16	6.0	7.7
1992	731.20	9.0	15.9
1993	1937.51	14.8	24.2
1994	2554.08	15.0	15.5
1995	3149.02	15.7	20.0
1996	3216.40	14.0	2.3
1997	3178.37	12.7	−1.9
1998	3614.23	12.7	12.6
1999	4103.20	13.7	33.8
2000	4984.05	15.1	28.8
2001	6344.11	17.0	31.7
2002	7790.92	17.9	23.0
2003	10153.80	18.3	19.6
2004	13158.25	18.7	20.1
2005	15909.25	17.9	15.0
2006	19422.92	17.7	16.6
2007	25288.84	18.4	21.5
2008	31203.19	18.1	16.7
2009	36241.81	16.1	9.7
2010	48259.40	19.2	22.5
2011	61796.89	19.8	22.6
2012	71803.79	19.2	15.8
2013	86013.38	19.2	19.6

Note: Contribution rate of real estate investment to total investment in fixed assets = (real estate investment of current year — real estate investment of the previous year) / (total investment in fixed assets of current year — total investment in fixed assets of the previous year) × 100%.

Source: Data on real estate investment are from *China Statistical Yearbook 2014*, p. 279.

1.2.4. *Contribution of real estate investment to economic growth*

The contribution of real estate investment to economic growth is calculated indirectly based on the contribution of GFCF to GDP by the expenditure approach.

GFCF refers to the total value of acquisitions minus the disposals of fixed assets by resident units within a certain period. Fixed assets are assets produced through production activities, excluding natural assets such as land. GFCF comprises tangible GFCF and intangible GFCF. Tangible GFCF refers to the acquisitions minus the disposals of construction projects, installation projects, and equipment and instruments completed in a certain period of time, as well as the value of land improvement, newly added draught animal, breeding stock, daily stock, fur-bearing animal and animals for entertainment purpose, and newly-added economic forest; intangible GFCF includes the acquisitions minus the disposals of mineral exploration and computer software, etc.[10]

Total investment in fixed assets is the basic data for accounting of GFCF. GFCF is calculated on the basis of the total investment in fixed assets, which mainly deducts the expenses of land and other items that do not form the fixed capital and adds the items that are not included in the total investment in fixed assets but need to be included in the GFCF. After necessary data adjustment, the GFCF is finally obtained.[11]

As an integral part of total investment in fixed assets, real estate investment is also important basic data for accounting of GFCF. However, there are two main differences in the scope of statistics. First, the purchase cost of land and old buildings is included in the real estate investment but not in the GFCF; second, the real estate investment does not include the value added of commercial housing sales, i.e. the difference between the sales value and investment cost of commercial housing, which is however included in the GFCF.

The analysis of the existing statistical data shows that "the proportion of GFCF to GDP calculated by the expenditure approach" and the proportion of real estate investment after deducting land acquisition fee to total investment in fixed assets after deducting land acquisition fee can be used to estimate the proportion of GFCF produced by real estate investment to GDP calculated by the expenditure approach; and "contribution rate of GFCF to the growth of GDP" and the proportion of real estate investment after deducting land acquisition fee to total investment in fixed assets deducting land acquisition fee can be used to estimate the contribution rate of real estate investment to GDP growth.

---

[10]The National Bureau of Statistics (2013). *National Statistical Survey Program (2013)* (I), p. 306.
[11]See Xu, X. (2013). Accurate understanding of China's income, consumption and investment. *Social Sciences in China*, Issue 2.

What is the reason to use proportion of real estate investment after deducting the land purchase cost to total investment in fixed assets after deducting the land purchase cost instead of directly using the proportion of real estate investment to the total investment in fixed assets? It is because the proportion of land purchase cost to real estate investment is much larger than that of land purchase cost to total investment in fixed assets, while the land purchase cost cannot be included in the GFCF. If the proportion of land purchase cost is not excluded, the proportion of GFCF produced by real estate investment to GDP calculated by the expenditure approach will be obviously overestimated, thus the contribution rate of real estate investment to GDP growth will be overestimated or underestimated.

The result shows that since 2004, the proportion of GFCF produced by real estate investment in GDP has been on the rise, from about 6% in 2009 and before, to 7.5% or above after 2009, and even 8% in 2013. From 2004 to 2013, GFCF produced by real estate investment accounted for an average of 6.8% of GDP (see Table 1.2).

Table 1.2. Proportion of GFCF produced by real estate investment to GDP by expenditure approach

Year	Proportion of real estate investment to total investment in fixed assets (%, deducting land purchase cost)	Proportion of GFCF to GDP by expenditure approach (%)	Proportion of GFCF produced by real estate investment to GDP by expenditure approach (%)
2004	15.9	40.5	6.4
2005	15.5	39.6	6.1
2006	15.0	39.5	5.9
2007	15.8	39.0	6.2
2008	15.4	40.5	6.2
2009	14.2	44.9	6.4
2010	16.4	45.6	7.5
2011	17.4	45.6	7.9
2012	17.1	45.7	7.8
2013	17.3	45.9	8.0

Note: Proportion of real estate investment to total investment in fixed assets (deducting land purchase cost) = (real estate investment − land purchase cost in real estate investment)/(total investment in fixed assets − land purchase cost in total investment in fixed assets) × 100%. Proportion of GFCF produced by real estate investment to GDP by expenditure approach = proportion of real estate investment to total investment in fixed assets (deducting land purchase cost) × proportion of GFCF to GDP by expenditure approach.

Source: Data on total investment in fixed assets and real estate investment are from *China Statistical Yearbook 2014*, p. 279; data on land purchase costs are from the National Database of the National Bureau of Statistics; data on GDP by expenditure approach and GFCF are from *China Statistical Yearbook 2014*, p. 69.

Table 1.3.   Contribution of real estate investment to GDP growth

Year	Proportion of real estate investment to total investment in fixed assets (%, deducting land purchase cost)	Contribution of GFCF to GDP growth calculated by the expenditure approach (%)	Contribution rate of real estate investment to GDP growth calculated by the expenditure approach (%)
2004	15.9	45.8	7.3
2005	15.5	41.5	6.4
2006	15.0	39.1	5.9
2007	15.8	37.1	5.9
2008	15.4	38.0	5.8
2009	14.2	93.7	13.3
2010	16.4	48.3	7.9
2011	17.4	42.9	7.5
2012	17.1	51.4	8.8
2013	17.3	53.4	9.3

Note: Contribution rate of GFCF produced by real estate investment to GDP growth by expenditure approach = proportion of real estate investment to total investment in fixed assets (deducting land purchase cost) × contribution rate of GFCF to GDP growth by expenditure approach.

Source: Calculations by the author based on data mentioned earlier.

The contribution rate of real estate investment to GDP growth has been above 5.8% since 2004, with some fluctuations between different years: less than 6.5% during 2005–2008; 13.3% in 2009 at the highest; continuously improved in 2012 and 2013, reaching 9.3% in 2013. From 2004 to 2013, the annual average contribution rate of real estate investment to GDP growth was 7.8% (see Table 1.3).

1.3. Contribution of Real Estate Production to Economic Growth

As defined in this report, real estate production activities include the production activities of the real estate industry itself and the production activities of other industries related to the real estate. The following is an analysis on the contribution of real estate production activities to economic growth from these two dimensions.

1.3.1. *Contribution of real estate industry to economic growth*

1.3.1.1. *Scope of the real estate industry*

According to *Industrial Classification for National Economic Activities (2011)*,[12] the real estate industry belongs to the tertiary industry, including five groups: real estate development and operation, property management, real estate intermediary services, operation activities of self-owned real estate projects, and other real estate activities. Real estate development and operation refers to the development of housing and infrastructure by real estate developers, as well as the transfer of real estate development projects or activities such as sale and renting of houses; property management refers to the repairs, maintenance, and management of housing and affiliated equipment and facilities and related sites, as well as the maintenance of environmental sanitation and related orders by property service enterprises; real estate intermediary service refers to real estate consulting, real-estate–related price evaluation, real estate brokerage, and other activities; operations of self-owned housing refer to the sale of self-owned real estate and rental activities for profit by units and resident households except real estate developers, real estate intermediary agencies and property management companies, as well as non-profit rental services provided by real estate management departments, enterprises, institutions, and organizations, and housing services provided by households living in their own houses.

1.3.1.2. *Calculation of the value added of the real estate industry*

The value added of the real estate industry, as an important component of GDP, measures the value added created by the housing services provided by the whole society (including rent and living), as well as the commercial services provided by real estate development and operation enterprises, property management and real estate intermediary companies during the

---

[12]Issued by the General Administration of Quality Supervision, Inspection and Quarantine of the People's Republic of China and the China Standardization Administration on April 29, 2011, implemented starting from November 1, 2011, and published by the Standards Press of China.

construction, utilization, and transaction of buildings. In calculating the value added of the real estate industry, the total output and value added of residents' self-owned housing service should be estimated virtually. That is because the ratios of residents' self-owned housing and rented housing vary among different countries and during different periods in the same country. If the total output and value added of residents' self-owned housing service are not virtually estimated, international and historical comparisons of the production and consumption of the housing services are meaningless.[13] When calculating the value added of the real estate industry, the income approach is adopted. The value added of real estate development and operation, property management, real estate intermediary services, and other real estate industries is obtained by adding up the four items: compensation of employees, net taxes on production, depreciation of fixed assets, and operating surplus. The total output of residents' self-owned housing services is calculated at cost price, including maintenance and repair cost, property management fee, and depreciation of fixed assets, with three items in value added, namely compensation of employees, net taxes on production, and operating surplus, being all zero, and only depreciation of fixed assets included, which is the virtual depreciation of residents' own housing. The formula is: virtual depreciation = value of resident's self-owned housing × depreciation rate, wherein the value of resident's self-owned housing is calculated according to housing cost, the depreciation rate of urban resident's own housing is 2%, and that of rural resident's self-owned housing is 3%.[14]

1.3.1.3. *Share of value added of the real estate industry in GDP on steady rise*

Since the reform and opening-up, especially since the reform of housing system, the value added of the real estate industry has increased rapidly with the continuous development of the real estate market. From 1978 to 2013, the value added of the real estate industry increased from 8 billion yuan to 3,329.5 billion yuan, showing a 39.6-fold increase at constant price

---

[13] For a detailed description of the virtual estimation of the value of self-owned housing services, see Xu, X. (2013). The current reform in priority statistical areas in China. *Economic Research Journal*, Issue 10.

[14] See the Department of National Account Statistics, National Bureau of Statistics (2008). *Method on Compiling Gross Domestic Product of China in the Non-census Years* (China Statistical Press, Beijing), pp. 64–70.

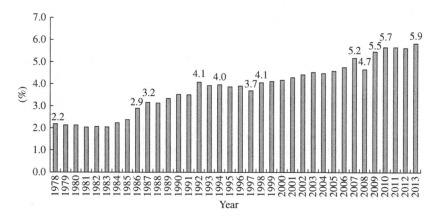

Figure 1.3. Proportion of value added of the real estate industry to GDP

Note: Calculated at current price.

Source: China Statistical Yearbook 2014, p. 50, 55.

and an average annual increase of 11.2%, or 1.4 percentage points higher than the average annual growth rate of GDP in the same period. With the continuous expansion of the total value added of the real estate industry, its share in GDP increased considerably from 2.2% in 1978 to 5.9% in 2013 (see Figure 1.3).

The pace of growth in the proportion of value added of the real estate industry to GDP coincides with the process of housing marketization, which can be divided into three stages. The years 1978–1986 featured the planned economy period of housing production and distribution, during which the proportion of value added of the real estate industry was less than 3%. Except for a share of 2.9% in 1986, the proportion of value added of the real estate industry did not exceed 2.4% in other years. The years 1987–1997 were the exploring period of housing marketization, during which the share of value added of the real estate industry was 3%–4.1%. The years after 1998 were the period of further development of housing marketization, during which the share of value added of the real estate industry rose from 4.1% in 1998 to 5.2% in 2007. Affected by the international financial crisis, this share dropped to 4.7% in 2008. The proportion remained above 5.5% after 2009 and reached 5.9% in 2013, demonstrating a growing share of value added of the real estate industry in GDP.

The proportion of value added of the real estate industry to value added of the tertiary sector showed an upward fluctuation, rising from 9.2% in 1978 to 12.7% in 2013 (see Figure 1.4).

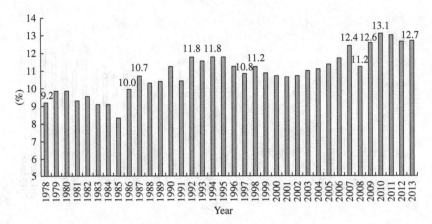

Figure 1.4. Proportion of value added of the real estate industry to value added of the tertiary sector

Note: Calculated at current price.

Source: *China Statistical Yearbook 2014*, p. 55.

1.3.1.4. *Contribution rate of the real estate industry to economic growth on the rise*

Based on data of GDP at constant prices, we can calculate the contribution rate of value added of the real estate industry to economic growth after deducting price factors. The formula is as follows: contribution rate of value added of the real estate industry to economic growth = Δ value added of the real estate industry at constant price/ΔGDP at constant prices $\times$ 100%. The results show that the average annual contribution rate was 1.7% from 1979 to 1988, 2.4% from 1989 to 2000, and 4.3% from 2001 to 2013. The highest contribution rate was 8.1% in 2007 (see Figure 1.5). It shows a growing contribution rate of value added of the real estate industry to economic growth and the important role of the real estate industry in promoting economic growth.

1.3.2. *Contribution of real-estate–related industries to economic growth*

Real estate is featured with a long industrial chain and involves many related industries. The production activities of industries closely related to real estate are the extension of real estate economic activities. On the one hand, real estate development is inseparable from production activities of the construction industry; on the other hand, it directly consumes a large

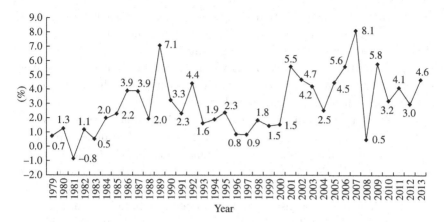

Figure 1.5. Contribution rate of the real estate industry to economic growth

Note: The contribution rate of the real estate industry to economic growth is calculated at constant prices.

Source: China Statistical Yearbook 2014, p. 52, 57.

quantity of building materials, which has led to the development of cement, steel, glass, hardware, metallurgy, ceramics, chemical, and other manufacturing industries. After buildings are sold, housing-related consumer activities have promoted the production of household appliances, furniture, home textiles, and other manufacturing industries. The development and sale of real estate will have a strong driving effect on logistics, finance, and other tertiary industries.

The input-output table is a powerful tool to study the relationship and interaction between different industries in the national economy. According to the national accounts system, China compiles a benchmark input-output table every five years through an input-output survey and prolonged input-output table on the basis of the benchmark table between two benchmark years. At present, the latest benchmark table in China is the input-output table in 2007, and the latest prolonged input-output table is the table published in 2010. Using the benchmark input-output model and the prolonged table of 41 sectors in 2010, the following input-output open model can be built:

$$\Delta X = [I - (I - \hat{M})A]^{-1}(I - \hat{M})\Delta F$$

where ΔX is the column vector of the total output change of each sector, ΔF is the column vector of the domestic final use change, $\hat{M}$ is the matrix formed through diagonalization of the proportion coefficient vector of the import volume of each sector to the domestic demand $(m_1, \ldots, m_n)$, and A is the direct consumption coefficient matrix.

Based on the column vector (ΔX) of the total output change of each sector multiplied by the value-added rate of each sector, the direct impact on the value added can be calculated.

In 2013, real estate investment was 8,601.3 billion yuan, of which 6,391.9 billion yuan was spent on construction and installation projects, 125 billion yuan on equipment and instruments, and 2,084.4 billion yuan as other expenses.[15] Most of the investment on construction and installation projects and the purchase of equipment and instruments constituted fixed capital, while other expenses mainly included purchase costs of land and old buildings, which did not directly form fixed capital and were deducted away. According to the above model, the analysis of the driving effect on real estate investment in various industries presented the following results. In 2013, real estate investment drove GDP by 5,384.8 billion yuan, accounting for 9.4% of GDP. Among them, the value added of the primary, secondary, and tertiary sectors was 165.1 billion yuan, 3,941.8 billion yuan, and 1,277.9 billion yuan, accounting for 2.9%, 15.8%, and 49%, respectively. It also drove imports by 1,132 billion yuan (assuming that the technology and price structure of each sector in 2013 changed little compared with 2010, the same assumption applies in the following). Among them, real estate investment has the greatest driving effect on the value added of the construction industry, amounting to 1,680.8 billion yuan, which accounted for 43.1% of the value added of the construction industry; it has noticeable driving effect on the value added of industries producing cement, glass, steel, chemical industry, hardware, household appliances, household supplies, furniture, and other products, stimulating the value added of all manufacturing industry by 2,261.1 billion yuan, which accounted for 10.7% of the value added of the manufacturing sector. It also has strong pulling effect on the value added of the tertiary industries such as transportation, wholesale, and retail trades and finance, stimulating the value added of the financial sector by 228.1 billion yuan, which accounted for 6.8% of the value added of the sector.

Estimation with the same method showed that the real estate investment drove the value added of related industries by 4,383.9 billion yuan

---

[15] *China Statistical Yearbook 2014*, p. 472.

in 2012. Estimates on this basis indicated the contribution rate of real-estate–related industries to GDP growth in 2013 was 24.8%.

By adding up the value added of the real estate industry and real-estate–related industries, we can see that the real estate production activities play an important role in economic growth. In 2013, the value added of the real estate industry was 3,329.5 billion yuan, and that of the related industries totaled 5,384.8 billion yuan (see Table 1.4). The total

Table 1.4. Value added of major industries in the national economy stimulated by real estate investment

(Unit: 100 million yuan)

Industry	Value added	
	2012	2013
Total	**43,839**	**53,848**
Primary sector	**1,344**	**1,651**
Secondary sector	**32,091**	**39,418**
Of which: Construction	13,683	16,808
Non-metal mineral products	3,382	4,155
Metal smelting and calendaring	2,516	3,090
Coal exploitation and cleaning	1,634	2,007
Production and supply of electric power and heat power	1,478	1,816
Chemical industry	1,450	1,781
Manufacture of general and special purpose machinery	1,176	1,444
Extraction of petroleum and natural gas	1,025	1,259
Processing of petroleum, coking, processing of nuclear fuel	919	1,129
Metal products	668	820
Mining and processing of metal ores	652	801
Mining and processing of non-metal and other ores	553	679
Manufacture of electrical machinery and equipment	536	659
Tertiary sector	**10,404**	**12,779**
Of which: Transportation and warehousing	3,220	3,956
Wholesale and retail trade	2,164	2,659
Finance	1,857	2,281
Information transmission, computer services and software	682	837
Integrated technology services	562	690
Hotels and catering services	548	673

Source: Data on real estate development and investment are from *China Statistical Yearbook 2014*, p. 279; data on input-output structure are from the National Statistical Database of the National Bureau of Statistics.

value added of the two was 8,714.3 billion yuan, accounting for 15.3% of the total GDP; the contribution rate of the real estate industry to GDP growth was 4.6%, and that of real-estate–related industries to GDP growth was 24.8%. The two added up to reach 29.4%.

1.4. Contribution of Real Estate Consumption to Economic Growth

It has been pointed out earlier in this report that real estate consumption activities refer to consumption activities of residential housing and related services. Real estate consumption is an important part of household consumption.

1.4.1. *Housing conditions of residents*

Since the reform and opening-up, especially with the reform and development of the housing system, China has continued to expand housing construction, which has resulted in increasing floor space of housing in urban and rural areas, much larger per capita floor space, and much better housing conditions for residents.

1.4.1.1. *Urban situation*

In 1978, the new urban housing space completed was only 38 million square meters. From 1986 to 1992, the new floor space completed averaged less than 240 million square meters per year, of which only 173 million square meters were built in 1990. From 1993 to 1998, the annual completed space increased from 308 million to 476 million square meters; from 1999 to 2004, the newly completed space averaged about 550 million square meters per year; and it began to grow rapidly, from 661 million square meters in 2005, to 1.212 billion square meters in 2013. The period from 2002 to 2012 witnessed a total of 8.1 billion square meters of new urban housing, and per capita housing construction space of urban households increased from 24.5 square meters to 32.9 square meters (see Figure 1.6).

1.4.1.2. *Rural situation*

In 1978, the new rural housing space was 100 million square meters, and in 1980 it quickly reached 500 million square meters. From 1985 to 2008, the newly completed housing space averaged 750 million square meters each year. In 2009, it exceeded 1 billion square meters, and until 2013, it was

Figure 1.6. Newly completed urban housing and per capita housing space of urban households

Source: China Statistical Yearbook 2014, p. 169.

about 1 billion square meters each year. With the new housing put into use, per capita housing space of rural households increased from 8.1 square meters in 1978 to 37.1 square meters in 2012 (see Figure 1.7).[16]

1.4.2. *Proportion of real estate consumption to GDP by expenditure approach*

Consumer expenditures consists of 10 categories, including food; clothing; housing; household facilities and services; health care; transportation and communications; cultural, educational, and entertainment goods and services; financial intermediary services; and insurance services and others. Among them, residential expenditures include rent, housing maintenance and management fees, utilities cost, and virtual expenditure of self-owned housing, which constitute real estate consumption.[17]

---

[16]The increase of per capita housing space of rural households is also related to the growing urbanization in China. On the one hand, the urbanization process reduces the number of rural residents; on the other hand, the process of urbanization is related to the level of regional economic development. Compared with the areas that have not yet been urbanized, the earlier urbanized areas are short of land resources, and their per capita housing space is often smaller.

[17]Household facilities and services in household consumption include the purchase of facilities and services related to households, and also related to real estate consumption.

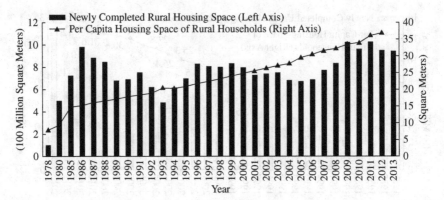

Figure 1.7. Newly completed rural housing and per capita housing space of rural households

Source: *China Statistical Yearbook 2014*, p. 169.

The results of the calculation show that the proportion of real estate consumption in household consumption expenditure, final consumption expenditure, and GDP by the expenditure approach remained basically stable from 2008 to 2011,[18] among which the proportion of real estate consumption in household consumption expenditure remained at about 17%, the proportion in final consumption expenditure at about 12%, and the proportion in GDP by the expenditure approach at about 6% (see Table 1.5).

From 2009 to 2011, the contribution rates of real estate consumption to GDP growth were 4.1%, 2.6%, and 2.8%, respectively. The contribution rates remained relatively stable (see Figure 1.8).

It has been estimated earlier that the GFCF produced by real estate investment in 2011 accounted for 7.9% of GDP by expenditure approach, i.e. 3,746.9 billion yuan. It totals 6,485.8 billion yuan together with 2,738.9 billion yuan of real estate consumption, accounting for 13.7% of GDP by the expenditure approach, and contributing 10.3% of GDP growth.

This report does not include this part when calculating real estate consumption expenditure.

[18] Due to the change of data sources and accounting methods, the data of household consumption expenditure was as of 2011.

Table 1.5. Real estate consumption during 2008–2011

	2008	**2009**	**2010**	**2011**
GDP by the expenditure approach (100 million yuan)	315,975	348,775	402,816	472,619
Final consumption expenditure (100 million yuan)	153,422	169,275	194,115	232,112
Household consumption expenditure (100 million yuan)	111,670	123,585	140,759	164,945
Rural households (100 million yuan)	27,677	29,005	31,975	37,395
Of which: Housing (100 million yuan)	5,006	4,851	5,042	5,792
Urban households (100 million yuan)	83,993	94,579	108,784	127,551
Of which: Housing (100 million yuan)	14,187	15,889	19,168	21,596
Real estate consumption (100 million yuan)	19,193	20,740	24,210	27,389
Proportion of real estate consumption to household consumption expenditure (%)	17.2	16.8	17.2	16.6
Proportion of real estate consumption to final consumption expenditure (%)	12.5	12.3	12.5	11.8
Proportion of real estate consumption to GDP by the expenditure approach (%)	6.1	5.9	6.0	5.8

Source: Data on household consumption expenditure are from *China Statistical Yearbook 2012*, p. 63.

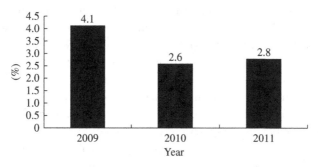

Figure 1.8. Contribution rate of real estate consumption to GDP growth
Source: Calculations by the author based on data mentioned earlier.

1.5. Summary

Since the reform and opening-up, China has gradually changed from a planned economic system to a market economic system. With the continuous development of the socialist market economy, the real estate economy plays an increasingly important role in China's economic growth.

According to the analysis mentioned above in this report, from the perspective of real estate production activities, the proportion of value added of the real estate industry and real-estate–related industries to GDP has steadily increased, and the contribution rate has been on the rise. In 2013, the value added created by real estate production activities was 8,714.3 billion yuan, accounting for 15.3% of GDP, and contributing 29.4% of GDP growth.

From 2004 to 2013, as an important part of investment in fixed assets, the GFCF produced by real estate investment has increased in its proportion to GDP and its contribution to GDP growth. From 2009 to 2011, the proportion of real estate consumption, as an important part of household consumption expenditure, and its contribution to GDP growth has remained basically or relatively stable. In 2011, the GFCF produced by real estate investment and real estate consumption totaled 6,485.8 billion yuan, accounting for 13.7% of GDP by expenditure approach and contributing 10.3% to GDP growth. Some of the expenditure on household facilities and services in household consumption expenditure is also the consumption activity stems from the real estate investment. If this is taken into consideration, the proportion of real estate investment and consumption to GDP by expenditure approach and the contribution rate to GDP growth could have been higher. This shows a noticeable contribution by the real estate economy to the economic growth through both real estate production activities and real estate utilization activities.

The real estate economy can either make important contribution to, or hinder the economic growth in, the fields of production, investment, and consumption. Take 2014 as an example. From the beginning of the year, the sales in terms of both floor space and value of commercial housing continued to decline, which first had an impact on the growth of real estate investment. From January to November, real estate investment rose by 11.9% year-on-year, down by 7.4 percentage points compared with the period from January to February and by 7.6 percentage points compared with the same period in 2013, which slowed down the growth rate of investment in fixed assets. From

January to November, investment in fixed assets increased 15.8% year-on-year, down by 2.1 percentage points compared with that during January to February, and by 4.1 percentage points compared with the same period in 2013, partly due to the decline in the growth rate of real estate investment.

The slowdown of growth in real estate investment has a direct impact on the production of building materials such as steel, cement, and plate glass. From January to November 2014, steel production increased by 4.5% year on year, 7 percentage points lower than the same period in 2013; cement production increased by 1.9%, 7.3 percentage points lower than the same period in 2013; and plate glass production increased by 2.4%, 9.2 percentage points lower than the same period in 2013. The drop of the growth rate of these products was partly due to the decline in the growth rate of real estate investment, which directly slowed down the growth rate of industrial value added.

The decline in the sales market of commercial housing also affects the decline of the growth rate of production and sales of related consumer products and further drags down the growth rate of household consumption. From January to November 2014, the output of washing machines for household use decreased by 4.5% year on year, whereas the same period in 2013 registered an increase of 8.5%. The output of household refrigerators showed no increase year-on-year, whereas the same period of 2013 registered an increase of 11.3%. From January to November 2014, the retail sales of household appliances and furniture goods in wholesale and retail businesses above the designated size had an increase of 8.7% and 14.0% year on year, respectively, which were 6.2 and 7.1 percentage points lower compared with the same period in 2013. The slower growth of production and sales of these consumer products was partly caused by the decline in the sales market of commercial housing, which directly slowed down the growth rate of household consumption.

The decline of the sales market of commercial housing also slows down the growth of the value added of the real estate industry. The value added of the real estate industry increased by 7.8% in the first quarter of 2013 and fell to 2.3% in the first three quarters of 2014, which played a role in dragging the growth of the national economy (see Figure 1.9).

In the process of economic development, too much reliance on real estate will result in many problems, such as an overheated real estate market, excessive rise of housing prices, real estate bubble, and real estate credit risk, which will have negative effects on the sustained, stable, and

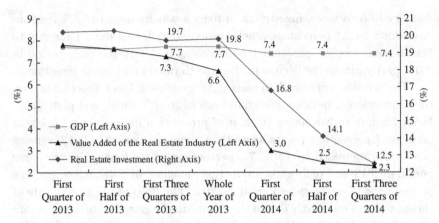

Figure 1.9. Growth rates of quarterly GDP, value added of real estate, and real estate investment since 2013

Source: The National Statistical Database of the National Statistical Bureau.

healthy development of the national economy. In the 1990s, Japan and China's Hainan province experienced economic recession caused by real estate bubble burst. The global financial and economic crisis triggered by the American subprime mortgage crisis in the 21st century was a case in point. The harm of overheated real estate economy is mainly reflected in three aspects.

(1) **"Drainage effect" on real economy:** In a market economy, the capital is naturally profit-driven. An overheated real estate market will attract large volume of capital to enter this lucrative industry and further drive up real estate prices. From 1998 to 2013, domestic loans in the paid-in investment of real estate development enterprises increased by 21.9% annually. The share of domestic loans in the real estate industry to total domestic loans rose from 21.4% to 33.5%, an increase by 12.1 percentage points. In the same period, the average annual growth rate of domestic loans in the manufacturing industry was 20.6%, which was 1.3 percentage points lower than that in real estate development. The proportion of domestic loans in the manufacturing industry to total domestic loans increased from 15.6% to 21.9%, and the gap with loans in real estate development widened from 5.8 percentage points in 1998 to 11.6 percentage points. The lack of credit in the real sector such as the manufacturing industry will hamper the healthy development of the national economy.

(2) **"Crowding-out effect" on household consumption:** An overheated real estate market may cause skyrocketing of housing prices, resulting in an abnormal price–income ratio for housing. Taking Beijing as an example, the price–income ratio in 2012 was 11.8,[19] which was far beyond the internationally recognized reasonable range of 3–6. In order to purchase housing, residents overdraft their own consumption capacity, which will have an obvious "crowding-out effect" on their consumption, and have a negative impact on the macrocontrol objectives of "transforming the growth model, making structural adjustments and improving people's wellbeing."

(3) **"Risk effect" on financial and economic performance:** In 2013, development loans of real estate developers and personal mortgage loans accounted for 27.6% of the paid-in investment for real estate development projects. According to data from the People's Bank of China, in 2013, the balance of real estate loans (including real estate development loans, housing purchase loans, and securitized real estate loans) totaled 14.61 trillion yuan, accounting for 21.0% of all loans in RMB granted by financial institutions. In recent years, part of the local government debt which caused great concerns went to real estate. The risks brought by the excessive growth of real estate may negatively affect China's financial industry, thus bringing latent risks to the performance of the entire national economy.

Therefore, we should have a clear understanding of the negative effects of the real estate economy and take serious precautions to develop a positive interaction between the real estate economy and the whole national economic development.

It is clear that the real estate economy is of great significance to the sound development of the national economy. If the growth rate of real estate economy is too low, it can adversely affect the steady growth of the national economy and hinder the improvement of people's lives. However,

---

[19]Price-income ratio for housing = total price of housing per household/total annual income per household. Wherein, total price of housing per household = average floor space per capita × average number of persons per household × average selling price per unit of floor space; annual total income per household = average number of persons per household × annual total income per person. Data were collected from Beijing Municipal Bureau of Statistics and Survey Office of the National Bureau of Statistics in Beijing (2013). *Beijing Statistical Yearbook 2013* [electronic edition] (China Statistics Press, Beijing).

if the growth rate of real estate economy is too high, it may lead to skyrocketing housing prices and real estate bubbles, thus causing financial risks and undermining social harmony and stability. Therefore, the real estate economy should maintain a reasonable growth, so as to effectively drive healthy and stable growth of the national economy, promote the improvement of people's livelihood, and avoid contradictions and problems in production, life, finance, and social stability.

Chapter 2

Economic Role of Automotive Industry and Future Quality Development

Xu Xianchun, Jiang Yuan, and Chen Yingting*

Abstract

After more than 60 years of development, China has become the world's largest automobile manufacturer in terms of production and marketing. Although its automotive industry is large in terms of volume, it does not possess the corresponding global clout. Automobiles of self-owned brands are not well recognized internationally. From the perspective of production, the contribution of the automotive industry to industrial value added is on the rise in general. The input-output analysis shows that the automotive industry plays an important driving role for growth in multiple sectors. From 2007 to 2012, the overall contribution of automobile consumption, investment, and export to the national economy was increasing. The contribution of the automotive industry to the national economy still has a lot of room to expand in terms of the proportion of the automotive industry to the total demand of domestic output, especially the proportion of the automotive industry to the domestic output of mid- and high-end raw materials, high-tech industry, and equipment manufacturing industries. At present, the automotive industry as a new driver is developing rapidly, and self-owned brands have great potential. The automotive industry, with its outstanding profitability, wide ranges of tax contributions, and a strong role in promoting employment, has made important contributions to improving the performance and upgrading of China's economy. The trend of deep integration of the automotive industry with intelligent manufacturing, high-end equipment manufacturing, and "Internet Plus" highlights the importance of independent development and innovation and industrial

---

*Xu Xianchun is a Professor at the School of Economics and Management, Tsinghua University; Jiang Yuan is a Senior Statistician at the National Bureau of Statistics; and Chen Yingting is an Intermediate Statistician at the National Bureau of Statistics.

collaboration. Starting with the basic and key technological innovation of the automotive industry and stimulating the independent development and innovation of the whole industry chain will help in effectively upgrading and developing the overall national economy and smoothly implementing the strategy of transforming China into a leading manufacturing power.

The automotive industry occupies a predominant position among all industries because it is a yardstick to measure a country's manufacturing strength. Countries with the title of "leading manufacturing power," including the United States, Germany, and latecomers Japan and Republic of Korea, all have their own global brands and unique comparative advantages in the automotive industry. Without exception, they all regard the automotive industry as a pillar industry and leading the long-term development of the automotive industry as a national priority strategy. After more than 60 years of twists and turns, China has become the world's largest automobile manufacturer and market, but while its automotive industry is large in terms of volume, it does not yet have the corresponding global prominence. As for the research on the development of the automotive industry, the current literature mostly observes from the perspective of industry and puts forward policy suggestions for the automotive industry itself but does not analyze the industry from multiple dimensions concerning the entire national economy. From the multi-dimensional perspective of the national economy, the automotive industry is highly relevant and occupies a decisive position in the production, investment, consumption, export, tax, and other aspects of the national economy, so it plays an important role in supporting GDP. Especially during China's economic transformation and upgrading, the prosperity of the automotive industry as a new driver, and the deep integration of the automotive industry with intelligent manufacturing and "Internet Plus," highlights the important role of the automotive industry in implementing the strategy of being a manufacturer of quality. The effective ways to promote China's strategy to develop into a leading manufacturing power through the revitalization of the automotive industry are strengthening top-level design and industrial collaboration, emphasizing talent utilization and resource integration, and interconnecting the independent development and innovation of the whole industry chain with that of the automotive industry.

2.1. The Course of Development of China's Automotive Industry and its International Position

2.1.1. *China's automotive industry: An overview*

China's automotive industry has gone through more than 60 years of development since construction commenced on the First Automobile Works of China in Changchun and the first mass-produced product, CA10 4-tonne Jiefang truck, successfully rolled off the production line in the 1950s. The output of automobiles increased from 100 units in 1955 to 41,000 units in 1965, 140,000 units in 1975, 437,000 units in 1985, and 1.453 million units in 1995. In the 21st century, the output of automobiles skyrocketed and reached 5.705 million units in 2005, exceeded the mark of 10 million units in 2009, and reached as much as 24.504 million units in 2015 (see Figure 2.1). The development of the automotive industry can be mainly divided into the following periods.

Before the reform and opening-up, China's automotive industry was mainly part of the planned economy. Except for some technical assistance from the Soviet Union in the early stages, Dongfeng 71 cars and Hongqi CA72 sedans were independently developed by state-owned enterprises. During this period, China's automotive industry mainly produced trucks and had a relatively weak technological foundation of cars. The assisted or contractual development of new factories by old ones was the main way to transfer and spread technology. Local automotive industries usually first

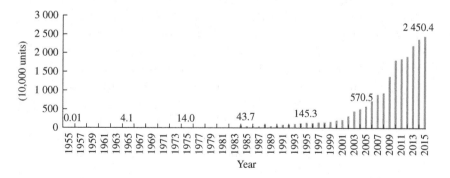

Figure 2.1. Annual output of automobiles

Source: China Automotive Industry Year book 2003, Table 2.4, p. 26.

developed a leading product, and then built a number of enterprises, making parts for the assembled vehicles. During this period, on the one hand, most automobiles were independently developed, thus creating some independent products, self-owned brands, and development platforms; on the other hand, because of the lack of market incentives and the decentralization of automotive enterprises in administrative divisions, there was a lack of stimulus of mass production, so it failed to develop any mass production mode characterized by assembly lines.[1]

Since the reform and opening-up, the demand for cars in the Chinese market has increased rapidly. The lack of mass production capacity has led to a geometric growth of car imports in the first half of the 1980s. In 1984 and 1985, the quantity of imported cars even exceeded the domestic output of cars.[2] In the mid-1980s, China's automotive industry began to introduce car-making technology through joint ventures, such as Beijing Jeep, SAIC Volkswagen, and Guangzhou Peugeot Automobile Company, which were established one after another. On the one hand, benefitting from the joint ventures and mass production, China's automotive production, especially car production, began to grow rapidly; on the other hand, the development of China's domestically produced cars has weakened due to more reliance on foreign technology.

From 2002 to 2003, due to lower import tariff on automobiles and parts after China's accession to WTO, the automotive industry faced a more open market, and the automobile market gradually changed from being truck-dominated to car-dominated. Before 2002, the output of trucks in physical terms took a larger share in total output of automobiles than that of cars. In 2002, the output of trucks and cars were both 1.092 million units. After 2002, the output and growth of cars obviously exceeded that of trucks and promoted the rapid growth of automobile production. In addition, the growing household consumption of cars has created a wider market for the automotive industry. Since then, China's automotive industry has ushered in a period of rapid development, and automobile production has increased quickly. After the promulgation of the *Auto Industry Restructuring and Revitalization Plan* from the end of 2008 to the beginning of 2009, measures such as reduction or exemption of automobile acquisition tax and subsidy

---

[1]See Lu, F., & Feng, K. (2005). *Policy Choice for Developing China's Automotive Industry with Own Intellectual Property Rights* (Peking University Press, Beijing), p. 7.
[2] *China Automotive Industry Yearbook 2003*, Table 2.4, p. 26.

for rural households to purchases new vehicles by trading in old ones effectively stimulated household consumption demand for automobiles. China's automotive industry has ushered in a period of rapid growth, with annual output exceeding 10 million units. China has become the world's largest automobile producer and seller since 2009.

2.1.2. *The course of development of self-owned automobile brands*

Up to now, the development of China's self-owned automobile brands roughly has gone through three stages. In the first stage (end of 1990s–2003), China's self-owned automobile brands started with the strategy of economic models, entered the low-end market that large joint ventures ignored by the virtue of their price advantages, and gradually accumulated related technologies. In the second stage (2003–2007), with the improvement of capacity of Chinese households in automobile consumption and the increasingly fierce market competition, the demand for the quality and performance of automobile has become increasingly prominent. Therefore, automakers with self-owned brands generally adopted the strategy of quality improvement. On the basis of the earlier technology accumulation, they gradually transformed and upgraded production process and increased their investment in R&D to improve the automobile quality. In the third stage (after 2007), due to the further intensification of market competition, user demand became increasingly diversified, and the direction of future development of China's self-owned automobile brands was then divided. Some brands still imitated international brands, or started joint-venture development, while some chose foreign acquisition. For instance, Geely Automobile grasped the opportunity to cooperate with internationally famous automakers such as Volvo, which provided the possibility to raise its technological power and improve its product quality relatively faster. There were some other automobile brands that strengthened their own R&D and began to introduce their products to joint-venture investors. For instance, Chang'an Automobile introduced the Alsvin V3 to Chang'an Ford, the new Benben to Chang'an Suzuki, and EADO EV to Chang'an PSA, and so on. Especially since SUVs and new energy vehicles became new consumption hotspots, some excellent Chinese self-owned brands have devoted themselves to the development of new models and achieved remarkable results, thus gaining a bigger share of the passenger-car market.

2.1.3. *Strategic position of China's automotive industry in the international market*

From the international perspective, China's automotive industry has developed rapidly since the start of the 21st century and has been the world's largest automobile producer and seller for seven consecutive years. In 2000, China produced 2.07 million vehicles, ranking the seventh in the world (after Spain and Canada). In 2002, China produced 3.251 million vehicles, surpassing the Republic of Korea and ranking fourth in the world. China became the world's largest automobile producer and seller in 2009 and has stayed on top ever since (see Figure 2.2).

However, the Chinese automotive industry does not yet possess the clout in commensurate with its volume, and its self-owned brands are not well-recognized internationally. The Global 500 list published in July 2015 included six Chinese automobile groups. SAIC Group ranked 60th with \$102.249 billion in revenue; FAW Group, 107th with \$80.195 billion; Dongfeng Motor Corporation, 109th with \$78.979 billion; BAIC Group, 207th with \$50.566 billion; GAC Group, 362nd with \$33.237 billion; and Geely Holding Group, 477th with \$24.986 billion. In terms of scale, most of the six Chinese automobile companies in the Global 500 list had a higher ranking than the previous year, yet none of them were among the top 50. In comparison, Germany, the United States, Japan, and other auto powers all have automobile companies among the top 50. Specifically, Volkswagen AG and Daimler AG of Germany ranked the 8th and 17th places, respectively; General Motors and Ford Motor of the United States

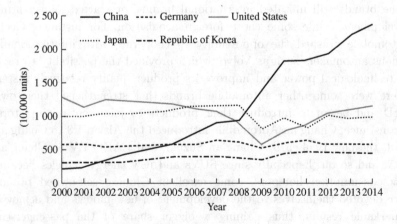

Figure 2.2. Annual automobile output in major auto-making countries

ranked the 21st and 27th places, respectively; and Toyota Motor and Honda of Japan ranked the 9th and 44th places, respectively. Moreover, the profits of German and Japanese automotive groups far exceeded those of Chinese automotive groups. In terms of automobile brands, all the foreign automotive enterprises in the Global 500 list had their self-owned brands, while the six Chinese automotive enterprises are mostly dominated by joint-venture brands, except Geely, whose self-owned brands and foreign brands have equal share. The SAIC Group sold more than 5 million cars in 2014, of which less than 1 million were of self-owned brands. In terms of export, most of the products of the top foreign automotive enterprises were exported, while most of the products of Chinese automotive enterprises were sold in the domestic market. From the perspective of brand awareness, Chinese automotive enterprises also fell behind (see Table 2.1).

An initiative to accelerate the implementation of *Made in China 2025*, unveiled by the State Council in 2015, pointed out that, in order to build China into a manufacturer of quality, it was necessary to seize the rare strategic opportunities, actively respond to challenges, strengthen overall planning, highlight innovation drive, formulate specific policies, give full play to institutional advantages, mobilize all social forces to strive hard, rely more on Chinese equipment, rely more on Chinese brands, and realize the transformation from made-in-China to created-in-China, from Chinese speed to Chinese quality, and from Chinese products to Chinese brands so as to accomplish the strategic task of upgrading China from a manufacturer of quantity to one of quality. Judging the current development of the automotive industry, there is still a long way to go to further boost China's self-owned brands and realize the transformation from made-in-China to created-in-China, and turn China from a manufacturer of quantity to a manufacturer of quality.

2.2. Production Characteristics of China's Automotive Industry and its Contribution to Industry

As a pillar of China's manufacturing industry, the automotive industry[3] has assumed an increasingly important status and role in recent years with an ever-growing output and increasing proportion. By observing the time series

---

[3]The automotive industry in this report, except noted otherwise, refers to the automobile manufacturing industry in the *Industrial Classification for National Economic Activities* (GB/T 4754–2011), i.e. industry category 36 in the classification standard.

Table 2.1. Automotive enterprises among 2015 fortune global 500

Automotive industry ranking	Total ranking in 2015	Total ranking in 2014	Company name	Operating revenue ($100 million)	Profit ($100 million)	Country
1	8	8	Volkswagen	2685.67	145.72	Germany
2	9	9	Toyota Motor	2477.03	197.67	Japan
3	17	20	Daimler	1722.79	92.35	Germany
4	19	24	Exor Group	1621.63	4.29	Italy
5	21	21	General Motors	1559.29	39.49	United States
6	27	26	Ford Motor	1440.77	31.87	United States
7	44	45	Honda Motor	1212.22	46.33	Japan
8	56	68	BMW Group	1066.54	76.91	Germany
9	59	61	Nissan Motor	1034.60	41.62	Japan
10	60	85	SAIC Motor	1022.49	45.40	China
11	99	100	Hyundai Motor	847.72	69.78	Republic of Korea
12	107	111	China FAW Group	801.95	42.48	China
13	109	113	Dongfeng Motor Group	789.79	16.00	China
14	128	119	Peugeot	711.11	−9.37	France
15	191	190	Renault	544.61	25.07	France
16	207	248	Beijing Automotive Group	505.66	8.20	China
17	242	246	Kia Motors	447.31	28.43	Republic of Korea
18	254	287	Tata Motors	429.75	22.87	India
19	268	258	Volvo	412.30	3.06	Sweden
20	362	366	Guangzhou Automotive Industry Group	332.37	2.84	China
21	429	449	Mazda Motor	275.94	14.44	Japan
22	436	414	Suzuki Motor	274.26	8.81	Japan
23	452	494	Fuji Heavy Industries	261.75	23.82	Japan
24	477	466	Zhejiang Geely Holding Group	249.86	2.76	China

Source: ChinaDaily.com.cn

data of automobile output and value added of the automotive industry, we can discover the characteristics of the production and output change, as well as the role of industrial policy of China's automotive industry.

2.2.1. *Short-term fluctuations and long-term trends of production in the automotive industry*

Monthly data from 2002 to 2015 show that automobile production has clear seasonal characteristics. Figure 2.3 shows the seasonal components (including seasonal factors and calendar factors) of automobile production in each month measured by seasonal adjustment software. The zigzag line represents the seasonal factors of each year from 2002 to 2015. The horizontal line represents the average of seasonal factors in the month of each year. A value smaller than 1 represents the off-season and a value larger than 1 represents the peak season. It can be seen that March and April are the traditional peak seasons of automobile production, and July and August are the traditional off-seasons. In recent years, however, November, December, and January of some years have become the peak

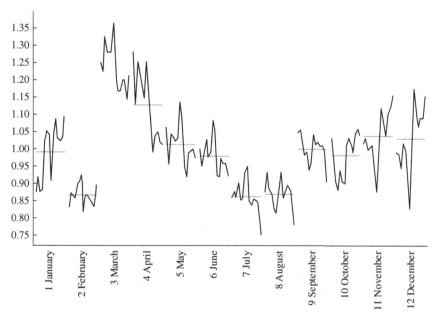

Figure 2.3. Seasonal factors of automobile production in each month from 2002 to 2015 (estimated by seasonal adjustment software)

season of automobile production (the last values of the zigzag lines in November, December, and January in Figure 2.3 are all greater than 1). This is because "make to order" has increasingly become the operational mode of automobile production. During New Year's Day and the Spring Festival, there is often have a stronger demand for car purchases, and the corresponding increase in orders drives output growth at the end of the year.

After removing the seasonal factors in the automobile output time series data by seasonal adjustment software, we can see the long-term trend of automobile output between 2002 and 2015. In Figure 2.4, the light-colored polyline shows the original data series of monthly automobile output, and the dark-colored flat curve shows the series and long-term trend of monthly automobile output excluding seasonal factors. It can be seen that, with the seasonal factors removed, the monthly output of automobiles shows a straight upward trend on the whole. From 2002 to 2007, the output increased steadily; during the global financial crisis of 2008, there was a noticeable fluctuation or even a decline in output. In 2009, the output increased rapidly and maintained a rapid growth in 2010. In 2011 and between the second half of 2014 to the third quarter of 2015, there were some fluctuations in automobile production, with a slowdown in the trend of growth. In the fourth quarter of 2015, automobile production considerably increased again.

The chain growth rate calculated using the seasonally adjusted time series can more clearly show the changes in the monthly output of automobiles. As shown in Figure 2.5, the seasonally adjusted chain growth

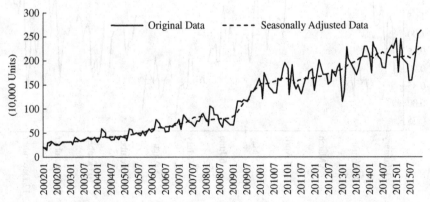

Figure 2.4. Seasonal adjustment results of time series of automobile output, 2002–2015 (estimated by seasonal adjustment software)

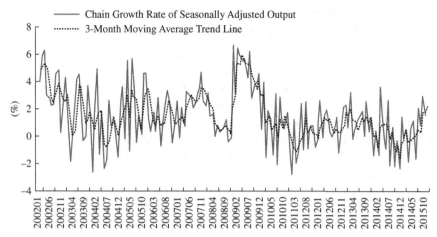

Figure 2.5. Chain growth rate of seasonally adjusted automobile production, 2002–2015

rate of automobile production has the same trend as that of the overall industrial production. From 2005 to 2007, a period in which industrial production grew relatively fast, the month-on-month growth rate of automobile production reached 2.09% on the average. During the global financial crisis of 2008, the growth rate of the overall industrial production dropped significantly, and so did the chain growth rate of automobile production, showing a negative growth for consecutive months. The effect of the automotive industry policy can also be clearly seen from the chain growth rate. From the end of 2008 to the beginning of 2009, the *Auto Industry Restructuring and Revitalization Plan* was issued, which covered the reduction or exemption of automobile acquisition tax and subsidy for rural residents' automobile purchases. With the issue of this policy, the chain growth rate of automobile output increased rapidly in early 2009. After the expiration of the two-year preferential policy, due to the elimination of the previous policy and the earlier arrival of purchasing demand, the chain growth rate of automobile production slowed down slightly in 2011 and 2012, and then recovered in 2013. In the case that the growth rate of automobile production slowed down again from the second half of 2014 to the third quarter of 2015, the chain growth rate of automobile production rebounded markedly in the fourth quarter, thanks to the introduction of tax incentives for small cars and policies to promote the development of new energy vehicles starting from October 1, 2015.

2.2.2. Contribution of the automotive industry to the growth of industrial production

From the production point of view, the share of the value added of the automotive industry to industrial value added above designated size has been on the rise (see Table 2.2), ranging from 4.0% to 4.9% between 2004 and 2009, and reaching 5.5% in 2010 and 6.2% in 2015. After 2006, the growth rate of the value added of the automotive industry was lower than that of the entire industrial sector only in 2008 when the global financial crisis broke out, and in 2011 and 2012, when the policy digestion period just began,[4] in which the contribution to industrial growth was 3.7%, 4.7%, and 4.4%, respectively. In other years, the growth rate was significantly higher than that of industry above the designated size, and its

Table 2.2. Share, growth rate, and contribution of the value added of the automotive industry to the growth of industry above designated size

(unit: %)

Year	Share of value added of automotive industry	Growth rate of value added of automotive industry	Growth rate of value added of industry above designated size	Contribution rate of automotive industry to growth of industry above designated size
2004	4.9	14.4	16.7	4.7
2005	4.2	9.3	16.4	2.7
2006	4.1	25.1	16.6	5.9
2007	4.1	26.4	18.6	5.6
2008	4.0	10.9	12.9	3.7
2009	4.8	20.3	11.0	7.5
2010	5.5	24.8	15.7	8.3
2011	5.1	11.5	13.9	4.7
2012	5.2	8.4	10.0	4.4
2013	5.5	14.9	9.7	8.0
2014	5.8	11.8	8.3	7.9
2015	6.2	6.7	6.1	6.5

---

[4]The growth of value added of enterprises above the designated size and the growth of value added of the automotive industry are the real growth rates calculated at comparable prices. Therefore, the contribution rate of value added growth is calculated based on comparable prices, which is the ratio of the increment of automobile value added above the designated size to the increment of industrial value added above the designated size at comparable prices. The statistics cover industrial enterprises with an annual main business income of over 20 million yuan. Data are the monthly data of industry above the designated size released by the National Bureau of Statistics.

contribution rate to industrial growth was also on the rise: 5.6% in 2007, 7.5% in 2009, 8.3% in 2010, 8.0% in 2013, 7.9% in 2014, and 6.5% in 2015, respectively.

2.2.3. *Analysis on production characteristics and development trend of the automotive industry*

Concerning the production characteristics of China's automotive industry at present, the following conclusions can be drawn from the above analysis:

First, the production of the automotive industry and the overall industrial production basically changed with similar trends. In the period of rapid growth of industrial production, automobile production generally grew faster; while in the period of noticeable declines of industrial production (such as during the 2008 global financial crisis), the growth rate of automobile production also declined correspondingly (see Figure 2.6).

Second, time series data show that industrial policies aiming at stimulating automobile consumption demand can significantly increase the automobile output during a certain period of time (2009 and 2010), indicating that automobile consumption has a relatively strong price elasticity. At the same time, due to the advance of automobile purchase demand, it will introduce a policy digestion period with a relatively low output growth after the policy withdrawal (2011 and 2012).

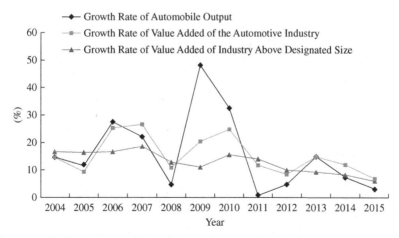

Figure 2.6. Comparison of growth rate of automobile production, growth rate of value added of automotive industry, and growth rate of value added of industry above designated size

Third, the trends of indicators on automobile output and value added of the automotive industry are basically the same, but there is a certain difference between the fluctuation of the quantity index and that of the value index, mainly due to the value structure of products. For example, the output grew obviously faster than the value added of the automotive industry in 2009 (see Figure 2.6), partly because the tax incentives for small cars brought about a faster growth of this type of cars with a lower unit price and lower contribution to value added; while in 2014 and 2015, the growth rate of value added of the automotive industry was faster than that of automobile output, due to the rapid growth of high-value products such as SUVs.

Fourth, with the gradual increase of automobile ownership, the year-on-year growth rate has slowed down for five consecutive years since 2011 (see Figure 2.7). In addition, the impact of resources, environment, and other factors will inevitably result in limited room for the growth of automobile production.

The above analysis indicates that the future development of the automotive industry cannot rely solely on the growth of automobile output. The industrial policy of tax reduction and other efforts to stimulate demand plays a role only during a certain period of time. In the future, the automotive industry will still need to explore greater room for development in improving quality and efficiency, building self-owned brands, and expanding its related industries.

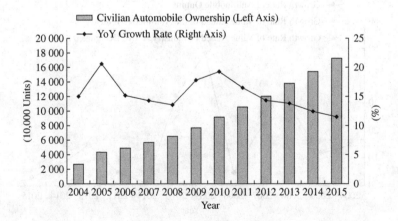

Figure 2.7.   Civilian automobile ownership and its YoY growth rate

Source: Statistical Communiqué of the People's Republic of China on the 2004–2015 National Economic and Social Development.

2.3. Contribution of China's Automotive Industry to the National Economy

Possessing a long industrial chain and a high degree of correlation, the automotive industry has a close tie with other industries and can drive the development of related sectors in the national economy and the development of the overall economy. The input-output table, as an important part of the national economic accounting system, describes the sources of input and the use direction of output of various sectors of the national economy during a certain period of time in the form of a matrix and reveals the quantitative relationship of interdependence and mutual restriction among various sectors of the national economy. According to the input-output table, we can quantitatively analyze the automotive industry's role in driving the output of various sectors and its contribution to the national economy.

2.3.1. *The linkage and driving role of the automotive industry and its development and change*

2.3.1.1. *Intermediate input and total output of the automotive industry rank high among all sectors*

According to China's Input-Output Table 2012, the intermediate input of the automotive industry[5] (including automobile, auto components, and accessories) was 4,015.38 billion yuan, ranking the 3rd among 138 sectors, behind only housing construction (6,235.12 billion yuan) and steel rolling (4,250.22 billion yuan)[6]; the value added of the automotive industry was 971.3 billion yuan, ranking the 13th; and the gross output of the automotive industry was 4,986.69 billion yuan, ranking the 4th, after

---

[5]According to the annotation to *Appendix I: Explanation and Code for Sector Classification* of *Input-Output Tables of China 2012* (p. 569), the automotive industry that has merged the two sectors: automobile (including automobile, modified cars, low-speed trucks, trolley cars, car body shell and trailers) and auto components and accessories in the input-output table has the same coverage as the automotive industry in the *Industrial Classification for National Economic Activities* (GB/T 4754–2011) (i.e. category 36 under the *Classification*).

[6]The estimates were made based on the 2012 input-output table. There are 139 sectors in the 2012 input-output table. In this report, the industry of automobile and the industry of auto components and accessories were merged into one industry, so there are only 138 sectors.

Table 2.3. Intermediate input, value added, and total output of the automotive industry and their share in all sectors

	2012		2007	
	Value (100 million yuan)	Proportion in the total of all sectors (%)	Value (100 million yuan)	Proportion in the total of all sectors (%)
Intermediate input in automotive industry	40,153.8	3.77	20,127.8	3.64
Value added of automotive industry	9,713.0	1.81	4,535.4	1.70
Gross output of the automotive industry	49,866.9	3.11	24,663.2	3.01

housing construction (8,512.73 billion yuan), wholesale and retail (7,215.53 billion yuan), and steel rolling (5,126.53 billion yuan).

In terms of proportion, the share of the intermediate input of the automotive industry to the total intermediate input of all sectors was 3.77% in 2012, up by 0.13 percentage points over that in 2007; the share of the value added of the automotive industry in the total value added of all sectors was 1.81%, up by 0.11 percentage points over that in 2007; and the share of the gross output of the automotive industry in the gross output of all sectors was 3.11%, up by 0.1 percentage point over that in 2007 (see Table 2.3).

2.3.1.2. *Total demand from final use of automobiles for the output of related product sectors*

The total consumption coefficient $\bar{b}_{ij}$ in the input-output table indicates the sum of direct and indirect consumption of goods or services in product sector i for each unit of final use supplied by product sector j.[7] The direct consumption coefficient matrix is represented by A and the unit matrix is represented by I. Then the formula for calculating the matrix of total consumption coefficient B is as follows:

$$B = (I - A)^{-1} - I$$

---

[7] See *Input-Output Tables of China 2012*, p. 7.

Among them, the matrix $\bar{B} = (I - A)^{-1}$ is the matrix of total demand coefficient (also known as Leontief inverse matrix), wherein elements $\bar{b}_{ij}(i, j = 1, 2, 3, \ldots, n)$ are called the total demand coefficients (also known as Leontief inverse coefficients), indicating the total demand for product sector i when sector j adds a unit to the final use.[8] From the formula, it can be seen that the total demand coefficient matrix can be obtained by adding the total consumption matrix and the unit matrix, i.e.

$$\bar{B} = B + I$$

The final use in the input-output table refers to the goods and services that have been withdrawn or temporarily withdrawn from the current production activities for the final demand. By multiplying the final use of the automotive industry by its total demand coefficient for each product sector, the total demand for the corresponding product sector of the automotive industry can be obtained. According China's Input-Output Table 2007, the final use of the automotive industry in 2007 was 1,047.35 billion yuan, and the total demand for the output of various sectors was 4,152.02 billion yuan, including 42.35 billion yuan for the primary industry, 3,717.1 billion yuan for the secondary industry, and 392.57 billion yuan for the tertiary industry. According to China's Input-Output Table 2012, the final use of the automotive industry in 2012 was 2,836.08 billion yuan, and the total demand for the output of various sectors was 10,762.09 billion yuan, including 113.44 billion yuan for the primary industry, 9,147.85 billion yuan for the secondary industry, and 150.08 billion yuan for the tertiary industry.

2.3.1.3. *Structural change of total demand for final use per unit in the automotive industry*

By using the input-output tables of China in 2007 and 2012 to calculate the total demand of each unit of the automotive industry for the output of each sector in 2007 and 2012, respectively, we can analyze the structural changes of the output of each sector consumed by the final use of each unit of the automotive industry in these two periods (see Table 2.4).

---

[8]The difference between the total demand coefficient matrix and the total consumption coefficient matrix is that the former includes the consumption of each product sector itself, while the latter does not include this part.

Table 2.4.   Total demand for output per unit of the automotive industry

	2012	2007	Ratio of 2012 to 2007
Total	**3.795**	**3.964**	**0.96**
Primary industry	**0.040**	**0.040**	**0.99**
Secondary industry	**3.226**	**3.549**	**0.91**
Mining	0.201	0.195	1.03
Manufacturing	2.900	3.194	0.91
Automobile manufacturing	1.572	1.646	0.96
Ferrous metal smelting and rolling	0.211	0.292	0.72
Non-ferrous metal smelting and rolling	0.191	0.149	1.28
Chemical raw material and products manufacturing	0.153	0.164	0.94
General-purpose equipment manufacturing	0.117	0.203	0.57
Rubber and plastic products	0.099	0.106	0.94
Petroleum processing, coking and nuclear fuel processing	0.088	0.093	0.94
Manufacturing of computers, telecommunications and other electronic equipment	0.076	0.065	1.17
Metal products	0.062	0.062	1.01
Electric machinery and equipment manufacturing	0.057	0.092	0.61
Textile	0.034	0.027	1.28
Leather, coat and feather products and shoemaking	0.017	0.027	0.63
Production and supply of power, thermal power, gas and water	0.117	0.157	0.74
Construction	0.008	0.002	3.23
Tertiary industry	**0.529**	**0.375**	**1.41**
Wholesale and retail trade	0.125	0.084	1.49
Transportation, storage & warehousing and postal services	0.120	0.092	1.31
Hotels and catering services	0.020	0.024	0.85
Information transmission, software and information technology services	0.010	0.016	0.64
Finance	0.090	0.047	1.92
Real estate	0.016	0.010	1.52
Leasing and business services	0.067	0.038	1.75
Scientific research and technology services	0.047	0.032	1.46
Services other than the above	0.033	0.031	1.06

Note: The ratio of 2012 to 2007 was calculated using the original data before retaining three decimal places, so the result will be slightly different from that of directly dividing the data in the table.

The results show that in 2012, the sum of total demand per unit of final use for the output of various sectors in the automotive industry was 3.795 units, which was lower than the level of 3.964 units in 2007.

Analyzed by industry, the total demand for the output of the primary industry in 2012 was 0.04 units per unit of final use the automotive industry, which was basically the same as in 2007; the total demand for the output of the secondary industry was 3.226 units, which was lower than that in 2007; and the total demand for the output of the tertiary industry was 0.529 units, which was 1.41 times as much as that in 2007, showing a clear rise.

Within the secondary industry, the main related industries of the automotive industry (except for itself) include raw materials industries such as steel, non-ferrous, chemical, rubber, and plastic products; energy industries such as power and petroleum processing; equipment manufacturing industries such as general-purpose equipment, electronics, metal products, electric machinery; and light industries such as textiles and leather. **The decline of the total demand for the output of the secondary industry per unit of final use in the automotive industry is partly due to the reduction of energy consumption in the automobile production process** (the total demand for the output of electric power, gas, and water per unit of final use in the automotive industry decreased from 0.157 units in 2007 to 0.117 units in 2012). From the perspective of the role that the final use of each unit in the automotive industry plays in driving the output of various sectors in the secondary industry, there are also several noteworthy trends: **First, the cost structure of basic raw materials for the automotive industry has changed.** In 2007 and 2012, the automotive industry (except for itself) had the highest total demand in the iron and steel industry, but its leading position was no longer obvious in 2012 (from 0.292 units to 0.211 units); and the total demand for output of the non-ferrous metal industry for each unit of the final use of the automotive industry was rapidly catching up, which was 1.28 times as much as that of 2007, and had reached 90% of the steel industry in 2012, reflecting the increasingly widespread use of light materials in automobile manufacturing. **Second, the demand of the automotive industry for the output of high-tech industry such as electronic communications is expanding.** In 2012, the total demand per unit of the automotive industry for the output of computer, communication, and other electronic equipment manufacturing was 1.17 times as much as that in 2007. From the perspective of subdivided industries, the total demand for the output of the electronic components sector was 1.22 times as much as in 2007, and that for the audio-visual equipment industry was 1.3 times as much. **Third, the demand of the automotive industry for the output of textiles and other industries of industrial consumer goods also increased rapidly.** In 2012, the total demand for textiles per unit of final use in the automotive industry was 1.28 times that in 2007. From the perspective of subdivided industries, the total demand of the automotive industry for main branches of the textile industry such as cotton, chemical fiber, knitting, or crochet knitting and their products in 2012 was more than 1.5 times as much as that in 2007, reflecting the rising demand for the output of interior decoration products.

In the tertiary industry, the demand of the automotive industry for the output of the main service industries was on a rise as a whole. The final use in the automotive industry had the largest total demand per unit for the output of the wholesale and retail trade industry and the transportation, storage, and postal services industry, which in 2012 was, respectively, 1.49 times and 1.31 times as much as that in 2007. The two sectors with the fastest growth in total demand in 2012 were the financial sector (1.92 times that of 2007) and the leasing and business services sector (1.75 times that of 2007). The total demand per unit of final use in the automotive industry for the output of scientific research and technological services also increased significantly, reaching 1.46 times in 2012 as compared with 2007.

It should be pointed out that the total demand of the automotive industry for various product sectors calculated by using the total demand coefficient in the input-output table includes not only the demand of the automotive industry for domestic product sectors but also the direct or indirect import demand of the automotive industry for foreign product sectors. Therefore, in order to measure the effect of the automotive industry in stimulating the output of domestic sectors, we need to further take into account and exclude the factor of import.

2.3.2. *Contribution of the automotive industry to the national economy*

The final use[9] in the input-output table can be divided into three parts according to the nature of use: final consumption expenditure, gross capital formation, and export. Among them, the final consumption expenditure

---

[9]Refer to *Input-Output Tables of China 2012*, p. 5.

is the consumption demand, the gross capital formation is the investment demand, and the export is external demand or export demand. Based on the three final demands of the automotive industry and excluding the influence of import factors, we can calculate the effect of the automotive industry in stimulating the output and value added of domestic sectors and then obtain the effect of the final demand of the automotive industry in stimulating GDP.

2.3.2.1. *Estimation method*

The output of various domestic sectors induced by a unit of final demand (consumption demand, investment demand, or export demand) of a given product sector can be calculated in the input-output table by using the production induction formula of the final demand.

The formula for the output of domestic sectors induced by the increase of unit consumption or investment demand in sector i is as follows:

$$K_i = [I - (I - \hat{M})A]^{-1} \times (I - \hat{M})S_i$$

Wherein, A is the direct consumption coefficient matrix; S_i is the column vector whose corresponding row elements of automotive industry are 1 and the rest elements are 0; $\hat{M}$ is the import coefficient matrix, which is a diagonal matrix. m_i is the element i on the main diagonal line of matrix $\hat{M}$, is the import proportion coefficient of sector i, which indicates the proportion of import in this sector to the domestic use of the industry (total intermediate use + sum of final consumption expenditures + sum of gross capital formations).[10] The K_i resulting from the above formula is a column vector, and its element j represents the effect of an additional unit consumption (or investment) demand in sector i on stimulating the output of domestic sector j (the driving force on the import is deducted through the import coefficient matrix).

Therefore, the induction formulas for the effect of a unit consumption and investment demand of the automotive industry on stimulating the output of domestic sectors are as follows:

$$K_i^C = [I - (I - \hat{M})A]^{-1} \times (I - \hat{M})S_i$$
$$K_i^I = [I - (I - \hat{M})A]^{-1} \times (I - \hat{M})S_i$$

---

[10]The implicit assumption of the matrix calculation is that the import ratio of the automotive industry to each product sector is equal to the import ratio of the product sector itself.

The formula for the output of domestic sectors induced by the increase of unit export in sector i is as follows:

$$K_i = [I - (I - \hat{M})A]^{-1} \times E_i$$

Wherein E_i indicates a column vector whose row-i element is 1 and all other elements are 0. The K_i resulted from the above formula is a column vector, and its element j indicates the effect of an additional unit of export in sector j on the output of domestic sector j.[11]

Therefore, the formula calculating the effect of unit export in the automotive industry on the output of domestic sectors is as follows:

$$K_i^E = [I - (I - \hat{M})A]^{-1} \times E_i$$

From the perspective of final demand, the total effect of consumption, investment, and export demand of the automotive industry on the output of domestic sectors is as follows:

$$K_i^C \times \text{automobile consumption demand}$$
$$+ K_i^I \times \text{automobile investment demand}$$
$$+ K_i^E \times \text{automobile external demand}$$

After calculating the effect of the final demand of the automotive industry on stimulating the output of domestic sectors, and then multiplying the output of each sector by the corresponding value added rate of each sector, we can get the effect of the final demand of the automotive industry on stimulating the value added of domestic sectors.

2.3.2.2. *Contribution of automobile consumption demand to national economy*

By using the input-output tables of China in 2007 and 2012, respectively, the report calculates the effect of automobile consumption demand on stimulating the value added of domestic sectors in 2007 and 2012 according to the induction formula (see Table 2.5). In 2012, automobile consumption demand drove the value added of various sectors by 414.59 billion yuan in total, accounting for 0.772% of GDP. Among them, it drove the primary industry by 8.73 billion yuan, the secondary industry by 292.31 billion yuan, and the tertiary industry by 113.55 billion yuan. The proportion of value added driven by the automobile consumption demand in GDP

---

[11] The implicit assumption here is that imports will not be used directly for exports.

Table 2.5. Effect of automobile consumption demand on stimulating value added of domestic sectors

	2012		2007	
	Value (100 million yuan)	Proportion to GDP of the year (%)	Value (100 million yuan)	Proportion to GDP of the year (%)
Total	4145.9	0.772	1220.4	0.459
Primary industry	87.3	0.016	26.7	0.010
Secondary industry	2923.1	0.545	953.0	0.358
Mining	231.5	0.043	69.6	0.026
Manufacturing	2568.1	0.478	833.4	0.313
Production and supply of power, thermal power, gas and water	112.9	0.021	49.3	0.019
Construction	10.7	0.002	0.7	0.000
Tertiary industry	1135.5	0.212	240.8	0.090
Wholesale and retail trade	395.3	0.074	67.3	0.025
Transportation, storage & warehousing and postal services	185.1	0.034	53.4	0.020
Hotels and catering services	32.7	0.006	10.5	0.004
Information transmission, software and information technology services	20.5	0.004	11.2	0.004
Finance	223.0	0.042	39.7	0.015
Real estate	51.0	0.010	10.9	0.004
Leasing and business services	87.4	0.016	13.7	0.005
Scientific research and technology services	70.5	0.013	18.9	0.007
Services other than the above	69.9	0.013	15.4	0.006

in 2012 increased by 0.313 percentage points compared with that in 2007. From the perspective of major industries, the effect of automobile consumption demand on the manufacturing industry increased by 0.165 percentage points; on the wholesale and retail trade industry by 0.049 percentage points; on the financial industry by 0.027 percentage points; on the transportation, storage & warehousing, and postal services industry by 0.014 percentage points; and on the leasing and commercial services by 0.011 percentage points (see Table 2.5).

Some data of automobile consumption can confirm the above conclusion. With the upgrading of consumption demand, automobile-related consumption involves not only the cost of automobile purchases but also the consumption of travel, tourism, maintenance, and repair services in the process of using automobiles, as well as financial consumption such as automobile insurance and credit, all of which have a strong role in driving the national economy. This trend was evidenced during the period from 2007 to 2012, and became more noticeable in recent years.

From the perspective of automobile purchase, the share of automobile retail sales above the designated size to the total retail sales of all consumer goods from 2012 to 2015 were 11.5%, 12.3%, 12.7%, and 12.0%, respectively, with their growth rates being 7.3%, 10.4%, 7.7% and 5.3%, and contributing 6.2%, 10.0%, 8.5%, and 6.2%, respectively, to the growth of total retail sales of all consumer goods (see Table 2.6).

From the perspective of consumption of automobile use, by the end of 2015, the total ownership of civilian automobiles in China reached 172.28 million units, an increase of 11.5% over the end of 2014. With more families having access to automobiles, the share of expenditure on automobile-related travel and tourism in household consumption expenditure kept increasing. According to data from the National Development and Reform Commission, the apparent consumption of refined oil reached 276.16 million tonnes in 2015, and automobile fuel consumption constituted the main part of refined oil consumption. The increase in automobile travel consumption significantly promotes tourism, logistics, and other industries. According to the Blue Paper *China's Tourism Performance: Review & Forecast (2015–2016)*, China accommodated more than 4.1 billion person-times of domestic and foreign tourists in 2015, with total tourism revenue exceeding 4 trillion yuan, showing an increase of 10% and 12%, respectively compared with 2014, of which more than 50% were self-driving tourists. Consumption of automobile services such as automobile maintenance and repair has also increased rapidly. Therefore, automobile consumption plays a strong role

Table 2.6.   Contribution rate of automotive retail consumption to total retail sales of all consumer goods

Year	Automobile retail sales of enterprises above designated size (100 million yuan)	Share in total retail sales of all consumer goods (%)	Growth rate of automobile retail sales (%)	Contribution rate of automobile retail sales to the growth of total retail sales of all consumer goods (%)
2012	23,803	11.5	7.3	6.2
2013	28,885	12.3	10.4	10.0
2014	33,397	12.7	7.7	8.5
2015	36,006	12.0	5.3	6.2

in stimulating petroleum processing of the manufacturing industry, and transportation, storage & warehousing, and postal services of the tertiary industry.

From the perspective of automobile financial consumption, automobile insurance, credit, and other services all grew rapidly, confirming a bigger role played by automobile consumption in promoting the financial industry. In China, automobile insurance accounts for the largest proportion of premium income of property insurance. According to the *China Motor Insurance Market Development Report (2014)*, China became the second largest automobile insurance market in the world in 2014. The premium income of automobile insurance reached 551.6 billion yuan, a year-on-year increase of 16.84%, accounting for 73.12% of the property insurance business. At the same time, automobile credit has also developed rapidly and become an important part of automobile finance. According to the *2015 China Auto Finance Almanac*, 26.00% of the respondents used automobile consumption credit in 2013, and it rose to 28.70% in 2014, and up to 34.40% in 2015.

2.3.2.3. *Contribution of automobile investment demand to national economy*

By using the induction formula on the effect of final demand on output, we can calculate the effect of automobile investment demand on the value added of domestic sectors (see Table 2.7). In 2012, automobile investment demand boosted the value added of various sectors by 1,438.32 billion yuan in total, accounting for 2.679% of GDP. Among them, it boosted the primary industry by 30.29 billion yuan, the secondary industry by 1,014.09 billion yuan, and the tertiary industry by 393.94 billion yuan. In 2012, the proportion of automobile investment demand in GDP increased by 0.734 percentage points compared with that in 2007. Analyzed by industry, in 2012, the proportion of the effect of automobile investment demand on the manufacturing industry to GDP increased by 0.332 percentage point compared with that in 2007. Among them, the proportion of its effect on the value added of the automotive industry itself, and on industries of non-ferrous metals, chemical, rubber, and plastic products, petroleum processing, metal products, building materials, textiles, telecommunications, and electronics industries to GDP all increased, while that on the value added of steel, common purpose equipment, and electric machinery declined. In 2012, the proportion of the effect of automobile investment demand on the

Table 2.7. Driving effect of automobile investment demand on value added of domestic sectors

	2012		2007	
	Value (100 million yuan)	Proportion in GDP of the year (%)	Value (100 million yuan)	Proportion in GDP of the year (%)
Total	**14,383.2**	**2.679**	**5,173.4**	**1.945**
Primary industry	**302.9**	**0.056**	**113.1**	**0.043**
Secondary industry	**10,140.9**	**1.889**	**4,039.7**	**1.518**
Mining	803.0	0.150	294.8	0.111
Manufacturing	8,909.2	1.660	3,532.9	1.328
Automobile manufacturing	5,356.6	0.998	1,917.3	0.721
Ferrous metal smelting and rolling	594.8	0.111	324.9	0.122
Nonferrous metal smelting and rolling	432.2	0.081	129.8	0.049
General-purpose equipment manufacturing	346.9	0.065	236.0	0.089
Chemical raw material and products manufacturing	305.8	0.057	125.0	0.047
Rubber and plastic products	283.1	0.053	108.8	0.041
Petroleum processing, coking and nuclear fuel processing	214.5	0.040	80.8	0.030
Metal products	182.3	0.034	64.9	0.024
Non-metal mineral products	180.3	0.034	51.9	0.020
Comprehensive utilization of waste resources	163.1	0.030	102.1	0.038
Electric machinery and equipment manufacturing	123.1	0.023	78.2	0.029
Textiles	94.0	0.018	26.4	0.010
Computer, communication and other electronic equipment manufacturing	92.0	0.017	30.5	0.011
Production and supply of power, thermal power, gas and water	391.5	0.073	209.1	0.079
Construction	37.2	0.007	2.8	0.001

(Continued)

Table 2.7.   (*Continued*)

	2012		2007	
	Value (100 million yuan)	Proportion in GDP of the year (%)	Value (100 million yuan)	Proportion in GDP of the year (%)
Tertiary industry	**3,939.4**	**0.734**	**1,020.6**	**0.384**
Wholesale and retail trade	1371.4	0.255	285.2	0.107
Transportation, storage & warehousing and postal services	642.2	0.120	226.2	0.085
Hotels and catering services	113.3	0.021	44.3	0.017
Information transmission, software and information technology services	71.2	0.013	47.7	0.018
Finance	773.6	0.144	168.2	0.063
Real estate	177.0	0.033	46.1	0.017
Leasing and business services	303.3	0.057	57.9	0.022
Scientific research and technology services	244.7	0.046	80.0	0.030
Services other than the above	242.6	0.045	65.1	0.024

service industry to GDP increased by 0.35 percentage points compared with that in 2007 (see Table 2.7).

Since 2012, the contribution rate of gross capital formation (including GFCF and inventory changes) to GDP growth has declined, which was 54.2%, 45.9%, and 41.7% from 2013 to 2015, respectively.[12] This had something to do with the slowdown of the growth rate of investment demand for fixed assets. Comparatively speaking, as a capital-intensive and technology-intensive industry, the automotive industry still has great room and potential for investment in fixed assets. In 2015, the investment in fixed assets of the automotive industry reached 1,152.7 billion yuan, showing a year-on-year increase of 14.2%, or 4.2 percentage points higher than the growth rate of the total investment in fixed assets, and contributing 2.9% to the growth of investment in fixed assets (see Table 2.8).

---

[12] *China Statistical Abstract 2016*, p. 38.

Table 2.8. Contribution of the automotive industry investment to total investment in fixed assets

Year	Investment in fixed assets in automotive industry (100 million yuan)	Share of investment in fixed assets in the automotive society to the total investment in fixed assets (%)	Growth rate of investment in fixed assets in the automotive industry (%)	Growth rate of total investment in fixed assets (%)	Contribution rate of investment in automotive industry to the growth of total investment in fixed assets (%)
2012	8,004	2.2	32.8	20.6	3.2
2013	9,272	2.1	15.0	19.6	1.7
2014	10,099	2.0	8.3	15.7	1.1
2015	11,527	2.1	14.2	10.0	2.9

In view of the type of investment, private investment was the main form of investment in the automotive industry, accounting for more than 70% of investment in fixed assets in the industry and maintaining a double-digit rapid growth in recent years. Although the private investment in the automotive industry accounted for only 3%–4% in the total private investment in China at present, it has a good momentum of development. In the first half of 2016, private investment in the automotive industry grew by 11% as compared with a 2.8% year-on-year increase in private investment in fixed assets, reflecting the strong willingness of private investors to enter into the automotive industry under the circumstances of low investment efficiency and low investment demand in the traditional industries, especially in the industries with excess capacity (see Table 2.9).

2.3.2.4. *Contribution of automobile export demand to national economy*

By using the induction formula on the effect of final demand on output, we can calculate the effect of automobile export demand on stimulating the value added of domestic sectors (see Table 2.10). In 2012, the driving force of automobile export demand on the value added of domestic sectors was 185.27 billion yuan, accounting for 0.345% of GDP. Among them, that on the value added of the primary industry was 3.9 billion yuan; of the secondary industry, 130.62 billion yuan; and of the tertiary

Table 2.9. Value and growth rate of private investment in the automotive industry

| | Private investment in automotive industry | | Total private investment | |
Year	Value (100 million yuan)	Growth rate (%)	Value (100 million yuan)	Growth rate (%)
2012	5,550	40.2	223,982	24.8
2013	6,685	19.5	274,794	23.1
2014	7,674	14.5	321,576	18.1
2015	8,626	12.4	354,007	10.1
First Half of 2016	4,214	11.0	158,797	2.8

industry, 50.74 billion yuan. In 2012, the proportion of GDP stimulated by automobile export demand dropped by 0.128 percentage points compared with 2007, mainly due to the decline in its share in driving the industrial sector as a whole.

From the perspective of export delivery value of the automotive industry, after the outbreak of the international financial crisis, the industry's export rate (i.e. the ratio of export delivery value to sales output value) has decreased (see Table 2.11), partly because of the return of automobile manufacturing in Europe and the United States. Some European and American parent companies of joint ventures relocated parts of their automobile production to offset the impact of the economic downturn on their employment after the outbreak of the international financial crisis. In recent years, the export rate of the automotive industry has been hovering between 4% and 5%. Due to the weak recovery of the world economy, the export growth rate of the automotive industry has also declined in recent years. In 2015, with the delivery value of all industrial exports falling by 1.8% year-on-year, it is not easy for the automotive industry to maintain a 1% increase in export delivery value.

As for the comparison of import and export products, the import and export of the automotive industry mainly includes automobiles, chassis, spare parts, and so on. According to customs statistics, in the export of major automobile commodities in 2015, the export value of automobiles and chassis was US$113 billion, and that of spare parts was US$468.2 billion, while in the import of major automobile commodities, the import value of automobiles and chassis was US$448.98 billion, and that of spare parts was US$274.81 billion. It can be seen that, at present, the export of

Table 2.10. Driving effect of automobile export demand on stimulating the value added of domestic sectors

	2012		2007	
	Value (100 million yuan)	Proportion to GDP of the year (%)	Value (100 million yuan)	Proportion to GDP of the year (%)
Total	**1,852.7**	**0.345**	**1,258.2**	**0.473**
Primary industries	**39.0**	**0.007**	**27.5**	**0.010**
Secondary industry	**1,306.2**	**0.243**	**982.5**	**0.369**
Mining	103.4	0.019	71.7	0.027
Manufacturing	1,147.6	0.214	859.2	0.323
Production and supply of power, thermal power, gas and water	50.4	0.009	50.9	0.019
Construction	4.8	0.001	0.7	0.000
Tertiary industry	**507.4**	**0.095**	**248.2**	**0.093**
Wholesale and retail trade	176.6	0.033	69.4	0.026
Transportation, storage & warehousing and postal services	82.7	0.015	55.0	0.021
Hotels and catering services	14.6	0.003	10.8	0.004
Information transmission, software and information technology services	9.2	0.002	11.6	0.004
Finance	99.6	0.019	40.9	0.015
Real estate	22.8	0.004	11.2	0.004
Leasing and business services	39.1	0.007	14.1	0.005
Scientific research and technology services	31.5	0.006	19.5	0.007
Services other than the above	31.3	0.006	15.8	0.006

automobile products in China is still dominated by automobile spare parts, with exports exceeding imports; and the imported products are mainly assembled vehicles and chassis, with imports larger than exports. The above data show that China's automobile export value is relatively low, and the export of assembled vehicles is still in its infancy.

Table 2.11. Driving effect of export in the automotive industry in stimulating export of industrial products

Year	Export delivery value of automotive industry (100 million yuan)	Export rate of automotive industry (%)	Growth rate of export delivery value in automotive industry (%)	Growth rate of industrial export delivery value of all enterprises above designated size (%)
2002	214.8	3.7	38.1	23.4
2003	302.6	3.7	31.3	30.7
2004	462.1	4.7	46.1	32.6
2005	738.3	6.7	50.9	26.1
2006	1,111.8	7.6	40.4	22.9
2007	1,572.5	8.1	41.6	21.5
2008	1,802.2	8.0	13.3	10.8
2009	1,365.8	4.7	−24.0	−10.1
2010	1,950.7	4.9	42.9	25.4
2011	2,432.5	5.3	28.6	16.6
2012	2,723.7	5.5	11.1	7.1
2013	2,948.8	5.0	7.4	5.0
2014	3,007.8	4.6	9.0	6.4
2015	3,062.2	4.4	1.0	−1.8

Table 2.12. Distribution of export destination of assembled vehicles

	Export volume (10,000 units)						Growth rate in 2015 (%)	Proportion in 2015 (%)
	2010	2011	2012	2013	2014	2015		
Asia	21.5	25.2	34.0	26.4	37.6	37.9	1	50
South America	11.6	26.9	23.1	27.4	22.2	19.3	−13	26
Africa	12.6	17.0	25.9	22.7	23.0	12.0	−48	16
Europe	7.4	12.9	14.9	14.3	9.4	3.1	−67	4
North America	2.4	1.4	2.1	2.8	1.8	2.6	46	3
Oceania	1.1	1.7	1.6	1.1	0.8	0.7	19	1

Exports, despite their small share, have a very important position. From the perspective of export destinations, Chinese automobiles are still mainly exported to Asian countries (see Table 2.12), accounting for about 50%, many of which are along the Belt and Road. Taking Chang'an Automobile as an example, its overall overseas market layout is "8 + 8 + 3," including eight major markets for its passenger cars: Chile, Peru, Colombia, Paraguay, Egypt, the Gulf countries, Algeria, and Azerbaijani; eight major markets for its commercial vehicles: Algeria, Egypt, Chile, Peru, Colombia,

Paraguay, Vietnam, and Malaysia; and three major bases: Russia, Iran, and India. About 80% of these markets are along the "Belt and Road." With its own advantages, self-owned brands have gradually entered the international automotive market. In addition to price advantages, they also benefit from the complete industrial system, the integrity of the automotive parts industry, the convenience of allocation and production, and the corresponding low transaction costs.

2.3.2.5. *Driving effect of final demand of the automotive industry on GDP*

Calculated by the production inducement formula of final demand, in the final demand of the automotive industry in 2012, the consumption demand stimulated the value added of domestic sectors by 414.59 billion yuan, investment demand by 1,438.32 billion yuan, and export demand by 185.27 billion yuan. In 2012, the final demand of the automotive industry stimulated the value added of domestic sectors by 2,038.18 billion yuan in total, accounting for 3.8% of GDP in that year. Compared with 2007, the proportion of the drive of automobile final demand to GDP rose by 0.9 percentage points in 2012. Among them, the drive of consumption demand increased by 0.3 percentage points, that of investment demand increased by 0.8 percentage points and that of export demand decreased by 0.2 percentage points (see Table 2.13).

Table 2.13. Driving effect of final demand of the automotive industry on GDP

	2012		2007	
	Value added of domestic sectors driven by automotive industry (100 million yuan)	Proportion to GDP in that year (%)	Value added of domestic sectors driven by automotive industry (100 million yuan)	Proportion to GDP in that year (%)
Total driving effect	20,381.8	3.8	7,652.1	2.9
Consumer demand	4,145.9	0.8	1,220.4	0.5
Investment demand	14,383.2	2.7	5,173.4	1.9
External demand	1,852.7	0.3	1,258.2	0.5

2.3.2.6. *Driving effect of final demand of automotive industry on GDP growth*

According to the production inducement formula of final demand, the report calculates the effect of three major demands of the automotive industry on the value added of domestic sectors in 2012 and 2007, respectively. The difference between the two is the increment of value added of domestic sectors driven by the automotive industry (1,272.97 billion yuan), and the GDP at current prices in 2012 was increased by 4.7% compared with that in 2007, which is the contribution rate of the three major demands of the automotive industry to the nominal growth of GDP from 2007 to 2012. Among them, the automobile consumption demand contributed 1.1% to nominal GDP growth, the investment demand contributed 3.4% to nominal GDP growth, and the export demand contributed 0.2% to nominal GDP growth. Based on the nominal growth of retail sales of automobile consumer goods, the nominal growth of fixed asset investment in the automotive industry and the nominal growth of export delivery value of the automotive industry in 2013, 2014, and 2015, we can calculate the consumption demand, investment demand, and export demand increment of the automotive industry. Specific methods are as follows: calculating the increment of automobile consumption demand by using the ratio of final consumption expenditure to the growth of retail sales of consumer goods and the growth rate of retail sales of automobile consumer goods; calculating the increment of automobile investment demand by using the ratio of the growth of gross capital formation to the growth of the total investment in fixed assets and the growth rate of investment in fixed assets of the automotive industry; and calculating the increment of automobile export demand by using the growth rate of automobile export delivery value. On this basis, the calculation of the ratio of the increment of value added driven by the three major demands of the automotive industry to the increment of GDP at current prices in the three years will result in the contribution rates of the automobile industry to the nominal growth of GDP in 2013, 2014, and 2015, which were 3.1%, 2.2%, and 2.3%, respectively (see Table 2.14).

2.3.3. *Stimulation of automotive industry to the national economy: Room for expansion*

The above calculation of the national economy stimulated by the automotive industry involves two dimensions: the total demand of the final use in the automotive industry for the output of various sectors (i.e. the total

Table 2.14. Rate of contribution of three major demands of the automotive industry to GDP growth

		Increment in 2012 over 2007	Year-on-year growth in 2013	Year-on-year growth in 2014	Year-on-year growth in 2015
Stimulated by three demands of automotive industry	Increment of value added (100 million yuan)	12,729.7	1,634.6	1,040.8	935.2
	Contribution to GDP growth (%)	4.7	3.1	2.2	2.3
Stimulated by automobile consumption demand	Increment of value added (100 million yuan)	2,925.5	354.8	268.2	173.6
	Contribution to GDP growth (%)	1.1	0.7	0.6	0.4
Stimulated by automobile investment demand	Increment of value added (100 million yuan)	9,209.8	1,142.8	593.5	739.9
	Contribution to GDP growth (%)	3.4	2.1	1.2	1.8
Stimulated by automobile export demand	Increment of value added (100 million yuan)	594.5	137.1	179.1	21.7
	Contribution to GDP growth (%)	0.2	0.3	0.4	0.1

demand coefficient multiplied by the final use of the automotive industry in the same year), and the output of domestic sectors stimulated by the final use of the automotive industry (i.e. the total output of domestic sectors stimulated by consumption, investment, and export demand of the automotive industry, and it does not translate into value added). Both are output stimulated by the final use of the automotive industry, and the difference lies in that the former includes the output of foreign sectors, while the latter is only the output of domestic sectors. Therefore, by comparing these two dimensions, we can see the amount of output that meets the total demand of the automotive industry is from domestic sectors, and the remaining part comes from direct or indirect imports, which is also the room for further development of the automotive industry in the future.

It is estimated that in 2012, the proportion of domestic output stimulated by the automotive industry to its total demand was 74.3% (see Table 2.15). The remaining output is about one quarter of the total demand. In this part, if imports can be replaced with domestic output, there will be considerable room for the automotive industry to stimulate the national economy. Analyzed by sectors, further developments are envisaged in the following areas to improve the effect of the automotive industry in stimulating the national economy.

The automotive industry should not only promote its own domestic production capacity but also strengthen the domestic production capacity of the whole automotive industry chain. The automotive industry's effect on stimulating its own output accounts for 87.4% of the total demand, ranking first among all industries, which indicates a relatively high proportion of domestic production of automobiles. This is due to the long-term national emphasis on localization of automobile production. However, from the relationship between automobiles and other product sectors, we can see that the independent production capacity includes the domestic production capacity of both the automotive industry itself and the whole automotive industry chain.

In the raw material industries involved with the automotive industry, improving the output of mid- and high-end and lightweight raw materials can significantly improve the development level of industries such as iron and steel, non-ferrous, etc. In 2012, the domestic output of the iron and steel sector stimulated by the automotive industry accounted for 78.8% of the total demand, and there was room for further development of mid- and high-end steel for automobiles. In 2012, the domestic output of the non-ferrous metals sector stimulated by the automotive industry only accounted for 61.1% of the total demand. The previous analysis of the output structure ratio of the total demand of the automotive industry shows that the use of light materials such as non-ferrous metals in automobile raw materials was increasing rapidly, and the phenomenon of excess production capacity of non-ferrous metals in China was serious. If high-end, non-ferrous metal products used in automobile production can be developed well to replace the low-end

Table 2.15. Proportion of domestic output stimulated by automotive industry to its total demand in 2012

	Total demand of automotive industry for the output of various sectors (100 million yuan) (estimated based on the induction formula on the effect of final demand on output)	Driving effect of the automotive industry to the output of domestic sectors (100 million yuan) (estimated based on the final demand production induction formula)	Proportion of the driving effect on domestic output to the total demand (%) (dividing column 2 by column 1 in this table)
Total	107,620.9	79,974.1	74.3
Primary industry	**1,134.4**	**716.8**	**63.2**
Secondary industry	91,478.5	68,180.8	74.5
Mining	5,691.4	2,414.8	42.4
Manufacturing	82,258.1	63,475.0	77.2
Automobile manufacturing	44,595.0	38,970.2	87.4
Ferrous metal smelting and rolling	5,984.1	4,714.4	78.8
Nonferrous metal smelting and rolling	5,430.6	3,315.5	61.1
Chemical raw material and products manufacturing	4,352.9	2,446.0	56.2
Common purpose equipment manufacturing	3,308.3	2,300.1	69.5
Rubber and plastic products	2,813.4	2,087.1	74.2
Petroleum processing, coking and nuclear fuel processing	2,489.1	1,523.0	61.2
Metal products	1,766.0	1,303.1	73.8
Electric machinery and equipment manufacturing	1,605.0	1,021.7	63.7
Non-metal mineral products processing	1,261.9	912.8	72.3
Manufacturing of computers, telecommunications and other electronic equipment	2,163.3	734.8	34.0

(*Continued*)

Table 2.15. (*Continued*)

	Total demand of automotive industry for the output of various sectors (100 million yuan) (estimated based on the induction formula on the effect of final demand on output)	Driving effect of the automotive industry to the output of domestic sectors (100 million yuan) (estimated based on the final demand production induction formula)	Proportion of the driving effect on domestic output to the total demand (%) (dividing column 2 by column 1 in this table)
Textile	968.9	705.1	72.8
Production and supply of power, thermal power, gas and water	3,310.2	2,134.5	64.5
Construction	218.8	156.5	71.5
Tertiary industry	**15,008.1**	**11,076.5**	**73.8**
Wholesale and retail trade	3,555.1	2,814.0	79.2
Transportation, storage & warehousing and postal services	3,414.3	2,478.2	72.6
Hotels and catering services	568.5	391.6	68.9
Information transmission, software and information technology services	286.8	197.2	68.8
Finance	2,566.5	1,819.0	70.9
Real estate	452.0	336.4	74.4
Leasing and business services	1,903.4	1,324.1	69.6
Scientific research and technology services	1,327.3	1,023.8	77.1
Services other than the above	934.1	692.2	74.1

production capacity that has insufficient demand, it will obviously promote the further development of China's non-ferrous metal industry.

In the equipment manufacturing and high-tech industry involved with the automotive industry, there is still considerable room of expansion for the output of high-tech products such as

electronic components. In 2012, the domestic output of general-purpose equipment, metal products, and electrical machinery stimulated by the automotive industry all accounted for less than 75% of the total demand. In particular, the domestic output of computer, communication, and other electronic equipment manufacturing sectors stimulated by the automotive industry accounted for only 33.5% of the total demand, mainly due to a relatively large import of electronic components. This shows that the automotive industry can play a bigger role in promoting China's high-tech industry.

If the automotive industry can increase the proportion of domestic output for the whole industry chain, it will also improve its driving role for energy, services, and other related industries. In 2012, the output of production and supply industry of power, thermal power, gas, and water driven by the automotive industry accounted for 64.5% of the total demand, mainly because of the impact from indirect imports (i.e. electricity and other energy consumed in the production of imported manufacturing products). The output of the tertiary industry driven by the automotive industry accounted for 73.8% of the total demand. Analyzed by industry, the output of wholesale and retail trade driven by the automotive industry accounted for 79.2% of the total demand of the automotive industry, that of transportation, storage and warehousing, and postal services, 72.6%; that of the financial industry, 70.9%; that of leasing and business services, 69.6%; and that of scientific research and technical services, 77.1%. According to the previous analysis, the automotive industry's total demand for the output of these service industries is in the process of witnessing a significant increase. If the proportion of domestic output in the whole automotive industry chain increases and the direct or indirect import of output in the service industry is translated into the output of the domestic service industry accordingly, the automotive industry will make a bigger contribution to the national economy.

2.4. Important Role of the Automotive Industry in China's Economic Transition and Upgrading and Implementation of the Manufacturing Power Strategy

The growing role of the automotive industry in economic growth, on the one hand, is a result of the rapid development of the automotive industry, and on the other hand, because of the slowdown and decline in the proportion of some industries with excess capacity in the current context of the transformation and upgrading of China's economy, and the traditional drivers being replaced by new ones, which further highlight the important role of the automotive industry.

2.4.1. *The role of the automotive industry in the replacement of economic drivers*

2.4.1.1. *Enhanced contribution of new driver to the growth of the automotive industry*

The automotive industry, as a technology-intensive industry, has continuity in technological accumulation. The automotive industries of the United States, Germany, and other Western countries have accumulated rich advanced experience and technical reserves in production, development, and design over the past 100 years. Japan, Republic of Korea, and other Asian countries, as the latecomers, also have leading advantages in cost control and branding strategy. It is not easy for China to catch up with these countries in the automotive industry, especially in the car industry. However, in recent years, SUVs and new energy vehicles have become popular among consumers. The annual output of SUVs increased from 520,000 in 2009 to 6,024,000 in 2015 (see Table 2.16), with an annual growth rate much higher than that of trucks and cars, and its share in the total output of automobiles increased from 3.8% to 24.6%. In 2015, the output of new energy vehicles reached 328,000, showing a year-on-year increase of 161.2%. New driving force is making a bigger contribution to the growth of the automotive industry and has also become a force supporting the transformation and upgrading of the whole industry and the national economy. In 2014, the expenditure on new product development of the automotive industry reached 92 billion yuan, accounting for 9.1% of the new product development expenditure of industrial enterprises above the designated size.

2.4.1.2. *Rapid progress of self-owned brands*

The product upgrading of the automotive industry provides opportunities for niche markets of fast-developing Chinese brands. As for SUVs, Chinese brands in great demand have greatly increased the share of SUVs in the passenger car market. The top five SUV brands in the Chinese automobile market in 2015, namely Harvard H6 of the Great Wall, Tiguan of SAIC Volkswagen, Refine S3 of JAC, Chery Tiggo, and Chang'an CS75, are

Table 2.16. Output of automobiles by subcategory
(10,000 units)

Year	Automobiles	By subcategory		
		Trucks	Cars	SUV
2002	325.1	109.2	109.2	—
2003	444.4	112.4	207.1	—
2004	509.1	111.6	227.6	—
2005	570.5	149.5	277.0	—
2006	727.9	179.8	386.9	—
2007	888.9	218.3	479.8	—
2008	930.6	202.7	503.8	—
2009	1379.5	308.0	748.5	52.0
2010	1826.5	391.6	957.6	96.6
2011	1841.6	324.7	1012.7	148.6
2012	1927.6	302.0	1077.0	200.0
2013	2212.9	321.5	1210.4	313.0
2014	2372.5	312.9	1248.3	419.0
2015	2450.4	272.9	1163.0	602.4

Source: China Industry Statistical Yearbook 2015, Statistical Communiqué of the People's Republic of China on the 2015 National Economic and Social Development.

all Chinese self-owned brands. With the rapid growth of SUV output and the increasing proportion of SUVs in automobiles, passenger cars of China's self-owned brands are gaining a significantly bigger share. In 2015, 8.7376 million passenger cars with Chinese brands were sold, a year-on-year increase of 15.27%, accounting for 41.32% of the total sales of passenger cars, and its share increased by 2.86 percentage points year-on-year.

Benefitting from the national policies and measures by the State Council, such as the *Decision on Accelerating the Cultivation and Development of Strategic Emerging Industries*, *Opinions on Accelerating the Development of Energy-saving and Environmental Protection Industries*, and the *Development Plan of Energy-saving and New Energy Automotive Industry* (2012–2020), new energy vehicles are also developing rapidly. In 2015, the output of new energy vehicles was 328,000 units, up 161.2% year-on-year. Self-owned brands have strengthened technological research and demonstration promotion, vigorously promoting the development of energy-efficient, low-emission, and energy-saving automobiles. At the beginning of 2016, 147 of the 1,179 cars exhibited at Auto China 2016 were new energy vehicles, of which the majority were self-owned brands. Automakers such as JAC, BYD, BAIC Motor, GAC Group, Chang'an, Geely, and others displayed several pure electric cars and SUVs. Even internet enterprises such as Letv released their electric super racing concept cars.

In terms of functional development and new function development of automobiles, Chinese brands have also made considerable progress. For example, Chang'an Automobile has reached or even surpassed the level of international famous brands in safety performance testing. It has successfully developed pilotless driving technologies such as auto-acceleration, auto-braking, auto direction control, auto-overtaking, and collision avoiding, as well as recognition of lane and speed signs, which have been validated. The success of Chinese brands indicates the great potential for the independent development of China's automobile industry.

2.4.2. *The role of the automotive industry in improving economic quality and efficiency*

The automotive industry has made key contributions in profit, taxation, employment, and labor productivity and has played an important role in improving economic quality and efficiency.

2.4.2.1. *Automotive industry ranked first in profit among all industrial sectors for three consecutive years*

In terms of profit-making, the automotive industry has become the most profitable industry in 41 industrial sectors from 2013 to 2015. Its proportion of gross profit to all industrial profit of enterprises above the designated size was 8.1%, 9.3%, and 9.6%, respectively, in the three years, with a profit margin of 8.44%, 8.99%, and 8.65%, respectively, noticeably higher than the level of 6.11%, 5.91%, and 5.76%, respectively, of all industries above the designated size. In the automotive industry, automobile manufacturing had the highest profit margin. From 2013 to 2015, automobile manufacturing had a profit margin between 9.99% and 10.76%, followed by automobile parts and accessories manufacturing, where the profit margin ranged from 6.81% to 7.39% from 2013 to 2015.

The automotive industry also topped among all industries in new profits. In 2013, its new profits ranked the second among 41 industries, accounting for 15% of the total new profits of all industries above the designated size. In 2014, its new profits ranked the first among 41 industries, accounting for 43.8% of the new profits of all industries above the designated size. In 2015, its profits increased by 1.5% despite a year-on-year decline of 2.3% in the total profits of all industries above the designated size.

From 2013 to 2015, the profits of all industrial enterprises above the designated size increased by 4.2% annually, while the profits of the automotive industry increased by 14.4%, and the average contribution rate of the automotive industry to the profit growth of all industrial enterprises above the designated size was about 25%.[13]

2.4.2.2. *Automobile-related tax revenue contributed significantly to national tax revenue*

National tax revenue can be divided by the categories of taxes into domestic value-added tax, domestic consumption tax, business tax, domestic enterprise income tax, foreign enterprise income tax, personal income tax, urban maintenance and construction tax, property tax, stamp duty, urban land-use tax, land value-added tax, vehicle purchase tax, vehicle and vessel tax, cultivated land occupation tax, deed tax, and other taxes.[14] Among them, the taxes directly related to automobiles are mainly vehicle purchase tax, and the industries directly related to automobiles are the automobile manufacturing industry and the wholesale industry of automobile and spare parts.[15] In addition, the refined oil processing industry is closely related to the use of automobiles, especially the refined oil consumption tax,[16] which mainly comes from the use of automobiles (see Table 2.17). From the perspective of tax revenue of different industries and categories in

---

[13]As the profit growth rates of all industries above the designated size and that of the automotive industry are the growth rates at the current prices, so the contribution rate of profit growth is calculated according to the current prices, which is the ratio of the new profit of the automotive industry at current prices to the new profit of industry above the designated sizeat current prices.

[14]Classification of tax categories comes from *China Taxation Yearbook*.

[15]The automobile manufacturing industry and the wholesale industry for automobile and spare parts in this section (automobile-related tax revenue contributed significantly to national tax revenue) is an industrial classification of *China Taxation Yearbook*. In order to distinguish from the automotive industry, which only includes the automobile manufacturing industry in the preceding sections, it is not called as the automotive industry in this section but as the automobile manufacturing industry, and the wholesale industry for automobile and spare parts respectively.

[16]Refined oil consumption tax refers to the consumption tax paid by consumers when they consume seven kinds of products such as gasoline, diesel oil, naphtha, solvent oil, aviation kerosene, lubricating oil, and fuel oil. Besides the oil for automobiles, it also includes oil used for other transportation equipment. However, there is no detailed tax information on different transportation equipment, and as gasoline for automobiles is the main part of refined oil consumption, so the refined oil consumption tax in this report is regarded as a part of automobile-related tax revenue.

Table 2.17. National tax revenue by category and by automobile-related industries, 2014

Tax category	National tax revenue (100 million yuan)	Automobile manufacturing industry		Wholesale industry of automobiles and parts		Refined oil processing	
		Tax revenue (100 million yuan)	Proportion to national tax revenue (%)	Tax revenue (100 million yuan)	Proportion to national tax revenue (%)	Tax revenue (100 million yuan)	Proportion to national tax revenue (%)
Total tax revenue	129,541.1	3,988.7	3.1	588.8	0.5	3,991.0	3.1
Domestic VAT	30,983.2	1,541.5	5.0	305.4	1.0	829.7	2.7
Domestic consumption tax	8,968.7	934.4	10.4	0.0	0.0	2,826.7	31.5
Business tax	17,778.9	8.3	0.0	2.5	0.0	3.3	0.0
Income tax of domestic enterprises	20,014.9	101.6	0.5	154.0	0.8	40.1	0.2
Income tax of foreign enterprises	6,426.9	907.9	14.1	22.1	0.3	8.5	0.1
Personal income tax	7,376.6	112.6	1.5	7.7	0.1	11.4	0.2
Urban maintenance and construction tax	3,641.9	141.1	3.9	13.2	0.4	183.3	5.0
Property tax	1,851.6	31.8	1.7	2.7	0.1	4.5	0.2
Stamp duty	1,542.3	21.4	1.4	6.1	0.4	5.6	0.4

(Continued)

Table 2.17. (*Continued*)

Tax category	National tax revenue (100 million yuan)	Automobile manufacturing industry		Wholesale industry of automobiles and parts		Refined oil processing	
		Tax revenue (100 million yuan)	Proportion to national tax revenue (%)	Tax revenue (100 million yuan)	Proportion to national tax revenue (%)	Tax revenue (100 million yuan)	Proportion to national tax revenue (%)
Urban land use tax	1,992.6	37.0	1.9	1.5	0.1	15.2	0.8
Land value added tax	3,914.7	15.4	0.4	0.3	0.0	0.4	0.0
Vehicle purchase tax	2,885.1	0.8	0.0	1.7	0.1	0.1	0.0
Vehicle and vessel tax	541.1	0.2	0.0	0.1	0.0	0.0	0.0
Cultivated land occupation tax	1,990.9	7.8	0.4	0.3	0.0	2.2	0.1
Deed tax	3,961.1	6.7	0.2	1.0	0.0	1.5	0.0
Other taxes	15,670.6	120.0	0.8	1.1	0.0	58.8	0.4

Note: Gray highlights in the table illustrate the automotive related taxes.
Source: China Taxation Yearbook 2015.

2014, automobile-related sources mainly include four types: (1) vehicle purchase tax, which was 288.51 billion yuan in 2014, accounting for 2.2% of the national tax revenue; (2) refined oil consumption tax, which was 282.67 billion yuan in 2014, accounting for 31.5% of the national domestic consumption tax and 2.2% of the national tax revenue; (3) tax revenue from automobile manufacturing, which totaled 398.87 billion yuan (of which 800 million yuan was the vehicle purchase tax of the automobile manufacturing industry itself), accounting for 3.1% of the national tax revenue; and (4) the total tax revenue from the wholesale of automobiles and spare parts, which was 58.88 billion yuan (of which 170 million yuan was the vehicle purchase tax of the wholesale industry of automobiles and spare parts itself), accounting for 0.5% of the national tax revenue. By deducting the duplication (i.e. vehicle purchase tax included in the automobile manufacturing industry and the wholesale industry of automobiles and parts) from the sum of tax revenue from the above-mentioned four areas, we can get the total automobile-related tax revenue, which was estimated to be 1,028.68 billion yuan (the sum of all tax revenue marked with grey shading in Table 2.17), accounting for 7.9% of the national tax revenue.

From the changes in tax revenue in these four categories over the years (Table 2.18 lists the annual automobile-related tax revenues from 2006 to 2014[17]), the vehicle purchase tax was the main source of tax revenue in 2006. In 2008, with the increase of automobile output, the total tax revenue of the automobile manufacturing industry exceeded the vehicle purchase tax and became the largest source of tax revenue. After the adjustment of the consumption tax policy of refined oil in 2009,[18] the consumption tax of refined oil increased from 37.16 billion yuan in 2008 to 202.47 billion yuan in 2009, while the relative growth of vehicle purchase tax slowed down due to preferential tax policies for small automobiles. From 2009 to 2013, the

---

[17]That is,the taxes in gray shading in Table 2.17 are classified into four categories: vehicle purchase tax, refined oil consumption tax, total tax of the automobile manufacturing industry (deducting the vehicle purchase tax), and total tax of the wholesale industry for automobile and parts (deducting the vehicle purchase tax).

[18]On January 1, 2009, the policy of refined oil consumption tax was adjusted. First, the unit tax of refined oil consumption tax was increased. The unit tax of gasoline, naphtha, solvent oil, and lubricant consumption tax was increased from 0.2 yuan per liter to 1.0 yuan per liter; the unit tax of diesel oil, aviation kerosene and fuel oil consumption tax was increased from 0.1 yuan per liter to 0.8 yuan per liter. Second, the consumption tax policy of refined oil for special purposes was adjusted.

Table 2.18. Automobile-related tax revenue, 2006–2014

(Unit: 100 million yuan)

Year	National tax revenue	Vehicle purchase tax	Refined oil consumption tax	Total tax revenue from automobile manufacturing (excluding vehicle purchase tax)	Total tax revenue from wholesale of automobiles and parts (excluding vehicle purchase tax)	Total automobile related tax revenue	Proportion to national tax revenue (%)
2006	37,637.0	687.5	298.8	548.5	47.2	1,581.9	4.2
2007	49,451.8	876.9	337.0	843.5	93.9	2,151.3	4.4
2008	57,861.8	989.9	371.6	1,203.0	159.9	2,724.3	4.7
2009	63,103.6	1,163.9	2,024.7	1,588.6	206.6	4,983.7	7.9
2010	77,394.4	1,792.6	2,403.1	2,321.5	312.4	6,829.6	8.8
2011	95,729.5	2,044.9	2,557.3	2,709.1	419.1	7,730.4	8.1
2012	110,764.0	2,228.9	2,811.0	2,970.6	361.5	8,372.0	7.6
2013	119,959.9	2,596.3	2,729.4	3,476.8	541.3	9,343.9	7.8
2014	129,541.1	2,885.1	2,826.7	3,987.9	587.1	10,286.8	7.9

Source: China Taxation Yearbook 2007–2015.

consumption tax revenue of refined oil exceeded the purchase tax revenue of automobiles. The share of tax from the wholesale industry of automobiles and its parts is relatively small, but it grew rapidly in 2013 and 2014. In general, from 2006 to 2008, the automobile-related tax revenue accounted for 4.2%–4.7% of the national tax revenue; and from 2009 to 2014, the automobile-related tax revenue accounted for 7.6%–8.8% of the national tax revenue.

2.4.2.3. *Automobile and related industries played an important role in promoting employment and improving labor productivity*

In terms of stimulating employment, the number of workers employed by the automotive industry itself reached more than 4.5 million in 2015, and the related industries at least created tens of millions of jobs. The per capita main business income of the automotive industry increased from 1.299 million yuan in 2012 to 1.562 million yuan in 2015, with an increase of 263,000 yuan in three years. Enterprises with self-owned brands not only attach importance to building their own human capital but also set up vocational and technical schools or collaborate with colleges and universities to carry out personnel training and engineer training. For example, Chang'an Automobile University and its Beijing Campus have established the Leadership Institute, the General Management Institute, the Strategic Research Institute, the Technical Institute, the Lean Manufacturing Institute, the Supply Chain Institute, the Marketing Institute, and so on, which have trained a large number of technical and managerial personnel for Chang'an Automobile. Zhejiang Geely Automobile Industrial School was appointed in 2003 by the Ministry of Education, Ministry of Transport, China Association of Automobile Manufacturers, and China Automotive Maintenance and Repair Trade Association as a school that undertakes training of scarce talents with professional skills in the automobile use and maintenance field, and awarded by the Ministry of Education the title of a state-level key secondary vocational school in 2006. As a 3A school located in Taizhou City, the school mainly trains high-quality skilled talents in automobile manufacturing, testing, sales, and maintenance for the automotive industry. Chery Automobile Vocational College, established in 2011, was invested and funded by Chery Holdings Ltd. The education and training system of self-owned brands, with a forward-looking vision in technical personnel, cultural environment, and management system, has effectively helped increase labor productivity and further improve the quality and performance of self-owned brands.

2.4.3. *The role of the automotive industry in implementing the manufacturing power strategy*

In terms of implementing the manufacturing power strategy, the R&D, innovation, and driving effect of the automotive industry, as well as the industry's role in promoting intelligent manufacturing and high-end equipment manufacturing, and the deep integration of industrialization and informatization of the automotive industry are all in line with the key directions of support as identified in *Made in China 2025*.

2.4.3.1. *R&D investment and R&D activities promoted by the automotive industry have played an important role in mid- and high-end transformation of the economy*

R&D activities and patents play important roles in the development of the automotive industry. In 2014, the full-time equivalent of R&D personnel in the automotive industry was 211,213 person-years, with 78.72 billion yuan worth of R&D expenditure and 18,840 effective invention patents. After merging with Volvo, an automotive giant, Geely developed a more open and innovative R&D model. Through the merger, Geely has acquired a series of intellectual property rights, such as the right to use Volvo's trademark, the technology of automobile chassis in the next 10 years, as well as a large number of high-tech talents and R&D experience. It has also established a few overseas innovation centers in developed countries in Europe and the United States to seek help from global wisdom to develop Chinese brands. Chang'an Automobile has established research institutes in nine locations in five countries for the independent development of its own brands in a more open environment.

In addition to its own R&D and innovation activities, the automotive industry also plays an important role in the economic transformation of parts and raw materials in the upstream as well as the tertiary industry in the downstream. For example, in the aspect of raw materials for automobiles, the development and production of Baosteel automobile sheet started in 1988, from mild steel based on low-carbon Al-killed steel to the vigorous development of Interstitial-Free steel (IF steel). Combined with the technology research based on user feedback, the technology content of the automobile sheet was further improved and gradually progressed to the production of galvanized and mid- and low-degree high-strength steel sheet. The development of the hot-dip galvanized steel sheet as the priority, and hot-dip galvanized steel sheet series, has approached or reached the level of similar products abroad. Baosteel has been engaged in automobile sheet development for decades and devoted to R&D activities at a time when the profit level of the steel industry was generally high, and when it was under a favorable situation with relatively good efficiency. However, in the current context of insufficient domestic demand, the slowdown of production growth, and higher trade barriers such as anti-dumping in the international market, Baosteel still maintains a certain profit margin, thanks to its long-term accumulation and sustained efforts in the technology development of automobile sheets.

2.4.3.2. *Automotive industry has played an important driving role in intelligent manufacturing and high-end equipment manufacturing*

Globally, the manufacturing industry is ushering in the Industry 4.0 era characterized by highly digital, networked, and intelligent manufacturing production. The initiative *Made in China 2025* proposes five major projects: (1) manufacturing innovation center, (2) consolidating foundation through industry, (3) green manufacturing, (4) intelligent manufacturing, and (5) high-end equipment manufacturing innovation, of which all are, to a certain extent, related to the automotive industry. For example, in the process of automobile production, the application of intelligent manufacturing is becoming increasingly popular. Automobile production workshops not only include many automation technology and equipment, flexible automobile production line, and engineering laboratory which can produce many kinds of products but also widely used industrial robots, such as grasping, welding, and rubber-extruding robots, which have exceeded manual handling in terms of precision and accuracy. There are nearly 400 industrial robots in a car factory with more than 3,000 employees in eastern China. Each industrial robot can replace two to three work stations. However, there are still some shortcomings in the equipment developed and manufactured independently in China. Industrial robots are still mainly imported from Germany (e.g. Kuka AG) or Japan. China's intelligent manufacturing still has much room for exploration and development in the future.

2.4.3.3. *Integration of "Internet Plus" and the automotive industry has promoted the collaborative development of secondary and tertiary industries*

In the "Internet Plus" era, automobile manufacturing will increasingly reflect the characteristics of scenarios, experience, and customization. The automotive industry will integrate with the applications of new-generation information technologies such as the Internet, big data, intelligent driving, and interactive entertainment. "Internet plus automobile" is not only a simple tool for travelling but also a mobile terminal with powerful information processing function. Users directly place orders online and select configurations and functions of automobiles and then producers provide services on demand. The source of raw materials, production process, and production progress in the plant are transparent to users. Users can follow up or even adjust their needs at any time. In this process, automotive enterprises can also accumulate big data resources of users to support decision-making in production. In the aspect of productive service industry, automotive enterprises have already brought experience service, which belongs to the tertiary industry, into their business scope. While inviting users to visit automotive enterprises and auto exhibitions, they also develop experience parks around automotive enterprises that integrate test driving experience with outdoor entertainment to attract tourists and consumers. The automotive industry is extending from manufacturing industry to service industry. It promotes the coordinated development between the secondary industry and the tertiary industry by means of information technology and the concept of transboundary integration.

2.5. Discussion on the Development Path of China's Automotive Industry Under the Strategy of Building a Manufacturer of Quality

By analyzing the history of China's automotive industry development, its important position in the national economy, its contribution to economic growth, especially its important role and potential in China's economic transformation and upgrading, we can see that the industry plays a significant role in the strategy of building a manufacturer of quality. The R&D, production, sales, and operation of the automotive industry directly or indirectly involve all sectors of the national economy, from the raw material industry, the energy industry, the equipment manufacturing industry, and other industries in the upstream to the marketing, transportation, finance, advertising, and other links in the downstream, and can play a great role in driving the national economy. Following is a preliminary discussion on the development path of China's automotive industry under the strategy of building a manufacturer of quality, taking into consideration of international experience and China's current situation.

2.5.1. *Path analysis*

From the perspective of the choice of development path, the 60-odd-year history of China's automotive industry development shows that independent development and innovation drive are both realistic needs and long-term strategic choice. According to the results of analysis based on the input-output table, the automotive industry has much room of expansion for "replacing imports by domestic production," including sectors of mid- and high-end light raw materials, equipment manufacturing, high-tech manufacturing, and relevant services. Through the observation of the current development of new driving forces, the transformation and upgrading of China's automotive industry is underway, and the new driving forces are increasing rapidly. The automotive industry will have a promising future if it grasps firmly the independent development and innovation as the main line.

2.5.1.1. *The domestic and international development of the manufacturing industry*

In the context of intensified competition in the world economy and changing international politics, the strategic position of the manufacturing industry lies more with the core equipment, key spare parts, strategic new materials and high-end manufacturing sectors, as well as transformation of S&T research and development achievements into new products. With the coordinated development of the primary, secondary, and tertiary industries, while the share of the manufacturing industry in the national economy decreases with the rapid development of the service industry, its pillar role lies more with the improvement of efficiency, quality, and technology. Under the circumstances of overcapacity, insufficient domestic demand, and slow growth of the industrial sectors, new materials, new energy, high-end equipment, intelligent manufacturing, and "Internet Plus," which represent the most advanced productive forces of the manufacturing industry, can integrate and interact with the automotive industry and promote mutual development, which more reflects the feasibility of promoting China's strategy of building a manufacturer of quality through revitalizing the automotive industry. In the new context, the promotion of the automotive industry will contribute to a balanced structure of supply and demand, the improvement of quality and efficiency, the enhancement of core competitiveness, and the cultivation of advanced technologies.

2.5.1.2. *Upgrading possibilities of one country's automobile industry*

The technological development of the automotive industry has its continuity. Ever since the invention of the automobile, the basic structure comprising the engine, chassis, and body has been retained. The development of new technology, new materials, and new functions is gradually carried out on the basis of the original development. Therefore, the manufacturing technology of automobiles represents the degree of industrial modernization. From the process of industrialization of developed countries, we can see that the vitalization of the automotive industry is an important factor contributing to a country's economic growth. During the Second Industrial Revolution, the rapid economic development of Germany and the United States was marked by the industrialization and modernization of their respective automotive industries. After World War II, Japan and the Republic of Korea became high-income countries, thanks to the rapid catching-up of their automotive industry. The economic rise of the major developed countries was not only attributed to their automotive industry but also to the transformation of their economic development mode and the improvement of their labor productivity brought about by the promotion of the automotive industry. This is because the accumulation of technical experience and talents in the automotive industry can drive the development of other sectors, thus greatly helping upgrade the technological capabilities of the overall manufacturing industry. The successful experience of Japan and the Republic of Korea in catching up with European and American countries in the automotive industry comes from the national strategy of independent development, and the strategic vision of enterprises to grasp the breakthrough point of the automotive market and to seek independent development.

A national strategy to encourage independent development and innovation based on technological accumulation can facilitate the nation to catch-up. The government of the Republic of Korea, as a leader of independent innovation investment, offers low-cost loans to large enterprise groups, establishes public technological research institutions, sets up new engineering R&D centers in universities, and encourages cooperation between universities and industrial sectors through providing tax incentives. In 1973, the Korean Government promulgated the "Economy Car" development plan, which clearly defined the goal of the relevant departments of the automotive industry to realize the localization, formulated specific products and schedules for the localization, and granted preferential treatment such as duty exemption to the import of necessary raw materials for the localization. Aiming at the development of automobile models with independent technology, the three automobile plutocrats were called by the government to compete in the development of the "Economy Car," ushering the era of independent research and design of automobiles of the Republic of Korea and gaining advantages arising from the manufacturing of small-sized, energy-saving automobiles for the country.

For an enterprise to catch up with and overtake others, the key experience is to understand the progressive characteristics of technological innovation and to grasp the breakthrough points in the details. The success case in Japan was mainly because it grasps the opportunity of the transformation of needs for economic models during the global energy crisis. After the outbreak of the global energy crisis in the 1970s, the high oil prices made it difficult for American automobiles with large engines to meet the needs of households. Japanese automobiles, with small engines, were featured as energy-saving, economical and practical, and highly cost-effective, and dominated the automotive market in the United States and Europe. The lucrative profit margin was mainly attributed to the new production system initiated by Toyota featuring just-in-time production and total quality control. The Republic of Korea's catching-up mainly relied on its development of European and American models by renovating them based on its own independent technologies. The Republic of Korea transformed and developed mature models through engineering redesign, based on European and American models, which placed more emphasis on practicality and less on decoration, to make the products more fashionable or provide more luxury at a lower cost. The Republic of Korea's automotive enterprise groups have established an efficient enterprise learning system, which does not depend on a complete set of imported product lines but introduces them in blocks and designs the product lines by themselves.

In the process of catching-up and overtaking, independent development always shows priority, without any shortcut. Only by accumulating technological experiences through independent development can we truly vitalize the automotive industry and accomplish the manufacturing power strategy.

2.5.1.3. *The independent development of the automotive industry and that of the whole industrial chain are the inevitable choice for China's automotive industry to implement the manufacturing power strategy, even the innovation-driven strategy and the "Belt and Road" initiative*

The transformation from "Made in China" to "Created by China," and from a big automotive maker to an automotive power must be achieved through the development of self-owned brands. The consumer reputation and market share of independently developed SUV and new energy vehicle brands show that China's self-owned brands also have the potential to overtake others through independent technological development. Through the establishment of product development platforms and work platforms, Chinese self-owned brands can also be competitive in terms of better quality, better performance, and advanced technology.

Innovation is the soul of the independent development of the automotive industry. It is important to strengthen the cultivation of independent innovation ability by seizing the time window of innovative talents. To become an innovative country, the first step is to cultivate a group of high-tech innovative talents, and provide appropriate posts for such talents, so as to achieve the accumulation and upgrading of high-tech production capacity, while the automotive industry can provide many technical innovation and R&D posts. At present, the age structure of China's labor force is changing. The proportion of a young labor force with strong innovation capability is at the edge of decline. Therefore, it is urgent to seize the current time window to develop innovative talents for the automotive industry.

At present, the Belt and Road countries are the main markets of China's automobile export, and some self-owned brands have invested and built factories in these countries. Although the share of export is still small, if we can gradually develop to participate in the longer automotive industry chain that is related to many other industries and promote the coordinated export of the raw materials and spare parts industries in the upstream and even the service industry in the downstream, we can widen the export channels of industrial goods and services in China.

2.5.2. *Analysis of competitiveness and its influencers*

The competitiveness of the automotive industry mainly includes manufacturing capacity, technical design capacity, equipment capacity, marketing service capacity, and so on. The manufacturing capability and the cost advantage are the traditional advantages of China's automotive industry. The marketing service capability through the use and the innovation of the mode of Internet is developing rapidly in recent years. Although the technological design capability and equipment capability are also gradually developing, to a certain extent, they are still the short board of China's automotive industry. Automotive enterprises in China are in a relatively disadvantageous position in terms of profit margin. All this shows that there are still shortcomings and some room for improvement in the current development of China's automotive industry.

First, there is a causal relationship between the dominant position of joint ventures and the insufficient R&D capability of the automotive industry. Joint ventures have played a role in a certain period. However, with the increasing demand for R&D capability in the development of the automotive industry, the mode of joint venture has increasingly shown its restrictive impacts. Due to the dependence of joint ventures on foreign technology and the lack of guidance and incentive mechanism for independent innovation, many Chinese automotive enterprises are at a lower level of processing, manufacturing, and assembly production, which has resulted in inadequate R&D and technological learning ability of the automotive industry, and hence the weak ability of development for self-owned brands.

Second, although the automobile consumption policy based on reduction and exemption of product tax can regulate demand, the top-level design of supply side is still needed in promoting the strategic objectives of automobile production and development. By analyzing the change of monthly output of automobiles, we can see that the two consumption policies based on product subsidies in 2009 and 2015 have effectively stimulated the recovery of demand and played a corresponding role in stabilizing growth, which is related to the greater price elasticity of demand of automobiles. However, if we want to enhance the development capacity of the automotive industry, we need top-level design on the supply side to encourage the development and research, especially research of basic key technology, from the level of national consideration.

Third, technology learning and catching-up mode need to follow some rules, and the successful experience of some other countries or other industries can be used as reference by China's automotive industry. Valuable lessons can be learned by China's automotive industry not only from the catching-up experiences of Japan and the Republic of Korea in the automotive industry but also from the experience of China's high-speed rail technology. Based on long-term technology accumulation and innovation practice, China's high-speed rail industry integrates the power of huge domestic market demand to increase the bargaining power for technology and product import; changes the industrial competitive structure and strength comparison; introduces a package of advanced technologies; and on this basis, digests, absorbs, and integrates innovations, so as to achieve technology catching-up and leap in a relatively short period of time. The development of China's high-speed rail industry illustrates the importance of resource integration at the national level for the whole process of technology introduction, learning, absorption, development, and innovation.[19]

2.5.3. *Policy recommendations*

The analysis of the development path and competitiveness of the automotive industry shows that it is the right policy choice to insist on independent development during opening-up, and to open up while insisting on independent development. To transform a country into a manufacturer of quality, we must strengthen top-level design and resource integration, strengthen collaborative innovation and cross-border application of technology in the automotive industry, and increase R&D investment and industrial innovation centered around user needs. Specifically, we propose the following policy recommendations.

First, in order to strengthen independent and innovation-driven development, the integrated strategy and top-level design should aim to enhance

---

[19]Wu, J. (2011). Reference and enlightenment of high-speed railway model to the development of strategic emerging industries *Fortune World*, Issue 15.

the domestic production capacity of the automotive industry and even the whole industry chain. Efforts should be made to create a high-level independent product development platform and work platform at organizational and technical levels, through resource integration and organizational coordination, to strengthen the collaboration between automotive enterprises and automotive talents, and to gather national efforts to carry out technological R&D, especially to promote research on basic key technology. We should improve not only the independent production of automotive products and the domestic capacity of raw materials and spare parts but also the independent development and manufacturing capacity of automotive technical equipment, high-end equipment, automation systems, and even industrial robots.

Second, we should pay attention to the cultivation of high-tech talents and high-tech posts so as to build an innovative team of automobile talents. At the integrated level, we should provide more incentives in the building of automobile technical talents, especially in the manufacturing, maintenance and design of high-end equipment, promote the cooperation between automotive enterprises and universities, seize the time window of innovative labor force, enhance the development of automobile talent team, and encourage more high-tech labor force to become industrial design and development talents in the automotive industry and its related industries.

Third, we should strengthen export competitiveness and industrial cooperation in the course of "going global," and explore the possibility of transition from automobile export to the coordinated export of the industrial chain. The international trade strategy should create a better trade environment for automobile export, especially the export of self-owned brands. In the implementation of the "Belt and Road" initiative, we should expand the foreign trade markets, promote the coordinated development of enterprises and industries, enhance the cooperation and complementation between the automotive industry and the upstream and downstream industries, and gradually develop the collaborative export advantages of industrial chain through increasing export competitiveness. For instance, we should strengthen the "going global" of information service by setting up overseas manufacturing chambers of commerce or trade associations, to enhance exchanges of geopolitical, financial, and legal information with enterprises in export destinations, and to provide better information and legal services to related enterprises for dealing with overseas investment disputes and business disputes.

The innovation drive requires profound accumulation, while structural optimization relies on gradual improvement. In order to accomplish the strategy of manufacturing power through revitalizing the automotive industry, we should make great efforts in promoting innovation drive and key driving forces, encouraging collaborative innovation of various industries with the technological innovation of the automotive industry in a strategic, gradual and systematic way, pushing forward the upgrading and development of the whole integrated economic system through the transformation and upgrading of the automotive industry and its related industries, in order to build a manufacturer of quality and to realize the "Chinese Dream" of great national rejuvenation.

Chapter 3

Research on the Role of Development of the High-tech Industry in Economic Growth and Employment Promotion

Zhang Zhongwen, Ye Yindan, Xu Xianchun, and Zhao Yanpeng*

Abstract

After the 2008 international financial crisis, despite the growing pressure of economic downturn and sluggish traditional industries, the new economy such as the high-tech industry has shown a good momentum. As the representative of the new industrial economy, the high-technology (high-tech) industry grew much faster than traditional manufacturing. This report provides a systematic and complete account of the impact of the development of high-tech industry on China's national economy from the perspectives of investment, production, and employment by using the theories and methods of statistics and national economic accounting. The results show that the average annual growth rate of investment in high-tech industry reached 25.17%, which has played a buffer role in restraining the excessive decline of investment in post-crisis era, and the average annual growth rate of value added at constant prices of the high-tech industry reached 19.18%, which is 9.19 percentage points higher than the average annual growth rate of GDP, and especially during the downturn of the economy, the contribution rate of high-tech industry to GDP growth reached 14.30%. Thus the high-tech industry played a clear driving role in the production and employment of other industries,

*Zhang Zhongwen is an assistant research fellow at Tsinghua China Data Center; Ye Yindan is a Ph.D. student at the Department of Business Technology and Operations, Vrije Universiteit Brussel, a postdoctoral researcher at the research institute of Bank of China and at Renmin University of China; Xu Xianchun is a Professor at Tsinghua China Data Center and at School of Economics and Management, Tsinghua University; Zhao Yanpeng is a researcher at Department of Finance of Henan Province.

especially traditional manufacturing. Promoting the rapid development of high-tech industry is of great significance to cope with the economic downturn and to change the mode of development.

After the 2008 international financial crisis, China's economy is facing greater downward pressure. After 2009, China's economic growth began to slow down, with the GDP growth rate even dropping to 6.9% in 2015. Despite the sluggish growth of traditional industries, the new economy represented by high-technology industry (high-tech industry), new energy sources, and "Internet Plus" showed a good momentum of development. In 2015, the value added of high-tech industry above the designated size (including manufacturing only[1]) increased by 10.2%, which was 4.1 percentage points higher than that of industries above the designated size. As the representative of the new industrial economy, the high-tech industry played a vital role in transforming the mode of economic development. In the context of supply-side structural reform, it is of great practical significance to study the impact of high-tech industry on the national economy.

Some scholars have discussed the relationship between high-tech industry and economic growth. Existing studies mainly adopt methods such as Grey Relational Analysis, the Cointegration Test, and the Granger Causality Test to explore the relationship between the two. The studies mainly focus on three aspects. The first aspect focuses on how the high-tech industry promotes economic growth, such as the research studies by Zhao and Fang[2] and Chen *et al.*[3] From a regional or a national perspective, the conclusions are basically that the development of the high-tech industry plays an increasingly prominent role in driving economic growth. The second aspect focuses how economic growth impacts the development of

---

[1]Because the statistics of high-tech industries (the services industry) still have problems, and the statistics of high-tech industries (the manufacturing industry) are relatively stable and reliable, the high-tech industries mentioned in this report only include the manufacturing industry.

[2]Zhao, Y., & Wei, F. (2006). Empirical analysis on the impetus function of high-tech industry development to the economic growth. *The Journal of Quantitative & Technological Economics*, Issue 6.

[3]Chen, T., Chen, S. & Shao, H. (2012). An empirical analysis of the linkage between high-tech industry and economic growth in Jilin Province. *Journal of Northeast Normal University (Philosophy and Social Sciences)*, Issue 3.

the high-tech industry, as evidenced by the research studies of Cai[4] and Li *et al.*[5] The conclusions of such research studies vary significantly due to different data, methods, and geographical scopes that are selected, and scholars have not yet reached a consensus on whether economic growth can effectively promote the development of the high-tech industry. The third aspect focuses on the interactive relationship between the high-tech industry and economic growth, such as the research studies by Chen *et al.*,[6] Zhang,[7] and Yao *et al.*[8] The conclusions of such research studies basically show a long-term stable equilibrium between the high-tech industry and economic growth.

However, up to now, the research studies on the impact of the high-tech industry on China's national economy are still neither systematic nor complete. Based on the theories and methods of statistics and national economic accounting, this report first examines the role of the high-tech industry in economic growth from the perspective of investment and production of high-tech industry and then estimates how the high-tech industry promotes the employment in various sectors of the national economy, so as to present a systematic and complete study of the impact of high-tech industry on the Chinese national economy.

3.1. The Role of Investment in High-tech Industry in National Economic Growth

3.1.1. *The concept of investment in high-tech industry*

The high-tech industry is a knowledge-intensive and technology-intensive sector. Drawing on the classification of Organisation for Economic Co-operation and Development (OECD) of high-tech industry, the National Bureau of Statistics (NBS) defines manufacturing with relatively high

---

[4]Cai, F. (2008). *Empirical Research on the Relation of High-tech Industry Development with Economic Growth: 1995–2004* (Party School of C.P.C. Jiangsu Committee).

[5]Li, H., Ren, N., Tao, M. *et al.* (2013). An empirical research on the relation between high-tech industry and economic growth. *Journal of Technical Economics & Management*, Issue 11.

[6]Chen, G., Xiao, X., Rui, X. *et al.* (2011). Co-integration study of China's high-tech industry and economic growth. *Technology Economics*, Issue 12.

[7]Zhang, H. (2013). An empirical analysis of the relationship between high-tech industry and economic growth. *Statistics & Decision*, Issue 10.

[8]Yao, S., Meng, F., Zhang, D. *et al.* (2015). Interaction between high-tech industry and economic growth: A case study of Sichuan Province. *Management World*, Issue 2.

R&D intensity (i.e. the proportion of R&D expenditure in the main business income) as the high-tech industry. In the *Catalogue of High-tech Industry Classification* published in 2002, eight categories of industries are defined as high-tech industries: nuclear fuel processing, manufacturing of electronic chemicals, pharmaceuticals, aircrafts and spacecrafts, electronic and communication equipment, computers and office equipment, medical equipment and instruments, and public software services. In the *Classification of High-tech Industries (Manufacturing Industry) (2013)*, high-tech industry includes six categories, namely: manufacturing of pharmaceuticals; manufacturing of aircrafts, spacecraft, and their equipment; manufacturing of electronic and communication equipment; manufacturing of computers and office equipment; manufacturing of medical equipment and instruments; and manufacturing of information chemicals.

Based on *the Classification of High-tech Industries (Manufacturing Industry) (2013)* and the *China Statistics Yearbook on High-tech Industry*, the manufacturing of the following products are defined as high-tech industry and analyzed in this report: pharmaceuticals, aircrafts and spacecrafts, communication equipment, radar and broadcasting equipment, household audio-visual equipment, electronic components, other electronic equipment, electronic computers, office equipment, and medical equipment and apparatus. The corresponding investment in the high-tech industry refers to the investment in fixed assets of these industries.

3.1.2. *Historical changes in the investment in high-tech industry*

With the increasing influence of science and technology in the fields of economy, culture, and society, many countries have incorporated the development of the high-tech industry into their national development programs. Since November 1986, China has launched the National High-tech Research and Development Program (863 Program for short), which has laid a foundation for the high-tech industry development in China. In the following years, the Chinese government approved the "Torch Plan," a guiding plan for the development of China's high-tech industry, and further promoted the investment and development of China's high-tech industry by issuing a series of documents, including the *Eleventh Five-Year Plan for the Development of High-tech Industry* and the *Decision of the State Council on Accelerating the Fostering and Development of Strategic Emerging Industries*.

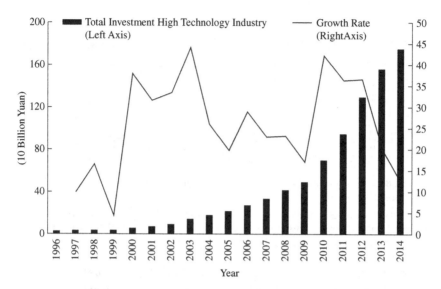

Figure 3.1. Investment and growth rate of high-tech industry, 1996–2014

Source: Data on investment in fixed assets of high-tech industry are from *China Statistics Yearbook on High-tech Industry* over the years.

In the aspect of statistics of high-tech industry, the National Bureau of Statistics began to develop standards for the high-tech industry in 2000. In 2002, it released the *Catalogue of High-tech Industry Classifications* and the *China Statistics Yearbook on High-tech Industry*. At present, the earliest investment data of high-tech industry from the *Yearbook* was only 30.66 billion yuan in 1996. After nearly 20 years of development, China's fixed investment in high-tech industry in 2014 reached 1,745.172 billion yuan (see Figure 3.1), or 60 times that of 1996, with an average annual growth rate of 25.17%.

The total investment in high-tech industry was increasing year by year. Except for the growth rate of 9.25% in 1997 and 4.25% in 1999, the growth rate in other years was over 10% but not stable. The growth rate hit the bottom at 4.25% in 1999 and reached the peak at 44.22% in 2003, and then declined to 17.00% in 2009. It rebounded to 42.24% in 2010, and then gradually declined in the following years, with a growth rate of 12.17% in 2014 (see Figure 3.2).

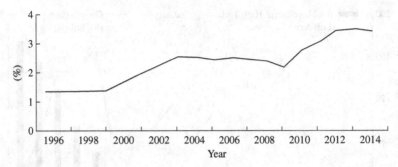

Figure 3.2.   The proportion of investment in high-tech industry to total investment in fixed assets, 1996–2014

Source: Data on investment in fixed assets of high-tech industry are from *China Statistics Yearbook on High-tech Industry* over the years, and data on total investment in fixed assets are from *China Statistical Yearbook* over the years.

3.1.3.   *Contribution of investment in high-tech industry to the growth of total investment in fixed assets*

The proportion of investment in high-tech industry to total investment in fixed assets during the past two decades can be roughly divided into four stages. In the first stage from 1996 to 1998, showing basic stability, the proportion rose slightly from 1.34% to 1.38%, with an average annual proportion of 1.36%. In the second stage from 1999 to 2003, which witnessed the first round of growth, the proportion increased from 1.37% in 1999 to 2.56% in 2003, with an average annual proportion of 1.98%. In the third stage from 2004 to 2009, showing mostly stability, the proportion declined slightly, except for a minor increase in 2006, and it was adjusted from 2.54% in 2004 to 2.17% in 2009, with an average annual proportion of 2.42%. In the fourth stage from 2010 to 2014, which witnessed a second round of growth, the proportion increased from 2.76% in 2010 to 3.49% in 2013, and slightly dropped to 3.41% in 2014, with an annual average proportion of 3.23% (see Table 3.1).

From the above analysis, we can see that the average proportion of investment in high-tech industry to the total investment in fixed assets during the four stages was 1.36%, 1.98%, 2.42%, and 3.23%, respectively, indicating that the proportion of investment in high-tech industry to the total investment in fixed assets was on the rise gradually.

The contribution rate of investment in high-tech industry to the growth of total investment in fixed assets remained stable from 1997 to 1999, with an average value of 1.41%; from 2000 to 2009, the contribution rate declined

Table 3.1. Contribution of investment in high-tech industry to the growth of total investment in fixed assets

Year	Investment in high-tech industry (100 million yuan)	Proportion to total investment in fixed assets (%)	Contribution rate to the growth of total investment in fixed assets (%)
1997	336.75	1.35	1.49
1998	391.88	1.38	1.59
1999	408.52	1.37	1.15
2000	562.95	1.71	5.04
2001	739.76	1.99	4.12
2002	986.78	2.27	3.93
2003	1423.13	2.56	3.62
2004	1790.49	2.54	2.46
2005	2144.09	2.42	1.93
2006	2761.02	2.51	2.91
2007	3388.35	2.47	2.30
2008	4169.23	2.41	2.20
2009	4882.24	2.17	1.38
2010	6944.73	2.76	7.61
2011	9468.46	3.04	4.22
2012	12932.65	3.45	5.48
2013	15557.68	3.49	3.67
2014	17451.72	3.41	2.88

Note: Contribution rate of investment in the high-tech industry to the growth of total investment in fixed assets = (investment in high-tech industry of current year − investment in high-tech industry of previous year) / (total investment in fixed assets of current year − total investment in fixed assets of previous year) × 100%.

Source: Data on investment in fixed assets of high-tech industry are from *China Statistics Yearbook on High-tech Industry* over the years, and data on total investment in fixed assets are from *China Statistical Yearbook* over the years.

from 5.04% in 2000 to 1.38% in 2009, with an average value of 2.99%; it climbed to 7.16% in 2010 and declined with fluctuations to 2.88% in 2014, with an average value of 4.77%. Although the contribution rate fluctuates, the average value of the three stages shows that the contribution rate of investment in high-tech industry to the growth of total investment in fixed assets was also on the rise. Especially after 2009, the contribution rate in this period was obviously higher than that in other periods. This was mainly due to the fact that the global financial crisis in 2008 had a great impact on China's economy, resulting in a sharp decline in the total investment in fixed assets as compared with the years before 2009.

Meanwhile, the growth rate of investment in high-tech industry during the same period increased significantly and was noticeably higher than the growth rate of total investment in fixed assets.[9] This has greatly increased the contribution rate and played a buffer role in restraining the excessive decline of investment in the post-crisis era.

3.1.4. *Contribution of investment in high-tech industry to national economic growth*

The contribution of investment in high-tech industry to national economic growth is estimated based on the contribution of gross fixed capital formation (GFCF) in expenditure-based GDP to the GDP growth.

The total investment in fixed assets is a general term of the workload of building and purchasing fixed assets and the related expenses in the form of currency in a certain period of time.[10] GFCF in expenditure-based GDP refers to the total value of fixed assets acquired by permanent resident units in a certain period of time minus the fixed assets disposed of.[11] GFCF is estimated on the basis of total investment in fixed assets through adjustments in the coverage and the overestimation of data.[12]

Referring to the method of Xu *et al.*,[13] this report uses "the proportion of GFCF in expenditure-based GDP" and "the proportion of investment in high-tech industry to total investment in fixed assets" to calculate the proportion of GFCF formed by investment in high-tech industry to expenditure-based GDP; and uses "the contribution rate of GFCF to expenditure-based GDP growth" and "the proportion of investment in high-tech industry to total investment in fixed assets" to calculate the contribution rate of investment in high-tech industry to GDP growth.

According to the results of the calculation, the proportion of GFCF formed by investment in the high-tech industry to expenditure-based GDP

---

[9]See Appendix I for the growth rate of total investment in fixed assets and the growth rate of investment in high-tech industries.

[10]See the definition of investment in fixed assets on NBS website: http://www.stats.gov.cn/tjsj/zbjs/201310/t20131029_449538.html.

[11]Xu, X. (2013). Accurate understanding of China's income, consumption and investment. *Social Sciences in China*, Issue 2.

[12]For the specific difference between the investment in fixed assets and the gross fixed capital formation in expenditure-based GDP, please see *ibid.*

[13]Xu, X., Jia, H., Li, J. *et al.* (2015). Research on the role of real estate economy in China's national economic growth. *Social Sciences in China*, Issue 1.

Table 3.2. The proportion of GFCF formed by investment in high-tech industry to GDP by the expenditure approach

(Unit: %)

Year	Proportion of investment in high-tech industry to total investment in fixed assets	Proportion of GFCF to expenditure-based GDP	Proportion of GFCF formed by investment in high-tech industry to expenditure-based GDP
1996	1.34	32.07	0.43
1997	1.35	31.39	0.42
1998	1.38	33.33	0.46
1999	1.37	32.95	0.45
2000	1.71	32.94	0.56
2001	1.99	33.80	0.67
2002	2.27	35.35	0.80
2003	2.56	38.54	0.99
2004	2.54	39.85	1.01
2005	2.42	39.53	0.95
2006	2.51	38.86	0.98
2007	2.47	38.08	0.94
2008	2.41	39.40	0.95
2009	2.17	44.14	0.96
2010	2.76	44.56	1.23
2011	3.04	44.49	1.35
2012	3.45	44.46	1.53
2013	3.49	44.60	1.55
2014	3.41	43.96	1.50

Note: Proportion of GFCF formed by investment in high-tech industry to expenditure-based GDP = proportion of investment in high-tech industry to total investment in fixed assets × proportion of GFCF to expenditure-based GDP.

Source: Data on investment in fixed assets in high-tech industry are from *China Statistics Yearbook on High-tech Industry* over the years. Data on expenditure-based GDP, GFCF, and total investment in fixed assets are from *China Statistical Yearbook* over the years.

showed a rise amid slight fluctuations. From 1996 to 2004, it rose from 0.43% in 1996 to 1.01% in 2004, with an average value of 0.64%; from 2005 to 2008, it remained stable at about 1%, with an average value of 0.96%; from 2009 to 2014, it experienced the second round of rapid growth, rising from 0.96% in 2009 to 1.55% in 2013, and slightly declined in 2014 (1.50%), with an average value of 1.35% (see Table 3.2). From the average proportion in the three stages, the proportion of GFCF formed by investment in high-tech industry to expenditure-based GDP was on the rise.

From the perspective of the contribution rate of investment in high-tech industry to GDP growth, 1997–2003 witnessed an increase, during

Table 3.3. Contribution rate of investment in high-tech industry to GDP growth

(Unit: %)

Year	Proportion of investment in high-tech industry to total investment in fixed assets	Contribution rate of GFCF to expenditure-based GDP growth	Contribution rate of investment in high-tech industry to expenditure-based GDP growth
1997	1.35	23.65	0.32
1998	1.38	54.90	0.76
1999	1.37	23.51	0.32
2000	1.71	36.22	0.62
2001	1.99	51.25	1.02
2002	2.27	55.04	1.25
2003	2.56	73.92	1.89
2004	2.54	58.86	1.50
2005	2.42	48.89	1.18
2006	2.51	43.49	1.09
2007	2.47	46.92	1.16
2008	2.41	52.48	1.27
2009	2.17	120.13	2.61
2010	2.76	67.78	1.87
2011	3.04	58.57	1.78
2012	3.45	67.38	2.33
2013	3.49	71.40	2.49
2014	3.41	48.99	1.67

Note: Contribution rate of investment in high-tech industry to expenditure-based GDP growth = proportion of investment in high-tech industry to total investment in fixed assets × contribution rate of GFCF to expenditure-based GDP growth.

Source: Data on fixed-asset investment in high-tech industry are from *China Statistics Yearbook on High-tech Industry* over the years. Data on expenditure-based GDP, GFCF and total investment in fixed assets are from *China Statistical Yearbook* over the years.

which the contribution rate rose from 0.32% in 1997 to 1.89% in 2003, with an average value of 0.88%. From 2004 to 2009, the contribution rate first declined and then increased, dropping from 1.50% in 2004 to 1.09% in 2006, and then gradually rising to 2.61% in 2009, the highest among all years, with an average of 1.47%. From 2010 to 2014, the contribution rate experienced large fluctuations, first decreasing from 1.87% in 2010 to 1.78% in 2011, then gradually increasing to 2.49% in 2013, and then decreasing to 1.67% in 2014, with an average value of 2.03%. From 1997 to 2014, the contribution rate of investment in high-tech industry to GDP growth showed an overall uptrend, averaging at 1.40% (see Table 3.3).

3.2. Contribution of Production of High-tech Industry to Economic Growth

3.2.1. *Proportion of value added of high-tech industry to GDP*

3.2.1.1. *Calculation of value added of high-tech industry*

In the years of compiling the input-output tables (2002, 2007, and 2012), the value added of high-tech industry was calculated based on the input-output tables, i.e. the value added was obtained by adding up the four components of enterprises: remuneration of employees, net taxes on production, depreciation of fixed assets, and operating surplus. Taking reference of the methods of Zhang and Gao[14] and in line with the *Classification of High-tech Industries (Manufacturing Industry)* published by NBS in 2013 and the *Industrial Classification for National Economic Activities* published by the NBS in 2011 and 2002 (GB/T4754-2011, GB/T4754-2002), we reorganize the high-tech industries in the input-output tables of 2002, 2007, and 2012 into the following 11 categories: medical and pharmaceutical products, aircraft and spacecraft, communication equipment, radar and broadcasting equipment, electronic components, household audio-visual equipment, other electronic equipment, medical equipment and apparatus, instruments, electronic computers, and cultural and office machinery (see Appendix II for corresponding items in the input-output table)

It should be noted that in the input-output tables of 2002, 2007, and 2012, the manufacturing of aircraft and spacecraft was included in the category of other transportation equipment, and medical equipment and apparatus in the category of other special equipment. Taking reference to the practice of Zhang *et al.*,[15] we took the proportion of the total output value of aircraft and spacecraft manufacturing[16] to the total output value of

---

[14]Zhang, T., & Gao, T. (2012). Fiscal and tax policy incentives, development of high-tech industry and adjustment of industrial structure. *Economic Research Journal*, Issue 5. The approach by Zhang and Gao also includes the software industry. This report only takes into account manufacturing among high-tech industries, so it does not include the software industry.

[15]Zhang, T., Liu, M., & Gao, T. (2011). Method and application of compiling input-output tables and social accounting matrix of China's high-tech industry. *Mathematics in Practice and Theory*, Issue 10.

[16]Data on the total output value of the aircraft and spacecraft manufacturing industry and the medical equipment, apparatus, and instruments manufacturing industry are from *China Statistical Yearbook*. Data on gross output value was replaced by data on

other transportation equipment manufacturing, and the proportion of the total output value of medical equipment and apparatus to the total output value of other special equipment manufacturing as weights respectively, and then separated aircraft and spacecraft, medical equipment and apparatus, and instruments from other transportation equipment and other special equipment, to get the approximate value added of aircraft and spacecraft manufacturing, and the value added of medical equipment, apparatus, and instruments manufacturing.

In the years when there are no input-output tables, the value added of high-tech industries was obtained by multiplying the gross output value of high-tech industries[17] by the rate.[18] Among them, the annual value added rate of the years when there are no input-output tables was derived from the linear extrapolation of the annual rate of value added of the two input-output years.[19]

When estimating the value added of high-tech industries at constant prices, because the specific sectors in high-tech industries are quite different, it is necessary to adjust the prices by using the corresponding producer

---

main business income since 2012, and in the years (2009–2011) in which the data of the gross output and the main business income were both available, the ratio of the gross output value to the main business income of these two industries was stable at about 1. Therefore, we used the ratio of gross output value to main business income of both industries in 2011 (0.9890 and 1.0160) and the data of main business income of both industries (232.990 billion yuan and 160.200 billion yuan) to estimate the gross output value, and the result showed that the gross output value of the aircraft and spacecraft manufacturing industry and the medical equipment, apparatus, and instruments manufacturing industry was about 230.420 billion yuan and 162.760 billion yuan, respectively.

[17]Data on gross output value of high-tech industries in 2002–2011 and data on main business of high-tech industries in 2002–2014 are all from the *China Statistics Yearbook on High-tech Industry*. Since 2012, the *Yearbook* only published the main business income, so the gross output value of high-tech industries in 2012 was from the input-output table in 2012, and the gross output value in 2013 and 2014 was obtained by multiplying the annual main business income by the average value of the ratio (1.0027) between the gross output value of high-tech industries and the main business income in 2002–2012. Because data on gross output value in 2012 came from the input-output table, the average ratio of gross output value to main business income in 2002–2012 was adopted here.

[18]Because the industrial classification in the prolonged input-output table is different from the classification of high-tech industries in this report, the error of approximate estimation is large, so the data in the prolonged input-output table was not used to estimate the value added of high-tech industries in corresponding years.

[19]Value-added rates of high-tech industries estimated by input-output tables in 2002, 2007, and 2012 were 0.2437, 0.1870, and 0.1890, respectively.

price index (PPI) of different sectors. First, we estimated the value added of each sector by multiplying the gross output value of each sector[20] by the value added rate of the high-tech industries published in *China Statistics Yearbook on High-tech Industry*. Then, we adjusted the prices by using the corresponding sector's PPI in the base year of 2000. Finally, we added the value added of each sector at constant prices to get the value added of the high-tech industries at constant price. The *China Statistics Yearbook on High-tech Industry* classified the gross output value of sectors into pharmaceuticals, aircraft and spacecraft, electronic and communication equipment, electronic computers and office equipment, medical equipment, apparatus, and instruments. Therefore, we adjusted the prices by taking the PPI of pharmaceuticals manufacturing, the PPI of transportation equipment manufacturing, communications equipment manufacturing, computer and other electronic equipment manufacturing,[21] and the PPI of instruments, cultural and office machinery manufacturing[22] on the base year of 2000 accordingly.

3.2.1.2. *Steady rise in the share of value added of high-tech industries to the value added of manufacturing and to GDP*

Since 2002, with the continuous development of high-tech industries, their value added increased rapidly, from 367.959 billion yuan in 2002 to 2,424.539 billion yuan in 2014. In terms of comparable prices, the value added at constant price in 2014 was about 8.21 times that in 2002, i.e. the annual average growth rate was 19.18%, which was 9.19 percentage points higher than the 9.99% average annual growth rate of GDP during

---

[20]In 2012, 2013, and 2014, there were only main business income data for each sector. The gross output value was estimated by multiplying the main business income of each sector by the average value of the ratio of gross output value to main business income of each sector from 2002 to 2011. Because the classification coverage of high-tech industries here is different from that of the input-output table in 2012, if the gross output value of each sector in 2012 was estimated with the input-output table, the error of estimation would be large, so it was also estimated with the ratio of gross output value to main business income as in 2013 and 2014.

[21]Price adjustments were made to the manufacturing of electronic and communication equipment and the manufacturing of electronic computers and office equipment.

[22]Of the value added of the medical equipment and instrument manufacturing industry, the value added of instrument manufacturing is much higher than that of the medical equipment manufacturing. Therefore, we adopted the PPI of instrument and cultural and office machinery manufacturing.

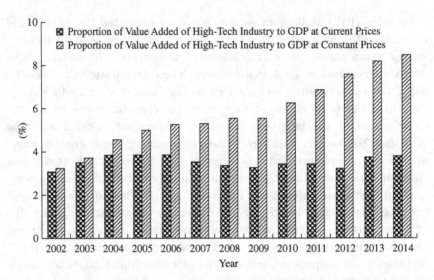

Figure 3.3. Proportion of value added of high-tech industries to GDP

Source: *China Statistical Yearbook* and *China Statistics Yearbook on High-tech Industry.*

the same period.[23] From 2002 to 2014, the proportion of value added of high-tech industries to GDP at current prices remained stable amid fluctuations (see Figure 3.3), basically within the range from 3%–4%. From 2002 to 2014, the change in the proportion of value added of high-tech industries to GDP at constant prices showed a trend of rise at the beginning and at the ending years of the period with flat years in between. Especially after 2009, the proportion of value added of high-tech industries at constant prices increased from 5.55% to 8.47%. It can be observed that in the years of relatively slow economic growth, high-tech industries played a more prominent role in the whole economy. By comparing the proportion of value added of high-tech industries at current prices with that of high-tech industries at constant prices, we can find that the proportion of value added of high-tech industries at constant prices is obviously higher than that at current prices. This is mainly because the price index of high-tech industries in the same period is much lower than that of

---

[23] In 2002, the GDP at constant price (with 2000 as the base year) was 11,787.970 billion yuan, and in 2014, the GDP at constant price (with 2000 as the base year) was 36,939.330 billion yuan.

GDP deflation index,[24] and the PPI has been falling all the time for the transportation equipment manufacturing, instruments, cultural and office machinery manufacturing, and telecommunication equipment, computer, and other electronic equipment manufacturing. In particular, the prices of telecommunication equipment, computer, and other electronic equipment manufacturing in 2014 were only 72% of that in 2000, representing a sharp decline. This also reflects the high-tech industries' characteristics of quick technology updates and declining product prices. Jorgenson *et al.*[25] drew a similar conclusion when studying the information and communication technology (ICT) industry in the United States.

The proportion of value added of high-tech industry to value added of the manufacturing industry is basically consistent with its proportion to GDP (see Figure 3.4). According to the comparable prices, the average annual growth rate of value added of the manufacturing industry in the

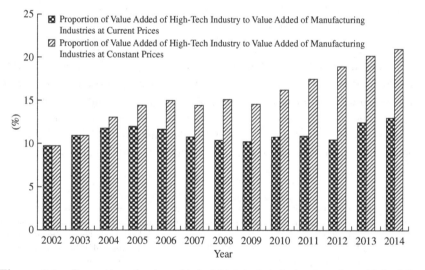

Figure 3.4. Proportion of value added of high-tech industry to value added of the manufacturing industry

Source: China Statistical Yearbook and *China Statistics Yearbook on High-tech Industry.*

---

[24]For a comparison of GDP deflation index and high-tech industry price index, see Appendix III.

[25]Jorgenson, D. W., Ho, M. S., & Stiroh, K. J. (2005). *Information Technology and the American Growth Resurgence, Productivity*, Volume 3 (Cambridge: MIT Press).

same period was 11.81%, which was 7.37 percentage points lower than that of high-tech industry. From 2002 to 2012, the proportion of the value added of high-tech industry at current prices to the value added of the manufacturing industry increased amid fluctuations, reaching 13.04% by 2014. After excluding price factors, the proportion of the value added of high-tech industry to the value added of the manufacturing industry basically stabilized at about 15% in 2005–2009, then rose rapidly during 2002–2005 and 2010–2014, and reached 21.02% in 2014, an increase of 11.24 percentage points over 2002. It can be found that in recent years, the development of the manufacturing industry encountered bottlenecks, and the high-tech industry played an increasingly important role in the manufacturing industry. (See Appendix IV and Appendix V for value added of high-tech industry, manufacturing industry,[26] and GDP[27] at current prices and constant prices and their respective proportions.)

3.2.1.3. *Rising trend in the contribution rate of high-tech industry to economic growth*

We calculated the contribution rate of the high-tech industry to the growth of the manufacturing industry and to economic growth by using the data of value added of the high-tech industry, value added of the manufacturing industry, and GDP after deducting price factors. The contribution rate of value added of high-tech industry to growth of manufacturing industry = Δ value added of high-tech industry at constant prices/Δ value added of the manufacturing industry at constant prices × 100%. The contribution

---

[26]Value added of the manufacturing industry at current prices is from the *China Statistical Yearbook*. As the value added of the manufacturing industry was not published before 2003, the 2002 and 2003 figures were estimated based on the value added of all industrial sectors of that year (4,731.07 billion yuan and 5,480.58 billion yuan, respectively) and the proportion of the value added of the manufacturing industry in the latest year (2004) to the value added of all industrial sectors (0.7956), while the value added of the manufacturing industry in 2014 was estimated based on the value added of all industrial sectors in 2014 (22,812.29 billion yuan) and proportion in 2013 (0.8147). The value-added of the manufacturing industry at constant prices was obtained based on the value added of that year adjusted by the industrial PPI in 2000 (obtained from *China Statistical Yearbook*) as the base year.

[27]GDP data at current prices are from *China Statistical Yearbook*. Through the relationship between GDP figures in the two base years, we adjusted the GDP data at constant prices of 2010 and 2005 as the base years published by NBS to data with 2000 as the base year.

rate of value added of high-tech industry to economic growth = Δ value added of high-tech industry at constant price/Δ GDP at constant price × 100%. The results showed that, on the whole, the contribution rate of the high-tech industry to manufacturing growth and economic growth is on the rise. During the period of rapid economic growth, the contribution rate of the high-tech industry to the manufacturing industry and the whole economy is relatively low, but during the period of slow economic growth, the contribution rate of the high-tech industry rises rapidly. From 2006 to 2009, the average contribution rate of the high-tech industry to the manufacturing industry and to the overall economic growth was 15.56% and 6.66%, respectively. From 2010 to 2014, however, the average contribution rate of high-tech industry to manufacturing growth reached 31.87%, and the average contribution rate of high-tech industry to economic growth reached 14.30% (see Figure 3.5). Both figures were double those during the period from 2006 to 2009. It can be seen that in recent years, with its rapid development, the high-tech industry has become an important engine for the growth of the manufacturing industry and played an increasingly important role in promoting economic growth.

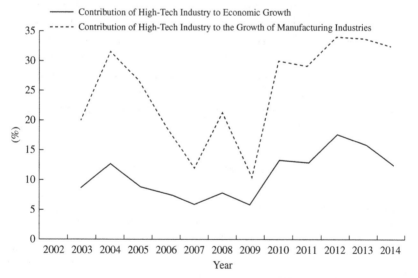

Figure 3.5. Contribution of high-tech industry to manufacturing growth and economic growth

Source: China Statistical Yearbook and China Statistics Yearbook on High-tech Industry.

3.2.2. *The driving effect of high-tech industry on other industries*

Using the above-mentioned method, we rearranged the input-output tables with 139 sectors in 2012, merged the high-tech activities of these sectors into high-tech industry as a whole, and rearranged and merged other industries with high-tech activities excluded. With the adjusted input-output table for 2012, we built the following model to calculate the output of other industries induced by the final demand of high-tech industry: $\Delta X = [I - (I - \dot{M})A]^{-1}(I - \dot{M})\Delta F$, wherein ΔX is the column vector of the change of total output of each sector, I is the unit matrix, A is the direct consumption coefficient matrix, $\dot{M}$ is the matrix formed through diagonalization of $(M_1, M_2, \ldots, M_n)^T$, which is the coefficient vector of the proportion of import volume of each sector to the domestic demand.[28] ΔF is the column vector for the change of final demand (consumption, investment, and export).[29] By multiplying the column vector of total output change by the corresponding rate of value added[30] of each sector, we can know the influence of high-tech industry on the value added of each sector.

Total output of all industries[31] driven by per unit of final demand of high-tech industry is 1.76 units. Although it is lower than that by traditional manufacturing, which is 2.69, the calculation shows that the proportion of the output of all industries driven by high-tech industry to the output of high-tech industry driven by itself is 1.89, while the proportion of the output of all industries driven by traditional manufacturing to the output of traditional manufacturing driven by itself is only 1.37. This means that the high-tech industry plays an evident role in driving other industries. By industry, the high-tech industry has a major role in driving

---

[28] Domestic demand = intermediate use + final use − export value.

[29] This report does not distinguish between domestic final demand and export. In the formula of output of each sector stimulated by export in the input-output table in 2012, it is assumed that export was entirely from domestic production. This report assumes that domestic production of export and domestic final demand was the same as that of import. Because most of China's export trade was processing trade, the domestic value-added rate is not high. Therefore, the hypothesis of this report was close to the reality, and the result in this report is the lower limit of stimulation effect. This report also calculates the export stimulation effect by using the formula in the input-output table of 2012. Readers may request it by emailing to the author at: yeyindan@163.com.

[30] From the input-output table of 2012.

[31] It refers to the output of other industries driven by one unit of the final demand of high-tech industry.

traditional manufacturing, and the output driven by per unit of final demand is 0.45, while traditional manufacturing has limited role in driving high-tech industry. Similar to traditional manufacturing, the high-tech industry can effectively drive the primary industry, and the other industries including wholesale and retail, finance, transportation, and storage and postal services, but traditional manufacturing plays a significantly bigger role in driving basic industries, such as mining, compared to the high-tech industry. The high-tech industry has little role in driving leasing and business services, scientific research and technology services.

As for the driving effect on value added, the value added of all industries driven by the final demand of high-tech industry in 2012 totaled 2,479.159 billion yuan, accounting for 4.59% of GDP at current prices; the value added of all industries driven by traditional manufacturing totaled 16,245.988 billion yuan, accounting for 30.07% of GDP at current prices (see Table 3.4). Because the size of the high-tech industry itself could not be compared with that of the traditional manufacturing, the proportion of value added driven by high-tech industry was significantly lower than that by traditional manufacturing. However, the share of the value added of high-tech industry at current prices to GDP in China in 2014 was only 3.81%, while in 2009, this figure in the United States already reached 8.57% and that in Japan was as high as 13.86%.[32] This shows that China's high-tech industry has a great potential for development but also indicates that during the downturn of traditional manufacturing, the rapid-growing high-tech industry with a strong driving role will make critical contribution to the economic growth.

3.3. The Role of High-tech Industry in Promoting Employment

3.3.1. *Compilation of non-competitive input-output tables*

In order to measure the role of the high-tech industry in promoting employment, this report built a non-competitive input-output table for quantitative analysis by referring to the method by the research team "Analysis and Application of China's Input-output Table of 2007."[33] Starting from the competitive input-output table of 2012 as the basis, we used

---

[32]Data are from the OECD Economic Survey (2013).

[33]Research group on "Analysis and Application of China 2007 Input-Output Table": Input-Output Analysis of the Impact of International Financial Crisis on Employment, *Statistical Research*, Issue 4, 2011.

Table 3.4. Output and value added of major industries of national economy driven by high-tech industry and by traditional manufacturing, 2012

Industrial classification	High-tech industry			Traditional manufacturing industries		
	Output driven by per unit of final demand	Value added in 2012 (100 million yuan)	Proportion of value added (%)	Output driven by per unit of final demand	Value added in 2012 (100 million yuan)	Proportion of value added (%)
Farming, forestry, animal husbandry and fishery	0.06	1977.68	3.78	0.14	17253.14	32.95
Mining	0.03	893.33	3.40	0.13	14222.26	54.17
High-tech industry	0.93	9484.15	54.40	0.03	1318.10	7.56
Traditional manufacturing	0.45	5002.98	3.35	1.97	88122.92	58.93
Production and supply of electricity, heating, gas and water	0.04	570.56	4.07	0.10	5568.99	39.74
Construction	0.00	56.46	0.15	0.01	317.97	0.87
Wholesale and retail trade	0.06	2215.05	4.44	0.07	11148.34	22.37
Communications and transportation, storage, post and telecommunication services	0.04	867.26	3.78	0.07	5967.36	26.02
Hotel and catering services	0.01	245.85	2.58	0.01	1196.25	12.54
Information transmission, software and information technology services	0.01	212.54	1.80	0.01	758.49	6.43

Table 3.4. (*Continued*)

Industrial classification	High-tech industry			Traditional manufacturing industries		
	Output driven by per unit of final demand	Value added driven in 2012 (100 million yuan)	Proportion of value added (%)	Output driven by per unit of final demand	Value added driven in 2012 (100 million yuan)	Proportion of value added (%)
Finance	0.05	1554.66	4.41	0.07	8588.82	24.41
Real estate	0.01	327.52	1.05	0.01	1688.09	5.40
Leasing and business services	0.03	600.12	5.35	0.04	2675.12	23.85
Scientific research and technology services	0.02	440.09	4.80	0.02	1593.31	17.36
Water conservancy, environment and public facilities management	0.00	25.89	1.01	0.00	233.56	9.14
Household service, repair and other services	0.01	178.68	2.20	0.01	1095.73	13.43
Education	0.00	28.76	0.18	0.00	159.22	0.99
Health and social work	0.00	6.43	0.08	0.00	46.59	0.52
Culture, sports and entertainment	0.00	59.09	1.67	0.00	319.99	9.07
Public administration, social security and social organizations	0.00	44.50	0.22	0.00	185.63	0.93
Total	1.76	24791.59	4.59	2.69	162459.88	30.07

Source: The Input-Output Table (2012) and China Statistical Yearbook 2014.

Table 3.5. Non-competitive input-output table

			Intermediate use	Final use			
			$1, 2, \ldots, n$	Final consumption expenditure	Gross capital formation	Export	Total output
Intermediate input	Domestic products	$1, 2, \ldots, n$	X_{ij}^D	Y_i^D		E_i	X_i
	Imported products	$1, 2, \ldots, n$	X_{ij}^M	Y_i^M		0	M_i
Initial input	Value added		V_j				
Total input			X_j				
Appropriation of labor force			L_j				

the proportional method to separate the imports consumed in intermediate and final use. The formulas for calculating domestic intermediate input X_{ij}^D, import intermediate input X_{ij}^M, final use of domestic products Y_i^D, and final use of imported products $Y_i^{M\,34}$ in the non-competitive input-output table are as follows: $X_{ij}^D = X_{ij} - X_{ij}^M, X_{ij}^M = X_{ij}\alpha_i, Y_i^D = Y_i - Y_i^M, Y_i^M = Y_i\alpha,$ where α_i is the proportion of import volume to domestic demand, that is, $\alpha_i = \frac{M_i}{X_i - E_i + M_i}(i = 1, 2, \ldots, n)$. Based on the above formulas, we can get the non-competitive input-output table of 2012 (see Table 3.5).

We know that the row balance model of the non-competitive input-output table is as follows:

$$X^D + Y^D + E = X$$
$$X^M + Y^M = M$$

Ensuring $A^D = X^D X^{-1}, A^M = X^M A^{-1}$, the above model can be expressed as follows, where A^D is the direct consumption coefficient matrix of domestic products, and A^M is the direct consumption coefficient matrix of imported products.

$$A^D X + Y^D + E = X$$
$$A^M X + Y^M = M$$

---

[34] The final domestic use (except export column vectors) is divided into two parts: the final use of domestic products and the final use of imported products.

3.3.2. *Calculation of direct non-agricultural employment coefficient and total non-agricultural employment coefficient*

On the basis of the above non-competitive input-output table, we also added L_i (see Table 3.5) to study employment absorption and role in driving various industries. Since there is no data on the number of employees with the same coverage as the input-output table, the basic idea of estimating the number of employees in various sectors is as follows: first, employee's remuneration C_i in the input-output table is used to estimate the number of employees in various sectors according to $L_i = C_i/W_i$, where W_i is the average wages of all industries, and then the number of employees in various sectors can be obtained after certain adjustments.

Under the hypothesis of no significant difference in average wages between urban and rural employers in all industries, we chose the average wages of employees and the number of people employed at the end of 2013 in the *China Labor Statistical Yearbook 2013* to estimate the average wages in different industries. In order to study the employment absorption and driving effect of high-tech industry, we divided the manufacturing industry into high-tech industry and traditional manufacturing. In addition to these two industries, the average wages in other 18 industries can be obtained directly from the *Yearbook*. The average wage in high-tech industry is equal to the weighted average of the average wage in each sub-industry of the high-tech industry, and the average wage of traditional manufacturing industry is equal to the weighted average of the average wage of all subindustries of the manufacturing, except high-tech industry (the weight is the number of employees at the end of the year in each subindustry). It should be noted that the industrial classification in the *Yearbook* is slightly different from that in the high-tech industry.[35] Taking cultural and office machinery manufacturing as an example, we assumed that the average wage of cultural and office machinery manufacturing is equal to that of other industries in the general equipment manufacturing industry. That is to say, the average wage of employees in the general equipment manufacturing industry can be

---

[35]The cultural and office machinery manufacturing industry is included in the general equipment manufacturing industry, the medical equipment and instrument manufacturing industry is included in the special equipment manufacturing industry, and the aerospace manufacturing industry is included in the railway, ship, aerospace, and other transport equipment manufacturing industry.

used as an estimate of the average wage of those in the cultural and office machinery manufacturing industry. When estimating the number of employees, assuming that the number of employees at the end of the year is proportional to GDP,[36] the number of employees at the end of the year in the cultural and office machinery manufacturing industry can be estimated based on the ratios of the two in GDP in the input-output table of 2012 and the number of employees at the end of the year in the general equipment ·manufacturing industry in the *Yearbook*. It is the same case with the other two industries.[37]

Considering significantly different actual wage levels of urban and rural employers, we use the total number of employees[38] in the primary, secondary, and tertiary industries in 2012 as the ceiling. Within each industry, the number of employees L_i obtained above is taken as the proportional weight, and the number of employees in the primary, secondary, and tertiary industries is allocated in the respective industries, so as to get the adjusted number of employees in the industries.

On this basis, we define the direct employment coefficient vector $A_L = [\alpha_{ij}] = [L_j/X_j]$, where element a_{li} represents the number of labor force absorbed by each unit of output value in sector j. Considering that agriculture is the "reservoir" of surplus rural labor force in China and the change in the number of employees is barely affected by output,[39] the agricultural sector in the vector of direct employment coefficient is set as 0, so the direct non-agricultural employment coefficient A_L^n can be obtained. According to the idea of input-output, we know that the formula for calculating the coefficient of total non-agricultural employment $B_L^n = A_L^n (I - A^D)^{-1}$, where element b_{ij}^N represents the sum of labor force absorbed directly by the unit output value of sector j and indirectly by consuming the products of other sectors. In addition, by multiplying the elements in the vector A_L^n with those in the corresponding position of

---

[36] It is obtained by subtracting import from the total output in the input-output table.
[37] In the input-output table, the methods of separating the medical equipment and instrument manufacturing industry from the other special equipment manufacturing industry, and separating the aerospace manufacturing industry from other transportation equipment manufacturing industry have been explained in the earlier section on the calculation of value added.
[38] Data are from *China Statistical Yearbook 2013*.
[39] Agricultural output is affected by many complex factors such as climate and environment.

column j in the matrix $(I - A^D)^{-1}$, we can get the total driving effect of the unit output value of sector j on the non-agricultural employment of various industries.

3.3.3. *Driving effect of high-tech industry on employment*

The driving effect of an industry on employment is mainly determined by its own production characteristics. Regardless of the direct non-agricultural employment coefficient or the total non-agricultural employment coefficient, on the whole, different industries have noticeably varying driving effects on employment (see Figure 3.6). The output value of 100 million yuan in education, public management, and household services can create more than 1,500 jobs for different industries, whereas the output value of 100 million yuan in real estate, production, and supply of power, heat, gas, and water can only create 500 jobs. Compared with manufacturing, the service industry is more capable of promoting employment. In the manufacturing industry, the high-tech industry and traditional manufacturing have similar capabilities in promoting employment, and the output value of 100 million yuan can create about 600 jobs. This indicates that, in the process of economic transformation and upgrading, vigorous development of the high-tech industry can alleviate the employment pressure brought by reducing the excess capacity of traditional manufacturing.

Specifically, when we look at the ratio between the employment of all industries stimulated by a particular industry and the employment of this particular industry stimulated by itself, the results of calculation show that the this ratio is 2.17 for high-tech industry and is only 1.59 for traditional manufacturing, which indicates that the high-tech industry has a clear role in driving employment of other industries. In addition to increasing its own employment, the high-tech industry has a relatively clear role in driving employment of traditional manufacturing, while traditional manufacturing has very limited role in driving the employment of high-tech industry (see Table 3.6). These two industries, both of which belong to the same manufacturing industry, have similar driving effects on the employment of other sectors of the national economy, and mainly drive the employment in wholesale and retail trade, communications and transportation, storage, post and telecommunication services, finance, leasing and business services, and scientific research and technology services. The difference lies in that the traditional manufacturing can have a relatively strong role in driving

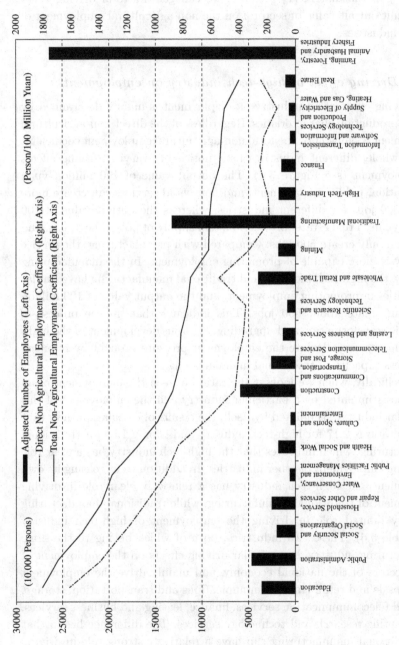

Figure 3.6. Employment in various industries, direct non-agricultural employment coefficient and total non-agricultural employment coefficient

Source: Input–Output Table 2012, *China Labor Statistics Yearbook 2013.*

Table 3.6. Employment driven by high-tech industry and traditional manufacturing

(unit: person/100 million yuan)

Industrial classification	Total non-agricultural employment coefficient of high-tech industry	Total non-agricultural employment coefficient of traditional manufacturing
Farming, forestry, animal husbandry and fishery industries	0	0
Mining	17	48
High-tech industry	275	7
Traditional manufacturing	124	386
Production and supply of electricity, heating, gas and water	8	14
Construction	3	3
Wholesale and retail trade	49	43
Communications and transportation, storage, post and telecommunication services	27	33
Hotel and catering services	18	16
Information transmission, software and information technology services	3	2
Finance	19	18
Real estate	3	3
Leasing and business services	19	15
Scientific research and technology services	12	8
Water conservancy, environment and public facilities management	2	3
Household service, repair and other services	12	13
Education	2	2
Health and social work	0	0
Culture, sports and entertainment	2	2
Public administration, social security and social organizations	3	2
Total	**596**	**615**

the employment of basic industries such as mining, production and supply of power, heating, gas, and water, while the high-tech industry does not have such an effect.

3.4. Conclusion

This report systematically examines the impact of the development of the high-tech industry on the national economy since the mid-1990s. It analyzes the role of high-tech industry in economic growth from the perspectives of investment and production and estimates the impact of the high-tech industry in promoting employment of various sectors of the national economy.

From 1996 to 2014, the investment in fixed assets of high-tech industry grew rapidly, with an average annual growth rate of 25.17%. Its share in the total investment in fixed assets also showed a rise. Especially after 2009, the growth rate of investment in high-tech industry was noticeably higher than that of total investment in fixed assets, which played a buffer role in restraining the excessive decline of investment in the post-crisis era. From 1997 to 2014, the contribution rate of investment in high-tech industry to GDP growth showed a general trend of rise, averaging 1.40%, yet with a relatively low contribution rate. The contribution rate of gross capital formation to GDP growth in 2014 was 46.9%. This also shows that, unlike the traditional manufacturing, the high-tech industry drives the economy with high-tech content which increases the efficiency, rather than relying on extensive investment.

According to data of three input-output tables from 2002 to 2012, value added of high-tech industry at current prices accounted for a relatively stable share in GDP, remaining at 3%–4%, whereas the proportion of value added of high-tech industry at constant prices to GDP at constant prices showed a rapid rise. In particular, after 2009 when the economy entered a downturn, the proportion of value added of high-tech industry at constant prices to GDP and value added of manufacturing at constant prices was 8.47% and 21.02%, respectively. On one hand, it shows that the growth rate of the high-tech industry is much higher, or 7.37 percentage points on the average, which is higher than that of traditional manufacturing. On the other hand, it shows that the prices of high-tech industry declines faster because of the high rate of technological progress. With the increase in the share of high-tech industry in the national economy, its contribution to economic growth is more prominent. From 2010 to 2014, the average contribution rate of high-tech industry to economic growth and manufacturing growth reached 14.30% and 31.87%, respectively, indicating that the high-tech industry has become an important engine for the growth of manufacturing. Using the adjusted input-output table of 2012, we find that the driving effect of high-tech industry on the national economy is prominent. Per unit of final demand in high-tech industry can drive 1.76 units of total output of all industries, which is 1.89 times the output driven by the high-tech industry itself. High-tech industry especially has an obvious role in driving traditional manufacturing, with per unit of total demand in high-tech industry driving 0.45 units of total output value of traditional manufacturing. In 2012, the proportion of value added of all industries driven by high-tech industry to GDP was 4.59%. As the size of the high-tech industry itself has great potential for development, and the industry will play an increasingly important role in promoting national economic growth in the future.

We obtained the direct non-agricultural employment coefficient and the total non-agricultural employment coefficient by making use of the competitive input-output table in 2012 to construct the non-competitive input-output table, and by including the number of employees in various industries into the input-output table. From the perspective of total non-agricultural employment coefficient, the high-tech industry and the traditional manufacturing have basically the same capability in driving employment, with every 100 million yuan worth of output value capable of creating about 600 jobs, which is less than the jobs than can be created by general service industry. The results of the calculation show that the ratio of employment in all industries driven by high-tech industry to the employment driven in high-tech industry itself is 2.17, while the same ratio for the traditional manufacturing is only 1.59. In addition to increasing its own employment, the high-tech industry plays a relatively clear role in driving traditional manufacturing. This means that in the process of economic transformation and upgrading, vigorous development of high-tech industry can alleviate the employment pressure brought by the effort in cutting excessive capacity of the traditional manufacturing industry.

With the economic development, the growth of the high-tech industry has made ever-increasing contribution to the national economic growth and can markedly drive up the production and employment of traditional manufacturing. As a technology-intensive industry, it does not need extensive investment. It is of great significance to promote the rapid development of high-tech industry, as it can help cope with the economic downturn and transformation of the development mode. However, China's high-tech industry still has a relatively low share, and the supporting high-tech services are relatively weak. Identifying the ways to direct the resources to inject the high-tech industry through further reform and open-up and by design of appropriate industrial policies is also an issue of concern.

Appendix I. Growth Rate of Total Investment in Fixed Asset and Growth Rate of Investment in High-tech Industry

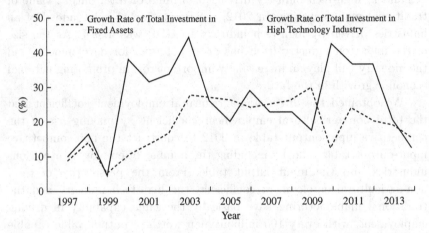

Appendix II. Comparison of High-tech Industry Categories in the Input-Output Table

Categories of high-tech industry	Items in the input-output table 2002	Items in the input-output table 2007	Items in the input-output table 2012
Pharmaceutical manufacturing	Pharmaceutical manufacturing	Pharmaceutical manufacturing	Pharmaceutical manufacturing
Aircraft and spacecraft manufacturing	Other transportation equipment manufacturing (sorting required)	Other transportation equipment manufacturing (sorting required)	Other transportation equipment manufacturing (sorting required)
Communication equipment manufacturing	Communication equipment manufacturing	Communication equipment manufacturing	Communication equipment manufacturing

(Continued)

Categories of high-tech industry	Items in the input-output table 2002	Items in the input-output table 2007	Items in the input-output table 2012
Radar and broadcasting equipment manufacturing	Other communication and electronic equipment manufacturing	Radar and broadcasting equipment manufacturing	Radio and television equipment and radar and accessory equipment manufacturing
Electronic components manufacturing	Electronic components manufacturing	Electronic components manufacturing	Electronic components manufacturing
Home audiovisual equipment manufacturing	Home audiovisual equipment manufacturing	Home audiovisual equipment manufacturing	Audiovisual equipment manufacturing
Other electronic equipment manufacturing	Other communication and electronic equipment manufacturing	Other electronic equipment manufacturing	Other electronic equipment manufacturing
Medical equipment and apparatus manufacturing	Other special equipment manufacturing (sorting required)	Other special equipment manufacturing (sorting required)	Other special equipment manufacturing (sorting required)
Instrument manufacturing	Instrument manufacturing	Instrument manufacturing	Instrument manufacturing
Electronic computer manufacturing	Complete electronic computer and other electronic computer equipment manufacturing	Electronic computer manufacturing	Computer manufacturing
Office equipment manufacturing	Cultural and office machinery manufacturing	Cultural and office machinery manufacturing	Cultural and office machinery manufacturing

Source: Basic flow tables of input-output tables in 2002, 2007, and 2012, National Economic Industry Classification (GB/T4754-2011, GB/T4754-2002), *Classification of High-tech Industries (Manufacturing Industry)*.

Appendix III. GDP Deflator Index and Price Indices of Various Categories of High-tech Industry

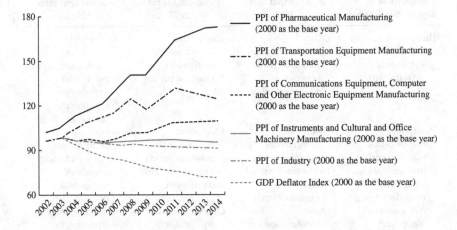

PPI of Pharmaceutical Manufacturing (2000 as the base year)

PPI of Transportation Equipment Manufacturing (2000 as the base year)

PPI of Communications Equipment, Computer and Other Electronic Equipment Manufacturing (2000 as the base year)

PPI of Instruments and Cultural and Office Machinery Manufacturing (2000 as the base year)

PPI of Industry (2000 as the base year)

GDP Deflator Index (2000 as the base year)

Appendix IV. Share of Value Added of High-tech Industry at Current Prices

Year	Value added of high-tech industry at current prices (100 million yuan)	Value added of manufacturing at current prices (100 million yuan)	GDP at current prices (100 million yuan)	Share of value added of high-tech industry at current price in value added of manufacturing at current prices (%)	Share of value added of high-tech industry in GDP at current prices (%)
2002	3679.59	37639.91	121002.00	9.78	3.04
2003	4776.32	43602.94	136564.60	10.95	3.50
2004	6137.22	51748.50	160714.40	11.86	3.82
2005	7205.78	60117.99	185895.80	11.99	3.88
2006	8329.00	71212.89	217656.60	11.70	3.83
2007	9435.54	87464.75	268019.40	10.79	3.52
2008	10697.91	102539.49	316751.70	10.43	3.38
2009	11349.12	110118.50	345629.20	10.31	3.28
2010	14061.25	130282.50	408903.00	10.79	3.44
2011	16680.67	153062.70	484123.50	10.90	3.45
2012	17431.84	165652.80	534123.00	10.52	3.26
2013	22043.16	177012.80	588018.80	12.45	3.75
2014	24245.39	185860.02	636138.70	13.04	3.81

Source: China Statistical Yearbook and *China Statistics Yearbook on High-tech Industry.*

Appendix V. Share of Value Added of High-tech Industry at Constant Prices

Year	Value added of high-tech industry at constant prices (100 million yuan)	Value added of manufacturing at constant prices (100 million yuan)	GDP at constant prices (100 million yuan)	Share of value added of high-tech industry at constant prices in value added of manufacturing at constant prices (%)	Share of value added of high-tech industry in GDP at constant prices (%)
2002	3811.99	38993.53	117879.70	9.78	3.23
2003	4836.84	44155.43	129693.70	10.95	3.73
2004	6499.62	49391.34	142763.20	13.16	4.55
2005	7923.12	54699.32	158963.90	14.48	4.98
2006	9442.51	62906.99	179129.94	15.01	5.27
2007	10887.26	74940.17	204565.42	14.53	5.32
2008	12436.17	82185.47	224246.61	15.13	5.55
2009	13584.65	93298.15	244958.22	14.56	5.55
2010	16995.43	104627.63	270995.45	16.24	6.27
2011	20291.66	115964.16	296705.30	17.50	6.84
2012	24280.63	127673.19	319692.69	19.02	7.59
2013	28134.50	139071.00	344262.17	20.23	8.17
2014	31292.21	148850.01	369393.30	21.02	8.47

Source: *China Statistical Yearbook* and *China Statistics Yearbook on High-tech Industry*.

Chapter 4

China's Investment Growth and Its Relation with Fiscal Policy*

Xu Xianchun, Wang Baobin, and Xu Xiongfei[†]

Abstract

This report expounds two indicators that reflect the development and change of investment in fixed assets in Chinese government statistics, i.e. the total investment in fixed assets and the gross fixed capital formation, as well as the relationship between them. It analyzes the performance of the growth of investment in fixed assets and the change in its contribution rate to economic growth since the reform and opening-up. It expounds how fiscal policy impacts the growth of investment in fixed assets. Through detailed statistical data, it specifically analyzes the impact of the two tightening fiscal policies, two expansionary fiscal policies, and one neutral fiscal policy on the growth of investment in fixed assets in China since the reform and opening-up. The practice indicates that fiscal policy has a direct and obvious impact on China's investment in fixed assets, but sometimes the policy effort goes too far. In the future, we should pay attention to the combination of fiscal policy and other economic policies, grasp the strength and timing of fiscal policy, and give full play to the role of fiscal policy in stabilizing the growth of investment in fixed assets.

4.1. Two Statistical Indicators of Investment in Fixed Assets and Their Comparison

In China's government statistics, there are two statistical indicators reflecting the development and changes of investment in fixed assets. They are

---

*This article was published in *Management World*, Issue 6, 2013.

[†]Xu Xianchun is a Senior Statistician of the National Bureau of Statistics (NBS) ; Wang Baobin is a Senior Statistician of the Department of Investment Statistics, NBS; and Xu Xiongfei is a Senior Statistician of the Department of National Accounts, NBS.

total investment in fixed assets in investment statistics and gross fixed capital formation (GFCF) in GDP by the expenditure approach. These two statistical indicators are different in definition, coverage, data source, calculation method and data presentation, as well as in their basic uses, so they need to be distinguished when they are used.

4.1.1. *Total investment in fixed assets in the investment statistics*

The total investment in fixed assets in investment statistics is mainly a statistical indicator designed from the perspective of demand on construction project management. It is the sum of the workload and related expenses of the fixed assets built and/or purchased by the whole society in a certain period of time in monetary form.[1] Total investment in fixed assets includes investment in construction projects of 5 million yuan or more,[2] investment in real estate development, and investment in fixed assets in rural areas. Statistics on investment in fixed assets comprehensively cover all construction projects with 5 million yuan or more, i.e. all construction projects with an investment of over 5 million yuan are to be included. Comprehensive survey is also used for the investment in real estate development, i.e. all enterprises and units engaged in real estate development and business activities are covered to collect data on investment in real estate development. Data on investment in fixed assets in rural areas are collected through sample survey, i.e. data on investment in fixed assets of selected households are collected.

Total investment in fixed assets comprises the cost of construction projects, the cost of installation projects, the purchase of equipment and instruments, and other expenses. Construction projects refer to the construction engineering of various houses and buildings; installation projects refer to the installation engineering of various equipment and

---

[1]National Bureau of Statistics (2010). *Explanation on Main Statistical Indicators of China* (China Statistics Press, Beijing).

[2]Before 2011, the threshold of a construction project to be included in investment in fixed assets statistics was 500,000 yuan. With the continuous expansion of the scale of construction projects, in order to reduce the workload of grass-roots statistical offices and to improve the quality of data, the threshold has been set at 5 million yuan since 2011.

devices, excluding the value of the installed equipment; purchase of equipment and instruments refers to the value of the equipment, tools, and instruments that are purchased or manufactured and meet the standards of fixed assets, including the purchase of used equipment; other expenses refer to the expenses that are incurred during the construction and purchase of fixed assets and should include the apportion of the cost of total investment in fixed assets other than the above-mentioned components, including purchase of land and purchase of used buildings.[3]

4.1.2. *GFCF in GDP by expenditure approach*

GFCF in GDP by the expenditure approach refers to the total value of fixed assets acquired by a resident unit within a certain period minus the fixed assets disposed of. Fixed assets are assets produced through productive activities, excluding natural assets such as land. GFCF comprises tangible GFCF and intangible GFCF. The tangible GFCF refers to the value of residential houses and non-residential buildings built; the purchase of machinery and equipment minus the disposal value; the value of land improvement; new livestock for draught, breeding, milk, wool, and recreational purposes; and new economic forest value during a certain period of time, whereas the intangible GFCF includes the value of acquisition minus the disposal of mineral exploration and computer software, etc.[4,5]

The internationally recognized indicator that comprehensively reflects the final demand is the GDP by the expenditure approach:

GDP by the expenditure approach

    = final consumption + gross capital formation

      + net export of goods and services = (household consumption

      + government consumption) + (GFCF + increase in inventory)

      + (export of goods and services − import of goods and services)

$$(4.1)$$

---

[3] National Bureau of Statistics (2012). *National Statistical Survey Program 2012.*
[4] National Bureau of Statistics (2003). *System of National Economic Account of China 2002* (China Statistics Press, Beijing).
[5] Department of National Accounts Statistics, National Bureau of Statistics (2011). *Method on Compiling Gross Domestic Product of China during the 2nd Economic Census Year.*

Therefore, the indicator that reflects the consumption demand is the final consumption in GDP by the expenditure approach, including household consumption and government consumption; the indicator that reflects the investment demand is the gross capital formation in GDP by the expenditure approach, including GFCF and the increase in inventory; the indicator that reflects the net export demand is the net export of goods and services in GDP by the expenditure approach, which is equal to the export of goods and services minus the import of goods and services. Therefore, the indicator reflecting the demand of investment in fixed capital is GFCF in GDP by the expenditure approach.

4.1.3. *Major differences between GFCF and total investment in fixed assets*

There are differences between GFCF and total investment in fixed assets in terms of coverage, data sources, calculation methods, basic uses, and data presentation. The differences in coverage mainly include the following aspects: First, total investment in fixed assets includes purchase of land and purchase of used buildings and used equipment, while GFCF does not include these cost. Second, total investment in fixed assets does not include investment in fixed assets in construction projects of less than 5 million yuan, while GFCF includes this part of investment. Third, total investment in fixed assets does not include the increment of the sales of commercial housing, i.e. the difference between the sales value and the investment cost of commercial housing, while GFCF includes this part of value. Fourth, total investment in fixed assets does not include intangible fixed capital expenditure such as mineral exploration and computer software, which is included in GFCF.

The differences between the GFCF and total investment in fixed assets in terms of data sources and calculation methods mainly lie in that total investment in fixed assets is calculated by directly utilizing data from the comprehensive survey of investment in fixed assets of construction projects of 5 million yuan or more, investment in real estate development, and data from sample survey of investment in fixed assets of rural households, while the GFCF is obtained by adjusting the total investment in fixed assets, including adjustments in the coverage and in overestimation of data. The adjustment of coverage is mainly aimed at the difference of coverage mentioned above. The adjustment of data overestimation is mainly aimed at adjusting the data of the overestimated investment in some places due to the unrealistic planning targets and performance appraisal, which leads to the overestimation of data on total investment in fixed assets.[6]

The main differences between GFCF and total investment in fixed assets in terms of basic use mainly lie in that total investment in fixed assets is basically used: (1) to serve the needs of construction project management, (2) to reflect the size and detailed structure of total investment in fixed assets, and (3) to provide basic information for the accounting of GFCF. GFCF is basically used: (1) to reflect the total demand for fixed capital investment in the final demand, (2) to calculate the proportion of fixed capital investment demand in the final demand structure, and (3) to calculate the contribution rate of fixed capital investment demand to economic growth.

The differences between GFCF and total investment in fixed assets in terms of coverage, data sources, and calculation methods will inevitably lead to the difference in data presentation between the two. As can be seen from Table 4.1, GFCF during 2009–2011 was less than 70% of total investment in fixed assets.

Figure 4.1 shows the data of GFCF and total investment in fixed assets from 1981 to 2011. As can be seen from the figure, before 2003, difference between the two was small, while after 2003, the gap between the two widened. In fact, in the 22 years from 1981 to 2002, except for the year 1988, GFCF was larger than that of the total investment in fixed assets. Since

Table 4.1. Comparison of the size of GFCF and total investment in fixed assets

Year	GFCF (100 million yuan)	Total investment in fixed assets (100 million yuan)	GFCF vs. total investment in fixed assets (%)
	(1)	(2)	(1)/(2)
2009	156680	224599	69.8
2010	183615	278122	66.0
2011	213043	311485	68.4

Source: GFCF data are from *China Statistical Yearbook 2012*, p. 62, and total investment in fixed assets data are from *China Statistical Yearbook 2012*, p. 158.

---

[6]For specific reasons and methods of adjustments in coverage and data overestimation, please refer to Xu, X. (2013). Accurate understanding of China's income, consumption and investment. *Social Sciences in China*, Issue 2, pp. 4–21.

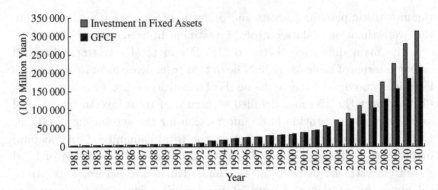

Figure 4.1. Comparison of GFCF and total investment in fixed assets, 1981–2011

2003, GFCF has been smaller than the total investment in fixed assets, and the gap has been widening. In 2003, GFCF accounted for 96.3% of the total investment in fixed assets, and in 2011, the proportion was only 68.4%.

Figure 4.2 shows the nominal growth rates of GFCF and total investment in fixed assets from 1981 to 2011. As can be seen from the figure, the nominal growth rate of GFCF in most years was lower than that of total investment in fixed assets. In fact, the nominal growth rate of GFCF was lower than that of total investment in fixed assets in 24 of the 31 years during the period. Especially after 2001, the nominal growth rate of GFCF was lower than that of total investment in fixed assets. From 2003 to 2007, the nominal growth rate of GFCF was lower by over 5 percentage points, and from 2009 to 2011, it was lower by over 6 percentage points. The gap between the two indicated a trend of widening.

Figure 4.3 shows the real growth rates of GFCF and total investment in fixed assets from 1981 to 2011. As can be seen from the figure, the real growth rate of the GFCF in most years was lower than that of total investment in fixed assets. In fact, in 23 of the 31 years, the real growth rate of GFCF was lower than that of total investment in fixed assets. Especially after 2001, the real growth rate of GFCF was lower than that of total investment in fixed assets. It was lower by over 5 percentage points during 2003–2008 and lower by over 7 percentage points during 2009–2011. On the whole, the gap between the two was obviously widening.

From the above discussion, we can see that GFCF is a component of GDP by the expenditure approach, while total investment in fixed assets is not. At the same time, as can be seen from Figure 4.1, the gap between GFCF and total investment in fixed assets was widening after

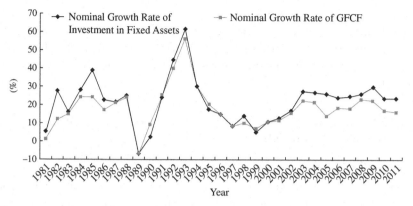

Figure 4.2. Comparison of nominal growth rates of GFCF and total investment in fixed assets, 1981–2011

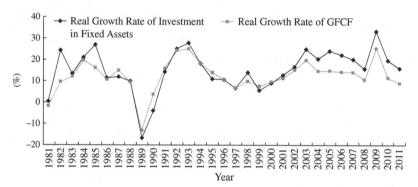

Figure 4.3. Comparison of real growth rates of GFCF and total investment in fixed assets from 1981 to 2011

2003. Therefore, when we analyze the share of demand of fixed capital investment in the final demand structure and the contribution rate of fixed capital investment demand to economic growth, we could not replace GFCF with the total investment in fixed assets. From Figures 4.2 and 4.3, it can be seen that after 2001, although the gap between the nominal growth rate of GFCF and that of total investment in fixed assets widened, the two had basically the same trend; although the gap between the real growth rate of GFCF and that of total investment in fixed assets widened more obviously on the whole, the two also had basically the same trend. Therefore, in the analysis of the growth rate of fixed capital investment demand, the growth rate of total investment in fixed assets can be used as an approximation of the growth rate of GFCF. Therefore, in the following analysis of the growth of fixed capital investment demand, we mainly use the growth rate of total investment in fixed assets, while in the analysis of the share and contribution rate of fixed capital investment demand, we use the indicator of GFCF.

4.2. Performance of China's Investment Growth since the Reform and Opening-up

4.2.1. *Growth of total investment in fixed assets*

Since the reform and opening-up, China's investment in fixed assets has maintained a trend of rapid growth in general, with an average annual nominal growth of 21.1%[7] from 1981 to 2011, from 91.1 billion yuan in 1980 to 31,148.5 billion yuan in 2011, an increase of 341 times. Massive investment and construction resulted in much improved infrastructure, much higher economic competitiveness, and much better housing conditions of urban and rural households in China. The long-term and rapid growth of total investment in fixed assets has made tremendous contributions to the development of the national economy and the improvement of people's livelihood.

In the over 30 years after the reform and opening-up, if we take the process of low-high-low growth as a cycle, then the nominal growth of total investment in fixed assets from 1981 to 2011 can be divided into three cycles, namely: 1981–1989, 1990–1999, and 2000–2011 (see Figure 4.4). The different characteristics of the growth rates of total investment in fixed assets in these three cycles not only reflect the change of economic environment in the transition from a planned economy to a market economy but also reflect the change of macrocontrol policies and the continuous improvement of regulations by the Chinese government.[8]

4.2.1.1. *First cycle, 1981–1989*

This was the initial stage of the development of China's investment in fixed assets. At the beginning of the reform and opening-up, China's economy

---

[7]The average annual growth rate in this report was calculated by geometric mean method.

[8]Department of Investment and Construction Statistics, National Bureau of Statistics (2009). *30 Years of Investment in China* (China Statistics Press, Beijing).

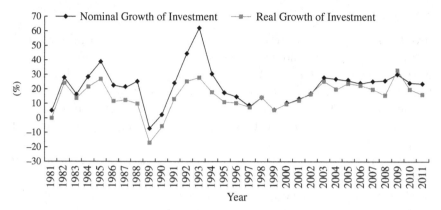

Figure 4.4. Nominal and real growth rates of total investment in fixed assets, 1981–2011

and society had many objectives that needed to be accomplished, and many fields needed additional investment in fixed assets in order to settle the historical debts. In this cycle, the nominal annual growth of total investment in fixed assets increased by 19.2%, and the value of investment increased by 3.8 times, from 91.1 billion yuan in 1980 to 441 billion yuan in 1989; the nominal growth rate climbed from 5.5% in 1981 to 38.8% in 1985, and then fell back to −7.2% in 1989, experiencing a relatively complete growth cycle. Due to the lack of experience in economic development in the early stage of the reform and opening-up, the too-tight policy regulation led to frequent fluctuations in investment growth during this period. In 1981, total investment in fixed assets increased by 5.5%, climbing up to 28% in 1982, falling to 16.2% in 1983, rising to 38.8% in 1985, declining by a large margin to 22.7% in 1986, remaining relatively stable in 1987 and 1988, and dropping sharply to −7.2% in 1989. This period witnessed a range of 46 percentage points between the highest and the lowest growth rates of total investment in fixed assets and recorded the only negative growth since the reform and opening-up.

After deducting the price factor, the annual real growth rate of total investment in fixed assets in this cycle was 10.7%. Because the prices of investment in fixed assets in each year were all on the rise, the real growth rate in each year was lower than the nominal growth rate, but the trend was basically consistent with that of the nominal growth.

4.2.1.2. *Second cycle, 1990–1999*

Investment in fixed assets in this period concentrated on coastal areas and development zones. The nominal annual growth of investment in fixed assets in this cycle was 21.1%, or 1.9 percentage points higher than that in the first cycle. It increased by 5.8 times from 441 billion yuan in 1989 to 2,985.5 billion yuan in 1999. In this cycle, the growth rate of total investment in fixed assets first climbed and then decreased, showing a typical inverted V curve.

The growth rate of total investment in fixed assets was 2.4% in 1990 and skyrocketed to 23.9% in 1991. In 1992 and 1993, total investment in fixed assets increased sharply by 44.4% and 61.8% respectively, with the growth rate in 1993 being the highest since the reform and opening-up. In order to cool down the overheated economy, the government adopted a series of macroregulation measures, resulting in a gradual decline in the growth rate of total investment in fixed assets, which was 30.4%, 17.5%, and 14.8% during 1994, 1995, and 1996, respectively. Influenced by the Asian financial crisis in 1997, the growth rate of total investment in fixed assets dropped to 8.8%. Since 1998, the government continuously issued long-term construction treasury bonds to strengthen investment in the infrastructure. In 1998, the growth rate of the total investment in fixed assets increased to 13.9%. However, private investment did not get actively involved due to the deep impact of the crisis, and the growth rate dropped to 5.1%, the lowest point of this cycle, in 1999.

The growth curve of this cycle illustrates the entire process of total investment in fixed assets from rapid warming to rapid cooling, which also reflects the instability of investment growth during the period of economic transition.

Excluding price factors, the annual real growth of total investment in fixed assets in this cycle was 12.3%, which was 1.6 percentage points higher than that in the previous cycle. In terms of the trend, the curve of real growth rate was also an inverted V-shape, but the curve of real growth rate was much smoother because the prices of investment in fixed assets rose by 15.3% in 1992 and 26.6% in 1993. In the last two years of this cycle, investment prices fell, so the real growth rate of investment was higher than the nominal growth rate.

4.2.1.3. *Third cycle, 2000–2011*

During this period, China's investment in fixed assets grew steadily and rapidly, and the rapid growth shifted from the eastern region to the central and western regions. In this cycle, the average annual nominal growth of total investment in fixed assets was 22.6%, which was 3.4 and 1.5 percentage points higher than the previous two cycles, respectively. In 2011, the total investment reached 31,148.5 billion yuan, a 9.4-fold increase over 1999.

In 2000, the investment in fixed assets picked up and entered a new round of growth. From 2000 to 2002, total investment in fixed assets increased by 10.3%, 13.1%, and 16.9%, respectively, showing a gradual uptrend, and reached 27.7% in 2003. Since then, it entered a track of stable and rapid growth. From 2004 to 2008, the investment increased by 26.8%, 26.0%, 23.9%, 24.8%, and 25.9%, respectively, with relatively small differences between different years. To cope with the shock by the international financial crisis, the Chinese government initiated a 4-trillion-yuan stimulus, pushing the growth rate of total investment in fixed assets to the highest point of 30% in this cycle in 2009. Due to the diminishing effect of the stimulus and the policy adjustment, as well as the lack of significant improvement in the international economic environment, the growth rate of total investment in fixed assets in 2010 and 2011 fell to 23.8%, significantly lower than that in 2009.

Compared with the previous two cycles, this cycle featured rapid growth, long duration, and small fluctuations in growth rate. However, more than 30 years of rapid growth had drained the potential growth capacity of investment in fixed assets and brought about more constraints on the rapid growth of investment. In the future years, the growth rate of investment would continue to slow down, and the growth rate in this cycle had not hit the bottom yet.

Excluding price factors, the annual real growth rate of total investment in fixed assets in this cycle was 19.4%, which was much faster than that in the previous two cycles. Besides the faster nominal annual growth rate, a more important reason was the relatively stable investment prices in this cycle, which increased at a much slower pace on the average than that in the previous two cycles.

4.2.2. *Growth of GFCF*

Similar to the total investment in fixed assets, since the reform and opening-up, China's GFCF has maintained a rapid growth trend, with an average annual nominal growth of 17.8% during 1981–2011, an increase of 160 times from 132.2 billion yuan in 1980 to 21,304.3 billion yuan in 2011.

According to the same division as the growth of total investment in fixed assets, the nominal growth of GFCF from 1981 to 2011 can

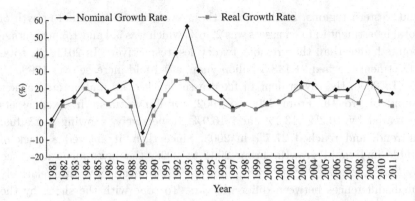

Figure 4.5.   Nominal and real growth rates of GFCF, 1981–2011

also evidently be divided into three cycles: 1981–1989, 1990–1999, and 2000–2011, which was completely consistent with the nominal growth cycles of total investment in fixed assets (see Figure 4.5).

In the first cycle, the annual nominal growth of GFCF was 14.3%, with the growth rate gradually increasing from 1.3% in 1981 to 24.6% in 1984, and then declining to −6.0% in 1989, the lowest point in this cycle.

In the second cycle, the annual nominal growth rate of GFCF was 21.3%. The growth rate increased gradually from 9.2% in 1990 to 56.3% in 1993, the highest point in the current cycle. After that, the growth rate dropped rapidly to 8.0% in 1997, rebounded slightly to 10.0% in 1998, and dropped to 6.9% in 1999, the lowest point in this cycle.

In the third cycle, the annual nominal growth of GFCF was 17.6%. The growth rate increased gradually from 10.9% in 2000 to 22.6% in 2003 and 14.0% in 2005. Then it gradually increased, reaching 23.2% in 2008, the peak in this cycle, and then dropped to 16.0% in 2011.

Excluding price factors, the real growth trend of GFCF was basically consistent with the nominal growth, but relatively stable. The annual real growth rates of GFCF in these three cycles were 8.1%, 13.2%, and 14.1%, respectively, showing a rising trend.

4.2.3. *Contribution of GFCF to economic growth*

Since the reform and opening-up, with the acceleration of industrialization and urbanization in China and its gradual development into a global manufacturing center, GFCF was featured by a rapid growth, a growing share in GDP, and greater contribution to GDP growth.

4.2.3.1. *Higher growth rate of GFCF than that of GDP*

(1) The nominal growth rate of GFCF was higher than that of GDP. Since the reform and opening-up, the nominal growth rate of China's GFCF has been generally faster than that of GDP. From 1981 to 2011, 18 years saw a higher nominal growth rate of GFCF than that of GDP during the same period, and another 13 years saw a lower nominal growth rate of GFCF than that of GDP in the same period. The annual nominal growth rate of GFCF was 17.8%, 1.6 percentage points faster than that of GDP in the same period. By different stages, the annual nominal growth of GFCF was 13.8% from 1981 to 1990, or 1.4 percentage points lower than that of GDP in the same period; the annual nominal growth of GFCF was 21.5% from 1991 to 2000, or 3.3 percentage points faster than that of GDP in the same period; and the annual nominal growth of GFCF was 18.2% from 2001 to 2011, which was 2.9 percentage points higher than that of GDP in the same period (see Table 4.2).

(2) The real growth rate of GFCF was higher than that of GDP. Since the reform and opening-up, the real growth rate of GFCF was generally higher than that of GDP. Between 1981 and 2011, 24 years saw a higher real growth rate of GFCF than that of GDP during the same period, and 7 years saw a lower real growth rate of GFCF than that of GDP in the same period. The annual real growth rate of GFCF was 12.0%, or 2.0 percentage points higher than that of GDP during the same period. Analyzed by the time frame, the annual real growth rate of GFCF was 7.6% during 1981–1990, or 1.7 percentage points lower than that of GDP during the same period; the growth of GFCF was 13.9% during 1991–2000, or 3.5 percentage points

Table 4.2. Comparison of nominal growth rates between GFCF and GDP
(Unit: %)

Year	Nominal growth rate of GDP	Nominal growth rate of GFCF	Nominal growth rate of GFCF — nominal growth rate of GDP
1981–1990	15.2	13.8	−1.4
1991–2000	18.2	21.5	3.3
2001–2011	15.3	18.2	2.9
1981–2011	16.2	17.8	1.6

Note: The nominal growth rate of GDP is calculated on the basis of data on GDP at current prices, which are from *China Statistical Yearbook 2012*, p. 44; and the nominal growth rate of GFCF is calculated on the basis of GFCF at current prices, taken from *China Statistical Yearbook 2012*, p. 62.

Table 4.3. Comparison of real growth rates between GFCF and GDP

(Unit: %)

Year	Real growth rate of GDP	Real growth rate of GFCF	Real growth rate of GFCF — real growth rate of GDP
1981–1990	9.3	7.6	−1.7
1991–2000	10.4	13.9	3.5
2001–2011	10.4	14.5	4.1
1981–2011	10.0	12.0	2.0

Note: The real growth rate of GDP is calculated according to the GDP index at constant prices, and data on the GDP index are from *China Statistical Yearbook 2012*, p. 48. The real growth rate of GFCF is calculated according to GFCF at constant prices, and data on GFCF at constant prices are from GDP by expenditure approach at constant prices of the National Bureau of Statistics.

higher than that of GDP during the same period; and the growth of GFCF was 14.5% during 2001–2011, or 4.1 percentage points higher than that of GDP during the same period (Table 4.3).

4.2.3.2. *Increasing share of GFCF in GDP*

GFCF is an important component of GDP by the expenditure approach. Since the reform and opening-up, the share of GFCF in GDP by the expenditure approach showed a general trend of rising. From 1981 to 2011, GFCF accounted for 34.0% of expenditure-based GDP on the average on annual basis. More specifically, the GFCF accounted for 26.7% of GDP by the expenditure approach in 1981, 26.9% in 1991, 34.6% in 2001, and 45.7% in 2011. The share in 2011 was 19.0, 18.8, and 11.1 percentage points higher than that in 1981, 1991, and 2001, respectively. The annual average share of GFCF in GDP by the expenditure approach was 28.2% in 1981–1990, 32.6% in 1991–2000, and 40.5% in 2001–2011 (see Figure 4.6).

4.2.3.3. *Rising contribution rate of GFCF to GDP growth*

The contribution rate of GFCF to GDP growth refers to the proportion of the increment of GFCF at constant prices to the increment of GDP at constant prices by the expenditure approach. Since the reform and opening-up, the contribution rate of GFCF to GDP growth has fluctuated greatly, but showed an upward trend as a whole. From 1981 to 2011, the annual average contribution rate of GFCF to GDP growth was 34.1%, with the

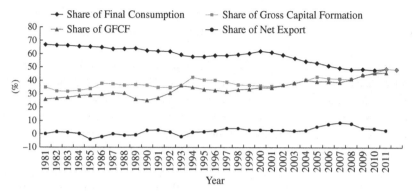

Figure 4.6. Composition of GDP by the expenditure approach, 1981–2011 (GDP by the expenditure approach = 100)

Note: The composition of GDP by the expenditure approach in this figure is calculated according to GDP by the expenditure approach and its components. Data on GDP by the expenditure approach and its components are from *China Statistical Yearbook 2012*, pp. 61–62.

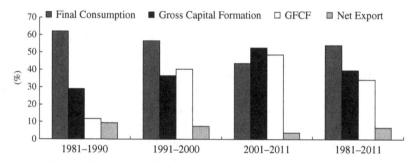

Figure 4.7. Annual average contribution rate of final demand from 1981 to 2011

highest in 2009 (93.7%) and the lowest in 1989 (−114.6%). Analyzed by different periods of time, the annual average contribution rate of GFCF to GDP growth was 11.7% during 1981–1990, 40.3% during 1991–2000, and 48.8% during 2001–2011 (see Figure 4.7).

4.3. The Impact of Fiscal Policy on China's Investment Growth

The fiscal policy mainly regulates economic operation by means of tax, subsidy, deficit, treasury bond, income distribution, and transfer payment. Together with monetary policy, it constitutes an important means of national macroregulation and is an important tool for smoothening economic peaks and troughs and maintaining stable and rapid economic growth.

According to the different directions of influence on economic performance, fiscal policy can be divided into expansionary fiscal policy, neutral fiscal policy, and austerity fiscal policy. Fiscal policy generally carries on the reverse adjustment when the economy fluctuates, i.e. when the economy is overheated, an austerity fiscal policy is carried out to restrain the growth of aggregate demand and achieve the stability of aggregate supply and demand; when the economy is depressed, an expansionary fiscal policy is adopted to stimulate aggregate demand and thus stimulate economic growth. Investment in fixed assets, as an important component of final demand, is a key area to be regulated by fiscal policy.

4.3.1. *How fiscal policy affects investment growth*

The impact of fiscal policy on investment in fixed assets is often achieved through reverse regulation. When the investment growth rate is too low, expansionary fiscal policy is adopted to stimulate investment growth. When investment is overheated, austerity fiscal policy is adopted to cool down the investment.

Expansionary fiscal policy mainly stimulates the growth of investment in fixed assets through the reduction of fiscal revenue and the increase of fiscal expenditure. In terms of fiscal revenue, the core measures to adjust investment are as follows. First, through tax reduction, enterprises can increase their profits, enhance their investment capacity, and expand their investment demand, thereby increasing the total investment and increasing the growth rate of investment. For example, various preferential tax policies for investment promotion and attraction issued by local governments can play a positive role in promoting investment growth. Second, preferential land policies can attract enterprise investment. As an expansionary fiscal policy, a land preferential policy is not issued nationwide by the central government, but as one of the main preferential policies of local governments for attracting investment, it has played a positive role in the rapid growth of investment in China for many years. In terms of fiscal expenditure, its impact on investment is first reflected in the increase of funds directly from the government budget for investment projects. The proportion of these funds in the total investment funds determines the direct impact on investment. With the increasing investment from non-government sources, the proportion of budgetary funds in all sources of investment funds is becoming smaller and smaller, so the direct impact is becoming less important. The second is the driving effect of government investment. Through government investment, bank loans and non-government capitals will be brought in, which will lead to an increase in the volume and growth of investment in the whole society. Compared with the direct role of government investment, its driving effect is more important. The effect of expansionary fiscal policy on investment depends mainly on whether it can effectively drive social capital into investment. It is clear that the process of impact of the expansionary fiscal policy on investment is as follows: tax reduction policy enhances the investment capacity of enterprises, and the land preferential policy enhances the investment enthusiasm of enterprises; the increase of government investment projects directly expands the size of investment and promotes the growth of non-government investment, thus promoting the growth of total investment in fixed assets.

The restrictive effect of austerity fiscal policy on investment in fixed assets is mainly achieved by increasing tax revenue and reducing fiscal expenditure. The mechanism of action is similar. Increased tax revenue will cut the profits of enterprises, reduce the investment capacity of enterprises, and then achieve the purpose of cooling down investment. Reduction of fiscal expenditure will cut the budgetary funds used as investment in fixed assets. Reduction of government investment will inevitably affect the duration of government investment projects and hence affect the availability of loans from banks, thus slowing down the growth of investment. Although an austerity fiscal policy can theoretically achieve the cooling effect on investment, there are many limitations in the process of implementation. First, the policy of increasing tax on enterprises, which has great impact on the economy, is seldom used. Second, reducing government investment can only affect government-invested projects, but has less impact on non-government investment projects, so the effect of cooling down investment is greatly compromised. Third, in order to achieve better results, austerity fiscal policy should generally be implemented with monetary and other policies, such as monetary policy to increase bank interest rates, deposit reserve rate, and capping on the scale of bank loans, or the adoption of some necessary administrative measures.

4.3.2. The practice of the impact of fiscal policy on China's investment growth

Since the reform and opening-up, China's economic system has undergone major changes. China's macroregulation mode has also undergone a transition from relying mainly on planning to the combination of planning and market, and then to market-oriented allocation of resources. As one of the key macroregulation measures, fiscal policy also shows different characteristics in different periods. In the early stage of the reform and opening-up, fiscal policy was the key measure to realize the national economic development plan, and fiscal investment was the important factor affecting the total demand and supply of the society. It mainly relied on the management of administrative plan. The use and function of its policy tools were constrained to a large extent by the planned economic system. Because it was difficult to hold the appropriate strength of the policy, although the goal of regulation was achieved after the implementation of the policy, it often led to the ups and downs of investment growth, resulting in greater fluctuations in economic growth. Since 1990s, with the continuous advancement of the reform of market economic system, the mode of financial regulation of the economy gradually changed from relying mainly on administrative measures to relying mainly on market means, focusing on the comprehensive use of various policy tools, which gradually improved the means of regulation and enhanced the stability of economic performance.

Since the reform and opening-up, the fiscal policy has undergone many changes in view of the macroeconomic and investment situations. China's fiscal policy was one of austerity (also called as adjustment at that time) in 1979–1981, expansionary in 1982–1987 (tightening a bit in 1985), austerity in 1988–1989, easing somewhat in 1990–1992, austerity in 1993–1997, expansionary in 1998–2003, neutral (or moderate) in 2004–2007, and expansionary in 2008–2010 (see Figure 4.8).

During this period, fiscal policy mainly had significant impacts on investment growth in five time spans, including two with austerity policies (1988–1989, 1993–1997), two with expansionary fiscal policies (1998–2003, 2008–2010), and one with neutral fiscal policy (2004–2007).

4.3.2.1. *The adoption of austerity fiscal policies for two time spans*

First time: the austerity fiscal policies implemented from 1988 to 1989. Since the second half of 1984, signs of overheating of the national

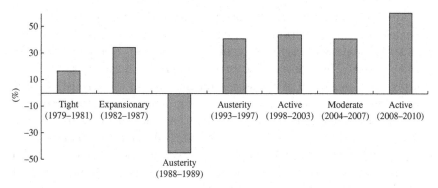

Figure 4.8. The impact of fiscal policy on the annual average contribution rate of GFCF in different periods

economy gradually emerged, with rapid growth in investment and GDP, and a sharp rise in the overall price level. From 1984 to 1988, the growth rate of total investment in fixed assets reached 28.2%, 38.8%, 22.7%, 21.5%, and 25.4%, respectively. GDP growth rates were 15.2%, 13.5%, 8.8%, 11.6%, and 11.3%, respectively. Consumer price index rose by 2.7%, 9.3%, 6.5%, 7.3%, and 18.8%, respectively. The contradiction between total supply and demand was very prominent.

In order to curb the excessive growth of investment in fixed assets, the Chinese government adopted an austerity fiscal policy in the second half of 1988, supported by tightening monetary policy and necessary administrative approaches. Specific measures of fiscal policy included tightening fiscal expenditure of the central government and reducing fiscal expenditure on investment; stopping financial subsidies for state-owned enterprises with poor operation and long-term losses; and rectifying and shutting down small enterprises with outdated technology. Administrative measures were adopted to reduce the scale of investment in fixed assets. At the end of September 1988, the State Council issued the *Circular on Liquidating Investment Projects in Fixed Assets in Construction, Reducing Investment Scale and Adjusting Investment Structure*, according to which some investment projects in fixed assets were required to be suspended or postponed, and extra-budgetary capital investment was controlled, and the scale of non-productive investment such as office buildings, large halls, and guesthouses as well as residential houses were controlled. Other measures included a big cut in administrative expenses, the pilot of tax-benefit diversion, the reform of tax system, etc.

After the implementation of the austerity policy, the budgetary funds allocated from the government finance for investment projects decreased by 13.0% and 15.3%, respectively, in 1988 and 1989, compared with the previous year. The growth rate of investment in fixed assets declined sharply, the momentum of excessive economic growth was curbed, and the price increase slowed down significantly. The growth rate of total investment in fixed assets dropped to −7.2% in 1989, and it only rose by 2.4% in 1990, down by 32.6 percentage points and 23.0 percentage points when compared with that in 1988. GDP grew by 4.1% and 3.8% in 1989 and 1990, respectively, down by 7.2 and 7.5 percentage points from 1988. CPI rose 18.0% in 1989 and 3.1% in 1990, down by 0.8 percentage point and 15.7 percentage points from 1988, respectively. However, the extreme policy led to a serious shortage of liquidity in enterprises, difficulties in normal operation of production, a marked decline in economic benefits, and a sluggish market to varying degrees.

Second time: the austerity fiscal policies implemented from 1993 to 1997. After Comrade Deng Xiaoping's Southern Tour in 1992 and the 14th National Congress of CPC, the reform of the economic system deepened gradually, the market-oriented mechanism kept improving, the vitality of enterprises was significantly enhanced, and China's economy developed rapidly. However, overexpansion of investment in real estate and development zones, rapid rise in the prices of means of production, and intensified "bottleneck" restrictions on basic industries and infrastructure also appeared. In 1992 and 1993, the total investment in fixed assets increased by 44.4% and 61.8%, respectively, of which the investment in real estate development increased by 117.5% and 165.0%, respectively. GDP grew by 14.2% and 14.0%, respectively. The consumer prices increased by 6.4%, 14.7%, 24.1%, and 17.1% from 1992 to 1995, respectively, indicating a really dire economic situation.

In 1993, in view of the overheated economy, the Chinese government launched a tightening fiscal policy. Specific measures of fiscal policy were as follows. First, it introduced 16 measures to strengthen regulation and control in 1993, and started the reform on the fiscal and taxation system in 1994. Second, it implemented a tight budgetary policy and strictly controlled the fiscal deficit. In 1994, *the Budget Law of the People's Republic of China* was approved by the National People's Congress. It stipulated that since 1994, the fiscal deficit of the central government would mainly be compensated by issuing treasury bonds, and there should be no more overdrafts or loans from the People's Bank of China. Third, measures were taken to liquidate and compress capital construction projects, control the excessive growth of investment in fixed assets, and implement the capital requirement system for investment projects in fixed assets. *The Circular on Continuing to Strengthen Macroeconomic Regulation and Control of Investment in Fixed Assets* was issued, requesting a concentration of financial and material resources to ensure key construction, giving priority to ensuring the completion and operation of key projects; stopping or suspending construction of projects that did not conform to industrial policies, projects without confirmed sources of funds, or projects with poor market prospect; and requiring that new large and medium-sized capital construction projects should be approved by the central government before they can start. Fourth, efforts were made to strengthen the management of the real estate market, to formulate real estate value-added tax and tariff collection policies, to stop resolutely speculation in real estate, and to take back the construction land if the development funds invested in the purchase of land within one year were less than 25% of the purchase cost.[9]

After the implementation of the above-mentioned policies, the growth rate of funds in the national budget for investment projects slowed down markedly, and increased by 9.5%, 17.3%, and 0.8% during 1994–1996, respectively, which was substantially lower than the growth rate of 39.2% in 1993. The demand for excessive growth was effectively curbed, the growth rate of investment in fixed assets declined sharply, and the growth rate of GDP and prices dropped considerably. From 1994 to 1997, the growth rate of total investment in fixed assets fell back to 30.4%, 17.5%, 14.8%, and 8.8%, respectively, while GDP growth slowed down to 13.1%, 10.9%, 10.0%, and 9.3%, respectively. CPI rose 2.8% in 1997, down by 21.3 percentage points when compared with 1994.

After the two rounds of austerity fiscal policies during 1988–1989 and 1993–1997, the overheated economy cooled down noticeably. However, seen from the regulatory effect on investment in fixed assets, the impact of policy was somewhat excessive, resulting in the ups and downs of investment growth.

---

[9]Jin, R. (2006). *Scientific Development and Fiscal Policy of China* (China Financial & Economic Publishing House, Beijing).

4.3.2.2. *The adoption of expansionary fiscal policies for two time spans*

Since the reform and opening-up, China's economy has experienced two severe shocks from international financial crises. In order to cope with the shocks, the Chinese government launched expansionary fiscal policies focusing on expanding fiscal expenditure, which played a positive role in reversing the sharp decline in economic growth.

First time: the expansionary fiscal policies implemented in 1998–2003. The Asian financial crisis that broke out in July 1997 hit the Chinese economy severely. China's exports declined, investment growth continued to decline, the speed of economic growth declined significantly, and the price level showed a negative growth. The growth rate of total investment in fixed assets decreased from 8.8% in 1997 to 5.1% in 1999; the growth rate of GDP declined from 9.3% in 1997 to 7.6% in 1999; and the CPI changed from a rise of 2.8% in 1997 to a drop of 1.4% in 1999.

In order to curb the further decline of economic growth and aggravation of deflation, the Chinese government implemented an expansionary fiscal policy since 1998, and strived to expand domestic demand and promote economic growth. Expansionary fiscal policy mainly includes the following contents:

(1) The first measure was issuing long-term construction bonds to step up infrastructure construction. From 1998 to 2000,[10] a total of 360 billion yuan of long-term special treasury bonds for construction were issued, to fund mainly infrastructure construction such as farming, forestry, water conservancy, transportation and communications, urban facilities, urban and rural power grids, and state-owned grain reserves. In these three years, the investment in fixed assets completed by treasury bond projects accounted for 9.7%, 8.1%, and 8.8% of total investment in fixed assets in 1998–2000, respectively, accounting for 79.9%, 165.9%, and 94.6% of total investment in fixed assets increment in the three years (see Table 4.4).

(2) From the second half of 1999, regulation tax on investment in fixed assets in specific industries was reduced by 50% (and the tax was suspended since 2000).

---

[10]From 1998 to 2004, a total of 910 billion yuan was issued.

Table 4.4. The impact of treasury bond on total investment in fixed assets from 1998 to 2000

Year	Total investment in fixed assets (100 million yuan)	Increment (100 million yuan)	Growth rate (%)	Investment in fixed assets funded by treasure bond (100 million yuan)	Share in total investment in fixed assets (%)	Share in the increment of total investment in fixed assets (%)
1998	28406	3465	13.9	2768	9.7	79.9
1999	29855	1449	5.1	2403	8.1	165.9
2000	32918	3063	10.3	2898	8.8	94.6

(3) Interest discounts on technological renovation projects were adopted to promote industrial upgrading and to accelerate the pace of structural adjustment.

(4) Since 1998, the imported equipment necessary for encouraging domestic investment projects and foreign investment projects was exempted from tariffs and import taxes within the prescribed scope.

(5) The purchase of domestic equipment for technological transformation projects of enterprises in line with the state industrial policies was allowed to be exempted from enterprise income tax at a rate of 40%.

(6) Adjustments and improvements were made on the fiscal management system to increase transfer payments to the central and western regions to support the large-scale development of the western region and the revitalization of the old industrial bases in northeast China.

Under the effect of expansionary fiscal policies, investment growth, GDP growth, and CPI growth began to recover steadily. From 2000 to 2003, investment in fixed assets increased by 10.3%, 13%, 16.9%, and 27.7%, respectively, with the growth rate continuing to rebound year by year. GDP growth rates were 8.4%, 8.3%, 9.1%, and 10%, respectively, which rebounded obviously compared with 1998 and 1999. CPI rose by 0.4%, 0.7%, −0.8%, and 1.2%, respectively, recovering somewhat from the −1.4% in 1999.

Second time: expansionary fiscal policies implemented in 2008–2010. In September 2008, the subprime mortgage crisis in the United States evolved into a global financial crisis, which accelerated its spread from virtual economy to real economy, from developed countries to emerging economies and developing countries, and its impact on China's economy accelerated. China's GDP grew by only 6.6% in the first quarter of 2009, the lowest quarterly growth rate since the 21st century; exports declined from 23.1% in the third quarter of 2008 to 19.8% in the first quarter of 2009. The CPI fell by 1.5% in the second quarter of 2009. In view of the severe economic situation, the Chinese government initiated expansionary fiscal policies with a 4-trillion-yuan stimulus.

The expansionary fiscal policies mainly included the following measures:

(1) To expand government public investment around the new 4-trillion-yuan stimulus. The central government allocated 924.3 billion yuan in 2009 and 1,071 billion yuan in 2010 for public investment, focusing on projects in agriculture and rural areas, and for farmers, projects to provide affordable housing to urban households, projects on education and health, energy conservation and emission reduction, environmental protection, etc.

(2) To implement the reform of value-added tax transformation in an all-round way, allowing enterprises to deduct the input tax on fixed assets of machinery and equipment purchased, so as to encourage enterprises to increase investment and promote technological transformation and technological innovation.

(3) To increase investment in rural infrastructure and public services, and to enhance support for poverty alleviation through development. The expenditures from central government budget on direct grain subsidy, comprehensive agricultural subsidy, improved seed subsidy, and agricultural machinery purchase subsidy for farmers totaled 119.6 billion yuan and 122.6 billion yuan in 2009 and 2010, respectively.

(4) To optimize the structure of financial expenditure by strictly controlling general expenditure, and significantly increasing investment in education, healthcare, housing, and other areas of livelihood. In 2010, construction was started on 5.9 million units of affordable housing and renovated shantytowns built or nationwide, with 3.7 million units basically completed.

(5) To improve the supporting measures and implementation rules to encourage and guide private investment, and to support private investment in railway, municipal, financial, energy, telecommunications, education, medical projects, and in other fields.

(6) To vigorously support scientific and technological innovation, promote industrial structure optimization and upgrading, and further push forward energy conservation and emission reduction.

(7) Approved by the State Council, the Ministry of Finance issued 200 billion yuan of local government bonds annually in 2009 and 2010 to meet the needs of local investment and construction.[11]

The implementation of expansionary fiscal policies has played an important role in stabilizing confidence, curbing the rapid decline of economic growth, and maintaining price stability. In 2009, total investment in fixed assets increased by 30%, 4.1 percentage points higher than that in 2008; GDP growth increased from 6.6% in the first quarter of 2009 to 12.1% in the first quarter of 2010; CPI rebounded to 2.2% in the first quarter of 2010, down by 1.5% compared with the second quarter of 2009.

The two rounds of expansionary fiscal policies implemented in 1998–2003 and 2008–2010 were both policies of expanding fiscal expenditure, mainly by issuing long-term construction treasury bonds (or increasing government investment) in response to the international financial crisis and preventing further decline in economic growth. These two rounds of expansionary fiscal policies effectively stimulated a large investment from bank credit funds by strengthening coordination with monetary policies and industrial policies, pooled together efforts in building a number of key strategic infrastructure projects, promoted the rapid growth of investment in fixed assets, reversed the rapid decline in economic growth, and avoided the intensification of deflation, hence recovering the economic growth.

4.3.2.3. *The adoption of neutral fiscal policies*

Neutral fiscal policies were implemented from 2004 to 2007. After years of expansionary fiscal policies implemented from 1998 to 2003, the Chinese economy gradually entered a new cycle of growth, and all macroeconomic indicators performed well. In 2003, the total investment in fixed assets increased by 27.7%, GDP by 10%, and CPI by 1.2%. Under the improved overall national economic situation, there were also some problems, such as the excessive growth of investment, the intensification of

---

[11]Xie, X. (2011). *China's Fiscal Reform and Development* (China Financial & Economic Publishing House, Beijing).

low-level duplicated construction projects, and the increasingly prominent contradiction between supply and demand of resources in some regions and some industries. The macroeconomy entered a new phase of general balance of supply and demand with increasingly prominent structural problems. In view of this, the expansion-oriented fiscal policies were gradually adjusted to neutral (or moderate) fiscal policies with moderate overall tightness and differential control in the structure.

Fiscal policy mainly includes the following:

(1) To appropriately reduce fiscal deficit and the scale of long-term treasury bond for construction and to convey the government's policy signal of reasonable control of investment to the society. From 2004 to 2006, the fiscal deficit accounted for 1.3%, 1.2%, and 0.8% of GDP, respectively, showing a declining trend. The fiscal balance in 2007 was 154 billion yuan.

(2) To increase investment on "agriculture, rural areas and farmers," innovate the policy system of benefiting agriculture, and vigorously support the construction of the new countryside. From 2004, government finance began to adjust the use of food risk funds and implement direct subsidies for grain growers.

(3) To increase investment in education, science and technology, health, social security, and other social undertakings to promote coordinated economic and social development.

(4) To strengthen the transfer payment and optimize its structure to promote the coordinated development of different regions.

(5) To increase support for ecological protection and environmental construction, vigorously promote the reform of the system for paid use of resources and environment, and promote the harmonious development of human and nature.

(6) To increase investment in railway construction funds to support the development of high-speed railway systems.

The implementation of the neutral fiscal policies combined maintaining macroeconomic stability with the promotion of structural optimization, thus effectively promoting the stable development of macroeconomy and investment. From 2004 to 2007, the total investment in fixed assets increased by 26.8%, 26.0%, 23.9%, and 24.8%, respectively, with relatively stable growth rate; the GDP growth rate was 10.1%, 11.3%, 12.7%, and 14.2%, respectively, which was accelerating year by year; and the CPI increase was 3.9%, 1.8%, 1.5%, and 4.8%, respectively, showing a rising trend after a decline.

4.3.3. *Correctly understanding the impact of fiscal policies on investment growth*

Practice since the reform and opening-up shows that fiscal policies have played an important role in stabilizing investment growth and smoothening investment fluctuations. However, we should also recognize the limitations of fiscal policy, constantly sum up experience and lessons, and bring the role of fiscal policy into full play in stabilizing investment growth and reducing negative impacts.

(1) Attention should be paid to the coordinated use of fiscal policy and other economic policies so as to achieve the optimal policy effect. Macroregulation involves not only fiscal policy but also monetary policy, industrial policy, and other related policies. Sometimes, certain administrative measures are needed. As the proportion of funds from government finance in all sources of investment funds is declining, the increase or decrease of financial funds will only affect government investment projects. To cool down investment, the fiscal policy needs to cooperate with monetary policies to increase the deposit reserve ratio or bank interest rates, as well as differentiated industrial policies to guide the flow of investment funds of enterprises. In the early stage of reform and opening-up, in order to cool down the rapid booming of investment while adopting fiscal and monetary policies, administrative means such as restricting project start-up were also used. Although the policy objectives were achieved, it also brought about enormous negative effects. With the continuous improvement of the market-oriented economic system, we should make more comprehensive use of various economic means and reduce the direct intervention of administrative means in the economy.

(2) The implementation of fiscal policy should take into account the intensity and timing of the policy to avoid the ups and downs of investment growth. To achieve better results, fiscal policy should not only be directed in the right direction but also grasp the intensity and timing of the policy. We should not wait until the economy or investment becomes obviously overheated (or supercooled) before introducing excessive austerity (or expansionary) policies. Otherwise, it will easily lead to

drastic fluctuations in the economy and investment, which will have a negative impact on economic development. Therefore, we should review the situation and start to adopt a mild fiscal policy to adjust flexibly when the economy is overheated (or supercooled), so as to achieve the goal of slowly cooling (or warming) the economy and reduce the negative effects.

(3) Expansionary fiscal policies should be applied to effectively stimulate rather than squeeze out social capital investment. As the financial investment cannot occupy a dominant position in the total investment, if the expansionary fiscal policies cannot effectively stimulate non-government investment, then the effect of the fiscal policies will be greatly reduced. Therefore, expansionary fiscal policies should make full use of government interest subsidies, financial guarantees and other means, give full play to the role of leverage, and use less capital investment to drive the growth of total investment in fixed assets.

(4) The regulation of fiscal policies should pay more attention to the adjustment and upgrading of industrial structure. More than 30 years of rapid growth has resulted in a very large total size of investment in fixed assets, saturated or excessive capacity of most industries, and little space for rapid growth of investment in fixed assets, and structural imbalance has become the main contradiction in the economic field. Therefore, the use of fiscal policies should aim at optimizing the industrial structure and improving the quality and efficiency of economic growth. First, government investment funds should focus on social security, education, culture, and related areas; gradually reduce government investment in competitive areas; break administrative monopoly; and leave more space to the private sectors for competitive investment. Second, government funds should be restricted for industries with high energy consumption or with excessive capacity. Third, structural tax reduction should be adopted to reduce the burden of enterprises and guide the flow of capital.

Chapter 5

Measurement and Analysis of Contribution of Opening-up to China's Economic Growth

Shi Faqi, Dai Minle and Zeng Xianxin[*]

Abstract

Since China's accession into the World Trade Organization (WTO), the scale of China's trade in goods surpassed that of Britain, France, Japan, Germany, and the United States, and rose to the first place in the world for the first time in 2013. China's utilization of foreign capital has ranked first among developing countries for 20 consecutive years. Outbound investment began to take shape, reaching US$ 90.17 billion in 2013. The calculation shows that the annual average contribution rate of domestic exports to economic growth was 11.4% during 2002–2013, and the annual average contribution rate of utilization of foreign capital to economic growth was 0.5%, adding up to 11.9%. The annual average proportion of factor income from abroad to GNI was 1.95% during 2001–2013. This report suggests that we should speed up the improvement of relevant laws and policies, better combine the opening-up with the integration of market resources, the introduction of technology management, the cultivation of competitive advantages and the optimization of economic structure, and further play the positive role of opening-up in "stabilizing growth, restructuring, and promoting reform."

Since China joined the WTO in 2001, China's opening-up has become wider and deeper, foreign trade has seen great strides, and the utilization of foreign capital and investment in foreign countries has expanded year

---

[*]Shi Faqi is Senior Statistician at the Department of National Accounts Statistics; Dai Minle is Statistician at the Department of Comprehensive Statistics; and Zeng Xianxin is Statistician at the Department of National Accounts Statistics, National Bureau of Statistics of China.

by year, which has added a strong impetus to the rapid economic growth of China. On the basis of briefly analyzing the new changes in opening-up since China's entry into the WTO, this report focuses on the measurement and analysis of the contribution of opening-up[1] to China's economic growth, and puts forward corresponding policy recommendations.

5.1. Great Changes in China's Opening-up Since its Entry into the WTO

Since China's accession into the WTO, China's foreign trade has achieved leapfrog development, the level of absorbing foreign capital has been continuously improved, the pace of foreign economic cooperation has been markedly accelerated, and great achievements have been made in economic development and various reforms.

The scale of trade in goods expanded rapidly. From 2002 to 2013, China's total import and export of goods amounted to US$ 27,398.6 billion, including US$ 14,675.5 billion of exports and US$ 12,723.1 billion of imports, which were 6.6 times, 6.9 times, and 6.4 times, respectively, that of 1978–2001 (the period of 24 years from the reform and opening-up to China's accession into the WTO). In the past 12 years, the annual growth of imports and exports was 19.1%, of which the annual growth of exports was 19.3%, and the annual growth of imports was 18.9%. In 2013, China's imports and exports reached an all-time high, with a total import and export value of US$ 4,160 billion, or 8.2 times that of 2001. Among them, US$ 2,209.6 billion was from exports, 8.3 times that of 2001, and US$ 1,950.4 billion was from imports, 8.0 times that of 2001.

In the 12 years after China's accession into the WTO, China's trade scale surpassed that of Britain, France, Japan, and Germany. In 2013, China surpassed the United States to rank first in the world for the first time. In terms of export, since China's accession into the WTO, it has been expanding its overseas demand market, expanding its export scale year by year, and its ranking and proportion in the world's total export volume was on the rise. In 2001, China's total export volume was similar to that of Britain, ranking the sixth in the world, surpassing Japan in 2004, the

---

[1]Opening-up mainly includes four parts: foreign trade, utilization of foreign capital, outbound investment, and labor service cooperation. According to the data sources, this report focuses on the first three parts.

United States in 2007, and Germany in 2009 to rank the first in the world. The proportion of China's total export volume in the world increased from 7.3% in 2001 to 11.8% in 2013. In terms of imports, China's domestic market was further internationalized, the scale of imports gradually expanded, and the ranking and proportion of imports in the world rose. In 2001, China's total value of imports was similar to that of Italy, ranking the sixth in the world, surpassing that of Japan, Britain, and France in 2003 and that of Germany in 2009, with the total imports rising to the second place in the world, becoming the second largest international market after the United States. The share of China's total imports in the world increased from 3.8% in 2001 to 10.3% in 2013.

Trade in services developed rapidly. In 2013, China's import and export of services (in terms of balance of payments, the same below) totaled US$ 539.6 billion, 7.5 times that of 2001. Among them, exports amounted to US$ 210.5 billion, 6.4 times that of 2001, and imports amounted to US$ 329.1 billion, 9.4 times that of 2001. China ranked the fifth in the world in terms of export of services (the top four in turn were the United States, Britain, Germany, and France) and the second in terms of import of services (the first was the United States).

Utilization of foreign capital has leapt to the second place in the world. During these 12 years, total foreign direct investment (FDI) in China reached US$ 998.48 billion, with an average annual growth of 8.7%. Its global ranking rose from the sixth in 2001 to the second (in 2012), and ranked the first among developing countries for 20 consecutive years (up to 2012). Even in 2009, when the impact of the international financial crisis was severe, FDI in China still exceeded US$ 90 billion, a decline far below the global average. In 2013, FDI in China reached US$ 117.59 billion, 2.51 times that of 2001.

Outbound investment grew rapidly. After its accession into the WTO, China deepened its "going global" strategy, and made new progress in outbound investment cooperation, further enhancing the scale and benefits of "going global." Despite the severe impact of the international financial crisis, China's outbound investment and foreign economic cooperation climbed against the trend, playing a positive role in promoting the steady and rapid development of the national economy. From 2003 to 2013, the flow of China's non-financial outbound investment increased by 36.9% annually, with a total value of US$ 90.17 billion in 2013, or 31.6 times that of 2002.

5.2. Measurement and Analysis of the Contribution of China's Opening-up to Its Economic Growth

5.2.1. *Contribution of foreign trade to economic growth*

Traditionally, there are two ways to measure the contribution of foreign trade to economic growth: one is to measure the proportion of annual incremental exports of goods and services at constant prices to incremental gross domestic product (GDP) by the expenditure approach at constant prices; the other is to measure the proportion of the annual incremental net exports of goods and services at constant prices to GDP by the expenditure approach at constant prices. The implicit assumption of the first approach is that all inputs in the exported goods and services of an economy are produced domestically. In fact, this assumption does not hold water, because in a modern open economy, the export value of an economy usually contains the value of components imported from other economies, which is more obvious in China. Therefore, this approach may over-estimate the role of foreign trade to the economic growth. The implicit assumption of the second approach is that all imports of an economy are for export, and similarly, this assumption does not hold water either, because imports of an economy usually contains investment and consumer goods, so this approach may under-estimate the role of foreign trade in economic growth. From Table 5.1, we can see that the contribution rate of exports of goods and services to economic growth was 32.48% in 2001–2013, while that of net exports of goods and services to economic growth was only 2.87%, with a difference of 29.61 percentage points between the two (see Table 5.1).

In order to eliminate the shortcomings of the above two approaches, we used the non-competitive input-output table to decompose imports of goods and services into investment goods, consumer goods, and intermediate inputs, then calculated the value of export after deducting imported intermediate inputs, and finally calculated its contribution rate to economic growth. This can be expressed in formula as the following:

$$\text{GDP}_t = C_t + I_t + \text{EX}_t - \text{IM}_t = C_t + I_t + \text{EX}_t - \text{IM}_t^c - \text{IM}_t^i - \text{IM}_t^{\text{int}}$$
$$= (C_t - \text{IM}_t^c) + (I_t - \text{IM}_t^i) + (\text{EX}_t - \text{IM}_t^{\text{int}})$$

Where, C_t represents final consumption expenditure, I_t represents gross capital formation, EX_t represents exports of goods and services, and IM_t represents imports of goods and services, which can be further decomposed into investment goods (IM_t^i), consumer goods (IM_t^c) and

Table 5.1. Contribution of foreign trade to economic growth in 2001–2013

(Unit: %)

Year	Contribution rate of net export to economic growth	Contribution rate of export to economic growth
2001	−0.10	23.11
2002	7.57	62.70
2003	0.85	61.38
2004	6.98	67.22
2005	22.22	53.58
2006	16.06	46.60
2007	18.03	35.68
2008	8.82	−1.03
2009	−37.38	−38.68
2010	3.95	66.42
2011	−4.22	13.42
2012	−2.12	10.33
2013	−3.35	21.50
Average	**2.87**	**32.48**

intermediate inputs (IM_t^{int}). ($C_t - IM_t^c$) refers to consumer goods supplied domestically, ($I_t - \text{IM}_t^i$) refers to investment goods provided domestically, and ($\text{EX}_t - \text{IM}_t^{\text{int}}$) refers to exports provided domestically.

The specific methods of categorizing imports of goods and services into investments goods, consumer goods, and intermediate inputs are as follows. For the import of goods, based on the 8-digit HS code from 2001 to 2013, we first distinguish investment goods, consumer goods, and intermediate inputs by using the Broad Economic Categories (BEC) of the United Nations Statistics Division and the 6-digit HS code comparison relationship; then we convert the aforesaid investment goods, consumer goods, and intermediate inputs calculated at the freight on-board (FOB) prices into investment goods, consumer goods, and intermediate inputs calculated at the cost, insurance, and freight (CIF) prices by using the proportional relationship between the imports of goods calculated at the FOB price in the balance of payments table and the imports of goods calculated at the CIF prices by the customs. For the import of services, we calculate the value of investment goods, consumer goods, and intermediate inputs using data on the balance of payments tables from 2001 and 2013 and the relevant proportion of service data in the input-output table of 2007 (see Table 5.2).

With the disaggregated data of imports of goods and services, we can easily calculate the export value of goods and services after deducting

Table 5.2. Breakdown of China's imports of goods and services, 2001–2013

(Unit: 100 million yuan)

Year	Import of goods			Import of services			Import of goods and services		
	Intermediate inputs	Consumer goods	Investment goods	Intermediate inputs	Consumer goods	Investment goods	Intermediate inputs	Consumer goods	Investment goods
2001	13847.8	871.2	4488.4	2006.5	1158.8	84.7	15854.4	2030.0	4573.1
2002	16839.8	1177.7	5280.9	2379.8	1353.5	117.8	19219.6	2531.3	5398.7
2003	23801.5	1518.9	7259.4	2935.5	1507.6	134.6	26737.0	3026.5	7394.0
2004	32607.0	2069.2	9555.9	3870.2	1944.1	156.0	36477.1	4013.3	9711.9
2005	38859.3	2439.1	10169.6	4458.3	2216.6	189.3	43317.6	4655.7	10358.9
2006	45214.2	2980.7	11748.0	5312.7	2501.8	223.7	50526.9	5482.5	11971.8
2007	52367.8	2914.4	13505.0	6635.6	2964.0	294.1	59003.3	5878.4	13799.1
2008	57224.3	3711.7	13648.7	7407.4	3235.1	394.9	64631.7	6946.8	14043.6
2009	50085.5	3169.2	11932.6	6990.4	3374.9	492.3	57076.0	6544.1	12425.0
2010	68219.3	5364.4	16263.6	8326.0	4328.0	432.8	76545.3	9692.4	16696.5
2011	80403.3	8592.8	18237.5	9714.6	5310.5	351.2	90117.9	13903.4	18588.7
2012	81320.7	10239.9	17979.6	10884.6	6525.3	339.6	92205.3	16765.3	18319.2
2013	84571.9	12724.8	17849.3	12352.8	7711.8	399.4	96924.7	20436.6	18248.7

Table 5.3.   Contribution of China's foreign trade to economic growth from 2001 to 2013

(Unit: %)

Year	Proportion of export to expenditure-based GDP	Proportion of net export to expenditure-based GDP	Proportion of domestically produced export to expenditure-based GDP	Contribution rate of net export to economic growth	Contribution rate of domestically produced export to economic growth
2001	22.73	2.13	8.19		
2002	25.10	2.57	9.15	7.57	23.29
2003	29.39	2.17	9.82	0.85	15.57
2004	33.85	2.63	11.19	6.98	21.93
2005	36.58	5.45	13.47	22.22	26.53
2006	38.00	7.48	15.32	16.06	23.73
2007	38.28	8.79	16.15	18.03	21.01
2008	34.77	7.67	14.31	8.82	5.19
2009	26.11	4.31	9.75	−37.38	−36.71
2010	29.30	3.75	10.30	3.95	21.46
2011	28.52	2.57	9.45	−4.22	2.86
2012	26.82	2.76	9.39	−2.12	4.61
2013	25.58	2.48	9.07	−3.35	6.73
Average	**30.57**	**4.40**	**12.90**	**3.11**	**11.35**

intermediate inputs from imports of goods and services. We might call it the export of domestically produced goods and services, and then we can calculate its proportion in GDP by the expenditure approach (expenditure-based GDP) and its contribution rate to economic growth (see Table 5.3). As can be seen from Table 5.3, in terms of the share in the expenditure-based GDP at current prices, that of exports is the highest, that of net exports the lowest, and that of domestically produced exports lies in between. From 2001 to 2013, the annual average proportion of domestically produced exports to expenditure-based GDP was 12.90%, which was 8.50 percentage points higher than that of net exports to expenditure-based GDP, but was 17.67 percentage points lower than that of exports to expenditure-based GDP. In terms of the contribution to the economic growth, that of exports was the highest, that of net exports the lowest, and that of domestically produced exports basically lies in between. From 2002 to 2013, the annual contribution rate of domestically produced exports to economic growth was 11.35%, 8.24 percentage points higher than that of net exports, but 21.91 percentage points lower than that of exports.

It should be noted that the above results do not fully or completely reflect the contribution of foreign trade, especially imports, to the economic growth. For example, imports can, on the one hand, make up for the gap of domestic products and promote the quality improvement and upgrading of our products; and on the other, introduce advanced technology and management expertise from abroad, so as to improve the technical level and management level of China. Unfortunately, these effects of imports on economic growth are difficult to quantify.

5.2.2. *Contribution of actual utilization of foreign capital to economic growth*

The contribution of actual utilization of foreign capital to economic growth is usually measured using the following method. According to the accounting identity of GDP by the expenditure approach, we can disaggregate the formation of fixed capital into domestic fixed capital formation and foreign fixed capital formation. The latter can be approximately replaced by the value of FDI, and the contribution of actual utilization of foreign capital to economic growth can be calculated. As can be seen in Table 5.4, from 2001 to 2013, the annual average proportion of FDI in expenditure-based GDP

Table 5.4. Contribution of China's foreign trade and FDI to economic growth, 2001–2013

(Unit: %)

Year	Proportion of domestically produced export to expenditure-based GDP	Proportion of FDI to expenditure-based GDP	Proportion of domestically produced export and utilizing foreign capital to expenditure-based GDP	Contribution rate of domestically produced export to economic growth	Contribution rate of utilizing foreign capital to economic growth	Contribution rate of domestically produced export and utilizing foreign capital to economic growth
2001	8.19	3.56	11.75	—	—	—
2002	9.15	3.62	12.77	23.29	4.07	27.36
2003	9.82	3.24	13.06	15.57	−0.25	15.32
2004	11.19	3.12	14.31	21.93	1.74	23.66
2005	13.47	2.64	16.10	26.53	−0.20	26.33
2006	15.32	2.26	17.57	23.73	−0.34	23.38
2007	16.15	2.13	18.29	21.01	1.40	22.40
2008	14.31	2.03	16.34	5.19	0.24	5.42
2009	9.75	1.76	11.51	−36.71	−0.33	−37.04
2010	10.30	1.78	12.08	21.46	1.77	23.23
2011	9.45	1.59	11.03	2.86	−0.62	2.24
2012	9.39	1.33	10.73	4.61	−1.64	2.97
2013	9.07	1.24	10.31	6.73	0.19	6.92
Average	**12.90**	**2.29**	**15.19**	**11.35**	**0.50**	**11.85**

was at 2.29%. This proportion began to decline annually after peaking in 2002, and further dropped to 1.24% in 2013, which was 2.32 percentage points lower than that in 2001. During this period, domestically produced exports and utilization of FDI (the sum of these two items is basically equivalent to opening-up) accounted for 15.19% of expenditure-based GDP on the average each year. This proportion gradually increased after 2001 and reached its peak in 2007. It gradually declined after 2008 and further dropped to 10.31% in 2013, a record low since the 21st century. From 2002 to 2013, the utilization of foreign capital made both positive and negative contribution to the economic growth, with an average annual contribution rate of 0.50%. The contribution rate of domestically produced exports and utilization of foreign capital to economic growth was 11.85% on the average, showing a trend of large contribution at first, then declining, and lingering at a low level especially in the recent two years.

5.2.3. *Contribution of "going global" to GNI*

Theoretically speaking, China's outbound investment and labor export drive the economic growth of other countries, rather than its own economic growth. It has impact on China's gross national income (GNI) through the acquisition of investment income and labor income, represented by the factor income from abroad. Therefore, in this report, we estimate the contribution of outbound investment and labor export to GNI of China by using the income credit-side data in the balance of payments statement (see Table 5.5).

Table 5.5 shows that from 2001 to 2013, the annual factor income from abroad accounted for 1.95% in GNI on the average. This proportion increased year by year after 2001 and reached the highest 2.47% in 2008. Then, it declined in fluctuations from 2009 and further dropped to 2.03% in 2013.

5.3. Policy Recommendations on Improving the Contribution of Opening-up to China's Economic Growth

Since China's accession into the WTO, the improving level of China's opening-up has effectively promoted the rapid development of the national economy. However, a series of problems in the development of foreign trade, such as being large but not strong and having unreasonable structure,

Table 5.5. Contribution of factor income from abroad to GNI, 2001–2013

Year	Factor income from abroad (100 million yuan)	Proportion of factor income from abroad to GNI (%)
2001	777.2	0.71
2002	690.7	0.57
2003	1332.2	0.98
2004	1701.5	1.06
2005	3217.1	1.74
2006	4349.7	2.01
2007	6347.5	2.39
2008	7763.7	2.47
2009	7394.6	2.17
2010	9641.4	2.40
2011	9318.0	1.97
2012	10127.9	1.95
2013	11506.0	2.03
Average	**5705.2**	**1.95**

have become constraints for the further development of China's foreign trade and even the national economy. The structure of utilization of foreign capital and the unfair competition between domestic and foreign capitals cannot meet the needs of current economic development. At present, profound changes have taken place in both the basic domestic conditions supporting foreign trade and even economic development, and in the international trade and financial situation. In order to better cope with these changes and problems, we need to have a holistic view in the process of "stabilizing economic growth, adjusting economic structure, and promoting further reforms," implement a more proactive strategy of opening-up, attach importance to the quality and efficiency of opening-up, grasp the strategic opportunity period, and comprehensively improve the level of open economy. To this end, we made the following recommendations:

(1) We should conscientiously implement various policies and measures for exports to achieve the goal of "steady economic growth and adjustment of the economic structure," take various measures to stabilize growth of foreign trade, accelerate the transformation and upgrading of foreign trade, and bring into full play a positive role of foreign trade in stabilizing the growth. First, we should closely follow the foreign trade situation and constantly consolidate and expand the international market. We should actively take advantage of the favorable situation in which the current external economic environment has improved, effectively deal with various risks and uncertainties, and actively and effectively deal with trade frictions. Second, we should intensify reform in relevant fields and further improve the institutional and policy environment for foreign trade development. We should make efforts to promote the construction of pilot free trade zones and explore new ideas and ways for China to expand its opening-up and deepen its reforms. We should further push forward the market-oriented reform of exchange rates, further improve the RMB exchange rate formation mechanism, accelerate the transformation of foreign exchange management concepts and methods, and deepen the reform of foreign exchange management system. Third, we should improve the level of trade facilitation and vigorously cultivate new competitive advantages in foreign trade. We should strive to improve the level of informatization in foreign trade, support the development of new trade modes such as cross-border e-commerce, encourage enterprises specialized in providing integrated services for foreign trade, and promote the construction of international business platforms and international marketing networks. Fourth, we should strive to change the mode of growth in foreign trade, strictly control the export of resource-intensive products, improve the level of technological innovation of export enterprises, increase the support for the export of products with own intellectual property right, and realize the leap from extensive to intensive development of foreign trade.

(2) We should continue to improve the import policy; optimize the import structure; increase imports of advanced technology and equipment, key components, resources in short supply, and energy-saving and environmental protection products; and promote the important role of imports in "transforming growth model, adjusting economic structure, and stabilizing economic growth." First, we should strive to narrow the trade surplus, promote the basic trade balance, and create a favorable external environment for macroeconomic management. Second, we should fully understand and pay attention to the important role of imports in "transforming growth model, adjusting economic structure and stabilizing economic growth," increase imports of key technologies and strategic resources in short supply, and ensure the basic trade balance.

(3) We should continue to improve the laws and policies related to the utilization of foreign capital, create a reasonable mechanism

of equal competition suitable for economic development, and give full play to the positive role of foreign capital in "stabilizing economic growth, adjusting economic structure and promoting reforms." First, we should unify domestic and foreign laws and regulations, implement "national treatment" for FDI, improve the investment environment, and promote stable growth of FDI. Second, we should integrate market opening and industrial policies with other relevant policies, and spare no time to promote orderly opening of service industries, including financing, education, culture, and health, and guide more foreign capital to invest in high-tech, advanced manufacturing, modern services, new energies, sophisticated processing and comprehensive utilization of resources, energy conservation, and environmental protection, so as to promote the upgrading of domestic industrial structure.

(4) We should clearly define the functions of government and give full play to the leading role of enterprises to combine the "going global" strategy with the integration of market resources, the introduction of advanced technology and management expertise, and the optimization of their own structure. First, we should rationally regulate the position and role of the government in the "going global" strategy, give full play to the functions of government in providing support and services, strengthen information service by providing timely investment information for domestic enterprises, such as laws and regulations, tax policies, market conditions and corporate credit. Second, we should improve the supervision and guarantee system as well as related laws and regulations concerning outbound investment. Third, we should encourage and help enterprises actively integrate domestic and foreign market resources according to their own development needs, bring in advanced technology and management expertise, optimize their production and technology structure, prevent investment risks, and avoid blind investment and expansion.

Chapter 6

Research on the Income Distribution of Chinese Residents

Wang Youjuan[*]

Abstract

This report systematically illustrates the income distribution of Chinese residents since the 12th Five-Year Plan (2011–2015), reviews the growth of residents' income and the change of its share in the gross national disposable income, analyzes the change in the composition of residents' income, reveals the multidimensional evolution of the income gap, and compares the relative level of the Gini coefficient of Chinese residents' income in the world.

Recent years have witnessed the stable and rapid growth of the Chinese economy, relatively rapid increase in residents' income, steady rise in the proportion of residents' income in the total disposable income, reduced income gap among residents, and generally improved income distribution situation. However, compared with the international community, the gap remains relatively large in the income distribution of China's residents, and further efforts are required to strengthen the reform on income distribution.

6.1. Rapid Income Growth of Chinese Residents and its Increasing Share

The CPC Central Committee proposes to double the per capita income of urban and rural residents by 2020 compared with that in 2010, to maintain synchronous growth of residents' income with the economic growth, and

---

[*]Wang Youjuan is a Senior Statistician at the Department of Household Surveys, National Bureau of Statistics.

to improve people's living standards and quality of life. It has effectively promoted the rapid growth of income of all residents, especially the income of rural residents, which outpaced the GDP growth in the same period, and increased the proportion of residents' income in the gross disposable national income.

6.1.1. *Higher growth rate in real terms of disposable income per capita of Chinese residents than that of GDP in the same period*

According to the national survey of income, expenditure and living conditions of residents by the National Bureau of Statistics, the disposable income per capita of all residents in China was 21,966 yuan in 2015. From 2011 to 2015, the real growth rates of disposable income per capita were 10.3%, 10.6%, 8.1%, 8.0%, and 7.4%, respectively, all of which were higher than the GDP growth in the same year. Over the past five years, the disposable income per capita of Chinese residents increased by 8.9% on the average annually, 1.1 percentage points higher than the GDP growth in the same period (see Table 6.1).

Table 6.1. Disposable income per capita and GDP growth, 2011–2015

(Unit: %)

	Real growth rate of disposable income per capita of residents	Real growth rate of disposable income per capita of urban residents	Real growth rate of disposable income per capita of rural residents	GDP growth rate
2011	10.3	8.4	11.4	9.5
2012	10.6	9.6	10.7	7.7
2013	8.1	7.0	9.3	7.7
2014	8.0	6.8	9.2	7.3
2015	7.4	6.6	7.5	6.9
Accumulated growth rate of "12th Five-Year Plan" period	53.0	44.7	58.2	45.7
Average growth rate of "12th Five-Year Plan" period	8.9	7.7	9.6	7.8

Note: Data on the disposable income per capita from 2013 to 2015 are from the national survey of income, expenditure, and living conditions of residents, while data of 2012 and before were estimated from historical data.

In terms of urban and rural areas, the real growth rate of disposable income per capita of rural residents in these five years outpaced that of GDP each year; the real growth rate of disposable income per capita of urban residents outpaced that of GDP in 2012, while in the other four years it was lower than GDP growth rate, and the growth rate for these five years as a whole did not outpace that of GDP. Part of the reason is that, in the process of urbanization, urban areas continued to expand, and the population of new and old urban areas continued to increase. The inclusion of rural migrants in cities and towns could in fact drag down the growth rate of urban residents' income, which caused a certain degree of incomparability between the years. However, the population of rural migrants, wherever they live, constitutes a part of the national residents. Therefore, in the statistics for the whole country, urbanization will not cause incomparability of the annual income of all residents between different years.

6.1.2. *Higher growth rate of per capita disposable income of rural residents than that of urban residents*

In 2015, the per capita disposable income of rural and urban residents was 11,422 yuan and 31,195 yuan, respectively. From 2011 to 2015, the real growth rates of rural residents' disposable income per capita were 11.4%, 10.7%, 9.3%, 9.2%, and 7.5%, respectively, which were higher than the real growth rates of per capita disposable income of urban residents in the same years. In these five years, the average annual real growth rate of per capita disposable income of rural residents was 9.6%, or 1.9 percentage points higher than that of urban residents in the same period.

6.1.3. *Higher income growth of residents in poverty-stricken rural areas than the average growth of all rural residents with a dramatic reduction of population in poverty in rural areas*

From 2013 to 2015, the real growth rates of per capita disposable income of rural residents in poverty-stricken rural areas were 13.4%, 10.7%, and 10.3%, respectively, with an average annual growth rate of 11.5%, or 2.8 percentage points higher than the overall growth rate of per capita disposal income of rural residents in the same period. The rapid growth of residents' income in poverty-stricken rural areas has accelerated the pace of poverty alleviation. In the three years, the total rural population in poverty decreased from 98.99 million to 55.75 million by 2015, with an average

Table 6.2. National income distribution in China from 2010 to 2013

(Unit: %)

	Share in gross national disposable income		
Year	Government	Enterprises	Residents
2010	18.0	23.6	58.4
2011	18.8	21.9	59.3
2012	19.2	20.6	60.2
2013	18.9	19.8	61.3

Source: China Statistical Yearbook 2015.

annual decrease of 14.41 million people and an average annual poverty alleviation rate of 17.4%.

6.1.4. *Increasing share of residents' income in the gross national disposable income*

According to data from the flows-of-funds table, the share of residents' disposable income in the gross national disposable income in 2010–2013 was 58.4%, 59.3%, 60.2%, and 61.3% respectively, showing a steady upward trend. In 2013, it was 2.9 percentage points higher than in 2010, with an average annual increase of nearly 1 percentage point (see Table 6.2).

6.2. Changes in the Composition of Chinese Residents' Income

With the continuous improvement of the socialist market economic system in China, as well as the increasing efforts of the government to regulate taxation, social security, and transfer payments, the net transfer and net property income, among the residents' income, have increased rapidly, while wage income still occupies the dominant position.

6.2.1. *Faster growth of net transfer income than that of wage income, net operating income and net property income*

According to the national survey of income, expenditure, and living conditions of residents, in 2015, the wage income per capita (12,459 yuan) increased by 19.7% over 2013, with an average annual growth rate of 9.4%; the net operating income per capita (3,956 yuan) increased by 15.2% over

Table 6.3. Per capita disposable income composition of Chinese residents from 2013 to 2015

(Unit: Yuan)

Indicator	2013	2014	2015
Disposable income per capita	18,311	20,167	21,966
1. Wage income	10,411	11,421	12,459
2. Net operating income	3,435	3,732	3,956
3. Net property income	1,423	1,588	1,740
4. Net transfer income	3,042	3,427	3,812

Source: National survey of income, expenditure, and living conditions of residents.

2013, with an average annual growth rate of 7.3%; the net property income per capita (1,740 yuan) increased by 22.2% over 2013, with an average annual growth rate of 10.6%; and the net transfer income per capita (3,812 yuan) increased by 25.3% over 2013, with an average annual growth rate of 11.9% (see Table 6.3). The average annual growth rate of net transfer income per capita was 2.5 percentage points, 4.6 percentage points, and 1.3 percentage points higher than that of wage income, net operating income, and net property income, respectively.

6.2.2. *Increasing share of net transfer and net property income with wage income still occupying the dominant position*

In 2015, wage income accounted for 56.7% of the per capita disposable income of residents, still occupying the dominant position but dropping by 0.1 percentage points when compared with 2013. Net transfer and net property income accounted for 17.4% and 7.9%, respectively, which increased by 0.8 percentage points and 0.1 percentage points compared with 2013. The proportion of net operating income was 18.0%, or 0.8 percentage points lower than that in 2013, showing the largest decline.

6.3. Narrowing Gap in the Income of Chinese Residents

In recent years, the income gap has been narrowing slowly among residents between urban and rural areas, regions, different income groups, and different industries. The Gini coefficient of income has been declining continuously. The fairness of income distribution has improved in general, but the income gap among rural residents fluctuated greatly.

6.3.1. *Narrowing gap in the income between urban and rural residents*

If we calculate the disposable income per capita of urban and rural residents using the same coverage, in 2015, the ratio of per capita income of urban residents and rural residents was 2.73, a drop of 0.17 compared to 2.90 in 2011. From 2011 to 2015, the trend was decreasing year by year (see Table 6.4).

If we look at the gap between urban and rural areas by region, the ratio of per capita disposable income between urban and rural residents in the eastern, central, western, and northeastern regions in 2015 was 2.57, 2.46, 2.91, and 2.38, respectively. The gap between urban and rural areas within the western region was significantly higher than that in other regions, and that in the northeastern region was the smallest.

6.3.2. *Narrowing gap in the income of residents between regions*

In 2015, the per capita disposable income in the eastern region was 28,233 yuan, up by 19.3% over 2013, with an average annual increase of 9.2%; in the central region, it was 18,442 yuan, up by 20.8% over 2013, with an average annual increase of 9.9%; in the western region, the figures were 16,868 yuan, 21.2% and 10.1%; and in the northeastern region: 21,008 yuan, 17.4% and 8.4% (see Table 6.5). The growth rate of per capita disposable income in the western region with a lower income level was the highest, which was 0.9, 0.2, and 1.7 percentage points higher than that in the eastern, central, and northeastern regions, respectively. In 2015, the ratio of per capita disposable

Table 6.4. Ratio of per capita disposable income of urban and rural residents, 2011–2015

Year	Urban residents (yuan)	Rural residents (yuan)	Ratio (rural = 1)
2011	21427	7394	2.90
2012	24127	8389	2.88
2013	26467	9430	2.81
2014	28844	10489	2.75
2015	31195	11422	2.73

Note: Data of per capita disposable income in urban and rural areas from 2013 to 2015 are from the national survey of income, expenditure, and living conditions of residents. Data of 2012 and before were estimated from historical data.

Table 6.5. Per capita disposable income of residents in different regions, 2013–2015

(Unit: yuan)

Region	2013	2014	2015
Nationwide	18311	20167	21966
Eastern region	23658	25954	28223
Central region	15264	16868	18442
Western region	13919	15376	16868
Northeastern region	17893	19604	21008

Source: National survey of income, expenditure and living conditions of residents.

income of all residents in the eastern, central, western, and northeastern regions was 1.67:1.09:1:1.25 (with the western region as 1). Compared with the ratio of 1.70:1.10:1:1.29 in 2013, the relative income gap between the eastern and western regions narrowed by 0.03.

Analyzed by region and by urban/rural residence, the ratio of per capita disposable income of urban residents in the eastern, central, western, and northeastern regions was 1.39:1.01:1:1.04 in 2015 (with the western region as 1). The income level of urban residents in the eastern region was outstanding, more than 35% higher than that of other regions. The income level of urban residents in the central, western, and northeastern regions was very close. In 2015, the ratio of per capita disposable income of rural residents in the eastern, central, western, and northeastern regions was 1.57:1.20:1:1.26 (with that of the western region as 1), down step by step from east to west. The gap in rural areas between the eastern region and the western region was larger than that in urban areas.

Analyzed by province, the ratio of per capita disposable income between the top five provinces and the bottom five provinces in 2015 was 2.51:1, which was 0.07 lower than that in 2013, and the inter-provincial disparity of per capita disposable income among residents narrowed.

6.3.3. *Narrowing gap between different income groups in general, with relatively large internal fluctuations in rural areas*

In terms of income quintiles, the year 2015 registered a per capita income of 54,544 yuan for the high-income group, up by 7.2% over 2013; 29,438 yuan for the upper-middle-income group, up by 9.9%; 19,320 yuan for the middle-income group, up by 10.9%; 11,894 yuan for the lower-middle-income group, up by 11.0%; and 5,221 yuan for the low-income group, up by 8.9% (see

Table 6.6.   Per capita disposable income by quintile group, 2013–2015

(Unit: yuan)

Group	2013	2014	2015
Per capita disposable income	18311	20167	21966
Low-income group (20%)	4402	4747	5221
Lower-middle group (20%)	9654	10887	11894
Middle-income group (20%)	15698	17631	19320
Upper-middle group (20%)	24361	26937	29438
High-income group (20%)	47457	50968	54544

Source: National survey of income, expenditure, and living conditions of residents.

Table 6.6). The average annual growth rates of per capita disposable income of the lower-middle, middle, and upper-middle groups were higher than that of high-income group and low-income group. In 2015, the ratio of per capita disposable income of high-income and low-income groups was 10.45:1, down by 0.33 when compared with that in 2013.

By urban and rural areas, the ratio of per capita disposable income between urban highest and lowest income groups was 5.32 in 2015, down by 0.52 over 2013 (5.84) and by 0.17 over 2014 (5.49). The ratio of per capita disposable income between rural highest and lowest income groups was 8.43 in 2015, up by 1.02 over 2013 (7.41) and down by 0.22 over 2014 (8.65). This indicates that in these three years, the income gap among different income groups of urban residents continued to narrow, while the income gap among different income groups of rural residents fluctuated greatly, and the income gap among rural residents was larger than that among urban residents.

6.3.4. *Narrowing gap of wage income of employees between industries*

The results of labor and wage statistics of the National Bureau of Statistics show that the relative gap of wage levels among industries has gradually narrowed in recent years. Among the 19 industries of the national economy, the average wage ratio of the highest to the lowest industries declined gradually from 2011 to 2014, and was 4.17 times, 3.96 times, 3.86 times, and 3.82 times, respectively.

Of the top 10 sub-industries with the highest average wage in 2014, 7 sub-industries had monopolistic nature to a certain extent, including other financial industries, capital market services, air transport, tobacco products, monetary and financial services, oil and gas extraction, and pipeline transportation; and 3 sub-industries were intensive in high-level human capital, including Internet and related services, software, information technology and technical services, and research and experimental development. Of the bottom 10 sub-industries with the lowest average wage, the lowest 5 sub-industries were farming, forestry, animal husbandry, fishery, and catering service, while the rest belongs to manufacturing (including lumber-processing, wood, bamboo, bine, palm, grass products, leather, coat and feather products, and shoe making), public facilities management, services for farming, forestry, animal husbandry and fishery, and other services. These facts demonstrate that the employees in the industries with the highest average wage generally have a higher education level, or those industries have monopolistic nature to certain extent; while the industries with the lowest average wage belong to the typical low-end labor-intensive industries, and the level of human capital is low.

6.3.5. *Declining Gini coefficient of per capita disposable income of Chinese residents year on year*

Gini coefficient is a common index used by the international community to measure the degree of inequality in income distribution. In 2012, the National Bureau of Statistics carried out the reform for the integration of urban and rural household surveys, established a unified indicator system for urban and rural income, and selected a coherent and integrated sample for the urban and rural household survey. Based on the basic information obtained from the household survey, the special survey data of rural migrant workers and personal income tax data, the National Bureau of Statistics adjusted the data of household income survey of urban and rural residents over the years, reconciled the incomplete income data of rural migrant workers and the low proportion of high-income households in urban areas, and estimated the Gini coefficient of disposable income of residents nationwide in 2012 and earlier years. After 2012, the Gini coefficient of disposable income of residents nationwide was calculated by using data from the national survey of income, expenditure, and living conditions of residents (i.e. the integrated urban and rural household survey).

Table 6.7. Gini coefficient of disposable income of Chinese residents nationwide, 2011–2015

	2011	2012	2013	2014	2015
Gini coefficient	0.477	0.474	0.473	0.469	0.462

Source: China Yearbook of Household Survey 2015.

From Table 6.7, we can see that the Gini coefficients of per capita disposable income of Chinese residents from 2011 to 2015 were 0.477, 0.474, 0.473, 0.469, and 0.462, respectively, showing a slow decline year on year.

In the past five years, the narrowing of income distribution gap among Chinese residents was closely related to the rapid growth of income of rural residents brought by the expansion of the scale of rural migrant workers, the rise of wages, the increase of grain output, and the rise of prices through fluctuation. It was a positive result of a number of national policies to benefit the people, including the increase of agricultural production subsidies, the implementation of targeted poverty alleviation, the improvement of social security system, the raise of individual tax threshold, the continuous increase of the income level of low- and middle-income groups, and the efforts to adjust the income distribution pattern.

6.4. High Level of Gini Coefficient of Income for Chinese Residents in the World

According to data released by the Organisation for Economic Co-operation and Development (OECD), the Gini coefficient of residents' income in 34 OECD member countries averaged at 0.314 in 2011. The Gini coefficient of 15 countries was below 0.3, that of 16 countries was between 0.3 and 0.4, and only 3 countries had a Gini coefficient above 0.4. According to data released by the World Bank, the Gini coefficient of Central and Eastern European countries has been less than 0.3 since 2005; the Gini coefficient of Asian countries, except the Philippines and Malaysia, was basically lower than 0.4; and that of some African and Latin American countries was higher than 0.5. According to data officially released by BRICS countries, South Africa had the highest Gini coefficient (0.640), followed by Brazil (0.500), China (0.462 in 2015) and Russia (0.420), and India at the lowest level (below 0.4) (see Table 6.8).

The calculation methods of Gini coefficient vary among international organizations and countries. Some use either pre-tax income or post-tax

Table 6.8. Comparison of Gini coefficient of residents' income in selected countries

Country	Year	Pre-tax Gini coefficient	Post-tax Gini coefficient	Adjustment intensity (%)
United States	2010	0.499	0.380	−23.80
Britain	2010	0.523	0.341	−34.80
Germany	2010	0.492	0.286	−41.90
France	2010	0.505	0.303	−40.00
Italy	2010	0.503	0.319	−36.60
Canada	2010	0.447	0.320	−28.40
Japan	2010	0.488	0.336	−31.10
Brazil	2012	—	0.500	—
Russia	2012	—	0.420	—
South Africa	2009	—	0.640	—
India	2010	—	0.339	—

Source: National data for India are from the World Bank database, data for other BRICS countries are from the *BRICS Joint Statistical Publication*, and data for G7 countries are from the OECD database.

income, while others use adjusted income or consumption expenditure data, so the results are not completely comparable. For example, in 2010, the Gini coefficient of residents' pre-tax monetary income in the United States was 0.499, and the Gini coefficient of post-tax monetary income was 0.380. India uses consumption expenditure to calculate the Gini coefficient, which was generally underestimated. China's Gini coefficient in 2007, published on the website of World Bank, was 0.425, using purchasing power parity (PPP) adjusted income. The Gini coefficient published by the National Bureau of Statistics was calculated using post-tax disposable income per capita without PPP adjustment.

From the international comparison, although the Gini coefficient of residents' income in China tends to decline in recent years, it is still at a high level, indicating that the unequal distribution of residents' income in China is still relatively high. The main reason is that the dual structure of urban and rural areas in China is still prevailing, the regional development is not balanced, and the income gap between different income groups is large. Especially in rural areas, the gap between regions and between different income groups is more prominent, which is noticeably larger than that in urban areas. It is also related to the current development stage of China.

From Table 6.8, we can see that the Gini coefficient of pre-tax income in some developed countries is relatively high, with most countries at around 0.5. However, after regulation through taxes, the Gini coefficient of post-tax income will decrease significantly, with a decline of more than 10 percentage points, with an adjustment intensity of about 30%–40%. According to estimation by relevant researchers, the degree of inequality of initial income distribution in China is not much different from that in OECD countries, but after redistribution, the Gini coefficient of residents' income in China is only a few percentage points lower than that in the initial distribution, and the adjustment intensity is only around 10%, which is weaker than that in OECD countries. The research results of some scholars indicate that indirect tax generally enlarges the income gap, while direct tax generally narrows the income gap. The proportion of direct tax in total tax revenue in China is too small to play a leading role in narrowing the income gap. At present, China has established a comprehensive social security system, but the level of social security is still at low level. For example, the original basic pension standard for rural resident was only 55 yuan per month and was increased to 70 yuan per month in 2015. This only accounted for about 9% of the average consumption of rural residents in that year, and about 30% of the poverty standard for rural residents in that year. The low level of overall security standard had very limited effect on narrowing the income gap. It is necessary to continue to enhance the adjustment intensity by increasing tax, social security, and transfer payments to narrow the income gap, to promote effectively the reform of the income distribution system, and to further narrow the income distribution gap among residents, so as to promote social fairness and justice.

Chapter 7

Changes and Challenges in China's Economic Structure[*]

Xu Xianchun, Zhang Yanzhen, Wang Xinxian, and Yao Aixing[†]

Abstract

This report expounds the changes in the key economic structure of China, including industrial structure, demand structure, regional structure, income distribution structure, and foreign trade structure; explores the severe challenges faced by these key economic structure; and proposes corresponding policy recommendations in response to these challenges.

The issue of economic structure is not only a prominent problem in China's current economic development but also a strategic issue of long-term economic development. In recent years, thanks to a series of economic restructuring policies and measures, positive changes are taking place in China's key economic structures such as industrial structure, demand structure, regional structure, income distribution structure, and foreign trade structure. However, the economic structure of China is still facing

---

[*]This report is a revised version of the research report of the fourth research group of the topic "Strategic Thinking and Leadership" of the 57th class for provincial- and minister-level officials of the Party School of the CPC Central Committee. The research group is led by Xu Xianchun, who is also responsible for the writing of the research report, and its members included Zhang Yanzhen, Wang Xinxian, and Yao Aixing, and this article was revised by Xu Xianchun. This report was published in the *Journal of Chinese Academy of Governance*, Issue 6, 2015.
[†]Xu Xianchun is the Deputy Commissioner of the National Bureau of Statistics; Zhang Yanzhen is the Vice-Minister of Justice; Wang Xinxian is the Vice-President of the China Disabled Persons' Federation; and Yao Aixing is the Vice Governor of the People's Government of Ningxia Hui Autonomous Region.

severe challenges. Using the latest statistical data, this report studies the changes and challenges of China's economic structure and puts forward some thoughts and recommendations for further adjustment of the economic structure.

7.1. Positive Changes in China's Key Economic Structure

Due to the reasons pertaining to, among other factors, history and nature, China's economic structures have long been plagued with some outstanding problems, such as the stagnation of the tertiary industry in terms of industrial structure; insufficient consumption demand and excessive dependence on investment demand and export demand in terms of demand structure; economic development in the central and western regions lagging behind the eastern regions in terms of regional structure; low proportion of household income and excessive income gap in terms of income distribution structure; and seriously delayed development of trade in services in terms of foreign trade structure.

The CPC Central Committee and the State Council attached great importance to the adjustment of China's economic structure. The report of the 18th National Congress of CPC identified strategic economic restructuring as the main direction of the transformation of the mode of economic development. The 3rd Plenary Session of the 18th CPC Central Committee adopted the *Decision of the Central Committee of the CPC on Some Major Issues Concerning Comprehensively Deepening the Reform*, which recognized promoting the coordination of major economic structures as one of the main tasks of macroregulation. In the section of "Situation and guiding ideas in the decisive stage of building a moderately prosperous society in all respects," the *Recommendations of the Central Committee of the Communist Party of China for the Thirteenth Five-Year Plan for Economic and Social Development* adopted at the 5th Plenary Session of the 18th CPC Central Committee, it was emphasized that "to achieve higher quality, more efficient, more equitable and more sustainable development, we need to speed up structural reform and transformation of the growth model by giving priority to economic construction and grasping the characteristics of development." The section on "Main objectives and basic concepts of economic and social development during the 13th Five-Year Plan period" outlined the requirement that the proportion of the service industry should be further increased and consumption should contribute more significantly to economic growth during the 13th Five-Year

Plan period; and the section on "Adhering to coordinated development and striving to form a balanced development structure" put forward the requirements of promoting the coordinated development between different regions and between the urban and rural areas. The section on "Adhering to open development and striving to achieve win-win cooperation" stated the requirements of speeding up the optimization and upgrading of foreign trade, consolidating export market share and developing trade in services. The section on "Adhering to shared development and striving to improve people's well-being" outlined the requirements of continuously increasing the income of urban and rural households, adjusting the distribution pattern of national income, and reducing income gaps.

In recent years, thanks to a series of economic restructuring policies and measures, positive changes have taken place in China's key economic structures such as industrial structure, demand structure, regional structure, income distribution structure, and foreign trade structure.

7.1.1. *Positive changes in the industrial structure*

The industrial structure consists of industrial structures at different levels, including the structure of the three industries, the structure of industrial sectors of national economy, and the structure of manufacturing.

7.1.1.1. *Proportion of the tertiary industry exceeded that of the secondary industry*

The structure of the three industries refers to the proportion of the value added of the primary, secondary, and tertiary industries to the gross domestic product (GDP). Figure 7.1 shows the changes in the structure of China's three industries since the reform and opening-up.[1] As shown in the figure, since the reform and opening-up, the proportion of China's tertiary industry has been on the rise, which, however, had always been lower than that of the secondary industry before 2012. In 2012, the proportion of the tertiary industry was 45.5% and that of the secondary industry was 45.0%, and this was the first time that the proportion of the tertiary industry exceeded that of the secondary industry. In 2013 and 2014, the proportion of the tertiary industry rose to 46.9% and 48.2%, respectively, and that of

---

[1] These are the changes in the structure of the three industries based on revised data after the third economic census.

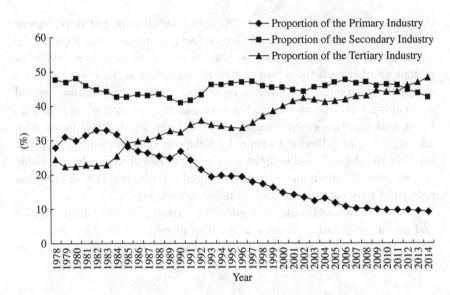

Figure 7.1.   Changes in the structure of three industries in China, 1978–2014

the secondary industry fell to 43.7% and 42.6%, respectively. In 2014, the proportion of the tertiary industry was 5.6 percentage points higher than that of the secondary industry.

In the first three quarters of 2015, the value added of the tertiary industry increased by 8.4% year-on-year, or 2.4 percentage points faster than that of the secondary industry; the proportion of the tertiary industry was 51.4%, up by 2.3 percentage points over the same period of the previous year and 10.8 percentage points higher than that of the secondary industry.

This change in the structure of the three industries is of great significance. It marks the accelerated transformation of China's economic growth from the dominance by the secondary industry to the dominance by the tertiary industry. The tertiary industry is characterized by low resource consumption, low environmental pollution, and strong capacity of creating jobs. Therefore, this change in the structure of China's three industries is conducive to reducing resource consumption and environmental pollution, to increasing employments, to improving the quality and efficiency of economic growth, and to improving people's livelihood.

7.1.1.2. *Proportion of high-tech industry and equipment manufacturing in the industry rose*

In recent years, encouraged by policies promoting the development of strategic emerging industries and advanced manufacturing and eliminating backward production capacity, industrial structures above the designated size[2] showed positive changes, with a growing proportion of technology-intensive, high-tech industry and equipment manufacturing and a declining proportion of energy-intensive industries and mining. The proportion of high-tech industry rose since 2011, from 8.9% in 2010 to 10.6% in 2014, and to 11.6% in the first three quarters of 2015; the proportion of equipment manufacturing increased since 2013, from 28.2% in 2012 to 30.4% in 2014 and to 31.4% in the first three quarters of 2015; while the proportion of energy-intensive industries declined from 30.7% in 2011 to 28.4% in 2014, and to 28.2% in the first three quarters of 2015; the proportion of the mining industry dropped since 2013, from 13.9% in 2012 to 11% in 2014, and to 8.8% in the first three quarters of 2015 (see Figure 7.2).

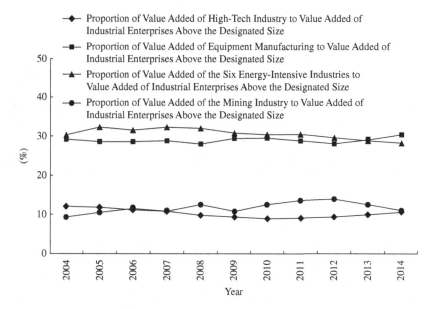

Figure 7.2. Changes in China's industrial structure, 2004–2014

---

[2]Industrial enterprises above designated size refer to industrial enterprises with annual main business income of over 20 million yuan.

7.1.1.3. *Strategic emerging service industries, the high-tech service industry, the culture and related industrial services industry developed rapidly*

In the first three quarters of 2015, in the context of greater pressure of economic downturn, the operating income of strategic emerging service industries above the designated size increased by 11.9% year-on-year, of which that of new material promotion service and specialized design service industries increased by 21.3% and 15.0%, respectively. The operating income of the high-tech service industry above the designated size increased by 8.9%, among which that of the Internet information service industry increased by 24.2% and that of information system integration service industry increased by 10.5%. The operating income of the culture and related industrial services industry increased by 11.4%, of which that of movie showing increased by 31.8%, and that of the conference and exhibition services increased by 15.4%.

7.1.2. *Positive changes in the demand structure*

In recent years, the structure of three major demands in China has been undergoing positive changes. From 2011 to 2014, the proportion of final consumption expenditure to GDP by the expenditure approach, i.e. the consumption rate, showed an uptrend; from 2012 to 2014, the proportion of gross capital formation to GDP by the expenditure approach, i.e. the investment rate, showed a downtrend; and from 2008 to 2014, the proportion of net exports of goods and services to the GDP by the expenditure approach, i.e. the net export rate, showed a downtrend. The excessive reliance of China's economic growth on investment demand and export demand is changing.

As shown in Figure 7.3, from 1983 to 2010, China's consumption rate showed a decline with fluctuation, and in particular, from 2000 to 2010, it basically showed a downtrend year by year. The consumption rate was 67.4% in 1983, 63.7% in 2000, and 49.1% in 2010. The consumption rate in 2010 was 18.3 percentage points lower than that in 1983, and 14.6 percentage points lower than that in 2000. From 2011 to 2014, the consumption rate increased year-on-year, from 49.1% in 2010 to 51.4% in 2014, with an increase of 2.3 percentage points in four years and an average annual increase of 0.6 percentage point.

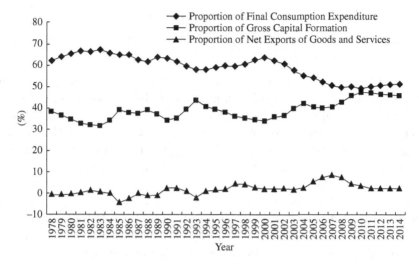

Figure 7.3. Changes in the structure of China's three major demands, 1978–2014

From 1983 to 2011, China's investment rate showed a growing trend with fluctuation, especially with a steep climb during 2000–2011. The investment rate was 31.7% in 1983, 33.9% in 2000, and 47.3% in 2011, which was up by 15.6 percentage points when compared with 1983 and up by 13.4 percentage points when compared with 2000. From 2000 to 2011, the average annual increase of investment rate was 1.2 percentage points. During 2012–2014, the investment rate decreased from 47.3% in 2011 to 45.9% in 2014, with a decline of 1.4 percentage points in three years, or an average annual decline of 0.5 percentage points.

From 1985 to 2007, China's net export rate zigzagged up. The net export rate was −4.0% in 1985, and 8.7% in 2007, the peak since the reform and opening-up, or since China's earliest GDP data by the expenditure approach for the year 1952. During the period, China's net export rate rose from a negative value to a peak of 4.5% in 1997. After the Asian financial crisis, it dropped year by year, and fell to 2.1% in 2001. After China's accession to the WTO, especially during 2004–2007, China's net export rate increased significantly, from 2.1% in 2001 to 8.7% in 2007. After the outbreak of the international financial crisis, China's net export rate kept declining from 8.7% in 2007 to 2.5% in 2011. From 2012 to 2014, China's net export rate maintained at a stable level of 2.7%, 2.5%, and 2.7%, respectively.

7.1.3. *Positive changes in the regional structure*

7.1.3.1. *Rise in the proportion of GDP in the central and western regions*

The lagging development of the central and western regions compared with the eastern region is one of the major structural contradictions in China's economic imbalance. As shown in Figure 7.4, from the initial stage of the reform and opening-up to 2006, the economic growth rate in the eastern region of China was higher than that in central and western regions for most of the years. Driven by regional development strategies such as the development of the western region, the revitalization of northeastern region, and the rise of the central region, the economic growth rate in the western region exceeded that in the eastern region after 2007; and after 2008, the economic growth rate in the central region exceeded that in the eastern region. Therefore, from the initial stage of the reform and opening-up to 2006, the proportion of the GDP of the eastern region to the total GDP of all regions in the country showed an uptrend, and the proportion of the central region showed a downtrend. After 2007, the proportion in the eastern region declined, while that in the central region showed an uptrend. From the initial stage of the reform and opening-up to 2005, the proportion of the western region showed a downtrend, and after 2006, the proportion of the western region showed an uptrend (see Figure 7.5).

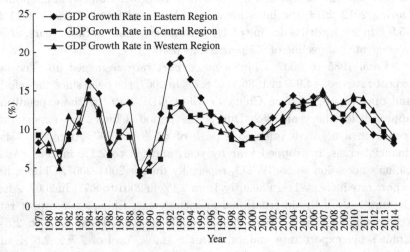

Figure 7.4. Changes in economic growth rates of eastern, central and western regions, 1979–2014

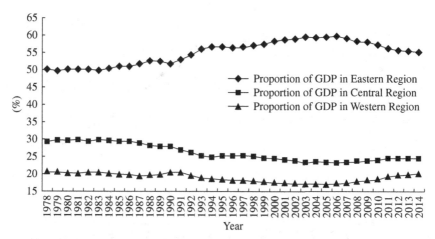

Figure 7.5. Changes in the economic structure of eastern, central, and western regions, 1978–2014

7.1.3.2. *Significant narrowing of the relative gap of per capita GDP between the most developed provinces in the eastern region and the least developed provinces in the western region*

As shown in Figure 7.6, from 1993 to 2000, the relative gap of per capita GDP between the economically most developed provinces in the eastern region and the least developed provinces in the western region showed an uptrend, rising from 9:1 in 1993 to 10.9:1 in 2000. From 2001 to 2014, the gap showed a downtrend, especially with a noticeable decline during 2005–2014, dropping from 10.4:1 in 2004 to 4:1 in 2014. It is obvious that the relative gap of per capita GDP between the economically most developed provinces in the eastern region and the economically underdeveloped provinces in the western region was significantly narrowing.

7.1.4. *Positive changes in the income distribution structure*

The income distribution structure described in this report mainly includes two aspects: one is the distribution structure of national disposable income among households, enterprises, and governments, and the other is the income distribution gap among households.

In China, the distribution of national disposable income between households, enterprises, and governments is calculated through the flow-of-fund tables in national accounts. The flow-of-fund tables divide income

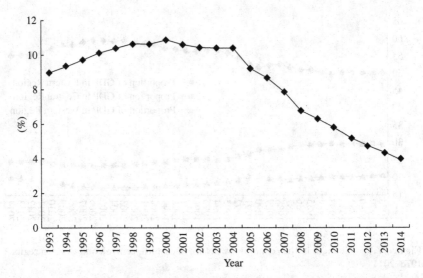

Figure 7.6. Ratios of per capita GDP in economically most developed provinces in eastern region to that in the least developed provinces in western region, 1993–2014

distribution into primary distribution and redistribution. The results of the primary distribution constitute the initial distribution of income among households, enterprises, and governments; and the redistribution yields the disposable income of households, enterprises, and governments. The sum of disposable income of households, enterprises, and governments are the national disposable income,[3] which is expressed as the formula below:

$$\text{National disposable income} = \text{disposable income of households}$$
$$+ \text{disposable income of enterprises}$$
$$+ \text{disposable income of governments}$$

$$(7.1)$$

Therefore, the flow-of-fund tables reflect how the national disposable income is distributed among households, enterprises, and governments, and the distribution structure therefrom.

---

[3] In the flow-of-fund tables, the disposable income of households, the disposable income of enterprises, the disposable income of governments and the national disposable income all include gross disposable income and net disposable income. The difference between them is that the former includes depreciation of fixed assets, while the latter does not. All disposable income in this report refers to gross disposable income.

The income distribution gap of households includes the income distribution gap between urban and rural areas, between regions, within cities, and within rural areas. This income distribution gap is reflected through the household survey.

7.1.4.1. *Picking up of the proportion of disposable income of households*

As shown in Figure 7.7, from 1997 to 2008, the proportion of disposable income of households in the national disposable income showed a down-trend, from 69.0% in 1996 to 57.2% in 2008, with a decline of 11.8 percentage points. The proportion of the disposable income of enterprises and that of governments to the national disposable income increased from 16.4% and 14.6% in 1996 to 24.5% and 18.3% in 2008, up by 8.1 and 3.7 percentage points, respectively. From 2009 to 2013, stimulated by a series of income distribution policies to strengthen social security and increase household income, the proportion of disposable income of households recorded a rebound, from 57.2% in 2008 to 61.3% in 2013, with a rise of 4.1 percentage points. The share of disposable income of enterprises declined from 24.5% in 2008 to 19.8% in 2013, down by 4.7 percentage points.

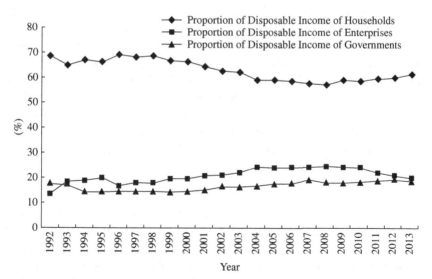

Figure 7.7. Changes in income distribution structure of three major economic entities, 1992–2013

Due to the source of the data, China's 2014 flow-of-fund tables has not yet been compiled, so the change in the distribution structure of national disposable income among households, enterprises, and governments in 2014 cannot be reflected by the flow-of-fund tables. However, the GDP data and household survey data showed that the income distribution in 2014 was further inclined to households significantly. Data from the household survey indicated that in 2014, the per capita disposable income of households nationwide increased by 8.0% in real terms, and the GDP increased by 7.3% in real terms, with the former being 0.7 percentage points higher than the latter. Therefore, one could expect that the proportion of disposable income of households in 2014 would further increase.

7.1.4.2. *Narrowing gap in the household income*

The following is a description of the trend of narrowing the relative gap in household income from three aspects: (1) income growth of urban and rural households, (2) relative income gap between urban and rural households, and (3) Gini coefficient of households.

(1) The growth rate of income of rural households was higher than that of urban households. As shown in Figure 7.8, from 1979 to 1988, due to the reform of the rural household contract responsibility system, farmers' production enthusiasm was greatly mobilized. Except for a few years, the growth rate of per capita net income of rural households was higher than that of urban households. From 1989 to 2009, the urban reform boosted the income of urban households. Except for a few years, the growth rate of per capita disposable income of urban households was higher than that of rural households. From 2010 to 2014, due to a series of favorable policies for farmers, such as the abolition of agricultural taxes, various subsidies for agricultural production, the establishment of a rural social security system, and the rapid growth of wages for rural migrant workers, the per capita net income of rural households grew faster than that of urban households.

(2) The relative income gap between urban and rural households was shrinking. As shown in Figure 7.9, from 2001 to 2009, the income ratio of urban and rural households, i.e. the ratio of per capita disposable income of urban households to per capita net income of rural households, increased from 2.79 in 2000 to the peak of 3.33 in 2009. From 2010 to 2014, the income ratio of urban and rural households declined from 3.33 in 2009 to 2.97 in

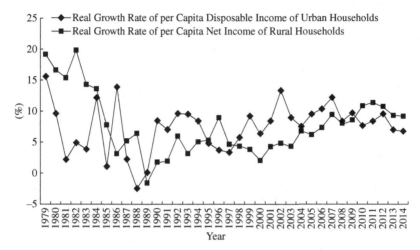

Figure 7.8.   Real growth rate of per capita disposable income of urban households and of per capita net income of rural households, 1979–2014

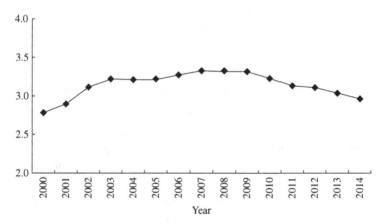

Figure 7.9.   Ratio of per capita disposable income of urban households to per capita net income of rural households, 2000–2014

2014. From this we can see that after 2010, the relative gap of income between urban and rural households was gradually narrowing.

7.1.5. *Falling Gini coefficient of households' income*

As shown in Figure 7.10, from 2005 to 2008, the Gini coefficient of household income in China increased from 0.473 in 2004 to 0.491 in 2008. From 2009

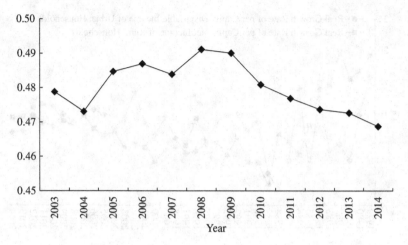

Figure 7.10. Gini coefficient of Chinese households' income from 2003 to 2014

to 2014, the Gini coefficient of household income decreased from 0.491 in 2008 to 0.469 in 2014, indicating that the relative income gap of Chinese households was narrowing after 2009.

7.1.6. *Positive changes in the foreign trade structure*

One of the outstanding features of the change in China's foreign trade structure is that technology-intensive industries have become more important than labor-intensive industries. From the export delivery value of major export industries in 2014, the export value of technology-intensive equipment manufacturing industry accounted for 64.5% of the export value of industrial exports above the designated size, which has become China's main export industry, and its proportion far exceeded that of traditional labor-intensive export industries such as textiles and light industry. In 2014, among the top 10 export industries, the export growth rate of technology-intensive, electronics and equipment related emerging industries accelerated compared with the previous year: the export delivery value of computer, communications, and other electronic equipment manufacturing increased by 5.8%, up by 0.2 percentage point; that of electrical machinery and equipment manufacturing industry grew by 6.1%, up by 3.9 percentage points; that of general equipment manufacturing industry grew by 2.4%, up by 1.9 percentage points; and that of metal products industry grew by 8.7%, up by 3.8 percentage points. On the other hand, the export growth rate of labor-intensive traditional industries like textile-based manufacturing fell from the previous year: clothing and apparel industry grew by 3.0%, down by 4.4 percentage points; textile industry grew by 1.0%, down by 6.3 percentage points; the manufacturing of leather, fur, feathers and their products, and footwear grew by 5.7%, down by 0.1 percentage point.

7.2. Severe Challenges Faced by China's Economic Structure

As mentioned earlier, thanks to a series of economic restructuring initiatives in recent years, China's key economic structures witnessed positive changes, such as in the industrial structure, demand structure, regional structure, income distribution structure, and foreign trade structure. However, China's current economic structure is still facing serious challenges.

7.2.1. *Challenges facing the industrial structure*

7.2.1.1. *Still very low proportion of the tertiary industry*

As mentioned earlier, since the reform and opening-up, the proportion of China's tertiary industry has shown an uptrend. In 2012, its proportion surpassed that of the secondary industry for the first time. In 2014, its proportion reached 48.2%, exceeding that of the secondary industry by 5.6 percentage points, thanks to China's industrial restructuring. However, the proportion of China's tertiary industry is still very low, and compared with the high-income countries and the world average, there is still a considerable gap, and it is true even when compared with the average of upper-middle-income countries, the group where China currently belongs to.

As shown in Table 7.1, in 2012, the proportion of the tertiary industry in the high-income countries was 73.7%, and the world average was 70.2%. In 2013, the proportion of the tertiary industry in the lower-middle-income countries was 55.1%, that in middle-income countries was 55.2%, and that in the upper-middle-income countries was 55.6%. At present, the proportion of China's tertiary industry is more than 25 percentage points lower than that of high-income countries, more than 20 percentage points lower than the world average, and more than 7 percentage points lower than that of upper-middle-income countries.

Table 7.1.   Composition of the three industries in the world, 2013

(Unit: %)

	Primary industry	Secondary industry	Tertiary industry
	Composition of the three industries		
World	3.08*	26.75*	70.18*
High-income countries	1.48*	24.82*	73.71*
Middle and low income countries	10.41	34.57	55.07
Middle-income countries	10.02	34.84	55.18
Upper-middle-income countries	7.65	36.73	55.63
Lower-middle-income countries	17.04	32.12	51.06
Low-income countries	25.80	23.63	50.50

*2012 data.

Source: World Bank Development Indicators Database.

7.2.1.2. *Still low proportion of high-tech industry versus still high proportion of energy-intensive industries*

As mentioned earlier, the proportion of high-tech industry to all China's industries above the designated size increased year on year since 2011 but was only 10.6% in 2014, whereas the proportion of energy-intensive industries to all industries above the designated size decreased year by year since 2012, but still stood at 28.4% in 2014. The low proportion of high-tech industry indicates the low content of China's industrial technology and weakness in innovation. The high proportion of energy-intensive industries is the most important reason for China's high energy consumption and high intensity of carbon dioxide emissions. According to the revised data after the third economic census, in 2013, the energy consumption of the six energy-intensive industries accounted for 79.8% of all industrial energy consumption above the designated size, the industrial energy consumption above the designated size accounted for 94.2% of the total industrial energy consumption, and the total industrial energy consumption accounted for 69.8% of the total energy consumption of the whole society. Therefore, more than half of the total energy consumption of the whole society was consumed by energy-intensive industries. As energy consumption is the main source of carbon dioxide emissions, the high proportion of energy-intensive industries is the primary culprit of the high intensity of carbon dioxide emissions in China.

7.2.2. Challenges facing the demand structure

As mentioned earlier, China's consumption rate rebounded from 2011 to 2014, China's investment rate kept declining from 2012 to 2014, and China's net export rate also kept declining from 2008 to 2014. The excessive reliance of China's economic growth on investment demand and export demand was alleviated. However, in 2014, China's consumption rate was only at 51.4%, which was 16.0 percentage points lower than the 67.4% in 1983, and 12.3 percentage points lower than the 63.7% in 2000. In 2014, China's investment rate was still as high as 45.9%, 14.2 percentage points higher than the 31.7% in 1983 and 12.0 percentage points higher than the 33.9% in 2000.

As shown in Table 7.2, in 2013, the average consumption rate in the world was as high as 77.6%, that in high-income countries was as high as 79.1%, that in middle-income countries was 69.8%, and that in upper-middle-income countries was 68.3%. China's consumption rate was over 25 percentage points lower than the world's average, over 27 percentage points lower than that of high-income countries, over 18 percentage points lower than that of middle-income countries, and over 16 percentage points lower than upper-middle-income countries. Therefore, whether it is a longitudinal comparison in history or a horizontal comparison with the world average, high-income countries, middle-income countries, and upper-middle-income countries, China's current consumption rate is quite low.

In 2013, the average investment rate in the world was only 22.3%, that in high-income countries was only 20.4%, that in middle-income countries was 31.2%, and that in upper-middle-income countries was 31.6%. China's investment rate more than doubled the world average, 25 percentage points

Table 7.2. Composition of the three major demands in the world, 2013

	Investment rate	Consumption rate	Net export rate
World	22.28	77.59	0.13
High-income countries	20.42	79.14	0.44
Middle- and low-income countries	31.04	70.27	−1.31
Middle-income countries	31.17	69.82	−0.99
Upper-middle-income countries	31.56	68.26	0.18
Lower-middle-income countries	25.45	78.64	−4.09
Low-income countries	26.07	88.32	−14.39

Source: World Bank Development Indicators Database.

higher than that of high-income countries, and more than 14 percentage points higher than that of middle-income countries and upper-middle-income countries. Therefore, whether it is a longitudinal comparison in history or a horizontal comparison with the world average, high-income countries, middle-income countries, and upper-middle-income countries, China's current investment rate is quite high.

Therefore, the low consumption rate and high investment rate are still major challenges facing China's demand structure. Consumer demand is not able to drive economic growth, which is still overly dependent on investment demand.

7.2.3. *Challenges facing the regional structure*

As mentioned earlier, driven by regional development strategies such as the development of the western region, the revitalization of northeast China, and the rise of the central region, the share of the western region kept rising after 2006; and the share of the central region kept rising after 2007. But until now, there is still a considerable gap in the economic development between the central and western regions with the eastern region. This is more evidenced by the absolute gap of per capita GDP between the economically most developed provinces in the eastern region and the least developed provinces in the western region.

From 2001 to 2014, the relative gap of per capita GDP between the economically most developed provinces in the eastern region and the least developed provinces in the western region showed a sharp decline from 10.9:1 in 2000 to 4:1 in 2014. However, the absolute gap of per capita GDP showed an obvious expansion. In 2000, the per capita GDP of Shanghai was 30,047 yuan, while that of Guizhou was 2,759 yuan, with a difference of 27,288 yuan. In 2014, the per capita GDP of Shanghai was 97,343 yuan, and that of Guizhou was 26,393 yuan, with a difference of 70,950 yuan. In 2014, the absolute difference in per capita GDP between Guizhou and Shanghai was 2.6 times that of 1993. Obviously, the absolute gap of per capita GDP between the economically most developed provinces in the eastern region and the least developed provinces in the western region has expanded significantly.

While there is still a considerable gap in economic development between the central and western regions with the eastern region, the central and western regions have encountered challenges from other developing countries in the process of development. Due to rising labor costs, the central and western regions have encountered fierce competition from developing countries with even lower labor costs in Southeast Asia, in the process of industrial transfer from the eastern region to the central and western regions. Therefore, the development of the central and western regions of China has encountered new problems.

7.2.4. *Challenges facing the income distribution structure*

As mentioned earlier, from 2009 to 2014, stimulated by a series of income distribution policies and measures such as strengthening social security and raising household income, the proportion of disposable income of households showed a recovery. However, compared with the year in which the disposable income of households was the highest in the 1990s, there was still a gap of 7–8 percentage points.

As shown in Table 7.3, the share of disposable income of households in China is lower than that of developed countries, especially that of the United States and Australia. Although the share of disposable income of households in other developed countries is not significantly higher than that of China, these countries often offer good welfare benefits to its citizens, and a considerable part of the government's disposable income is spent on the welfare of households, such as free education and free medical care. In fact, the government provides a large volume of social transfers in physical terms to the households, which are the beneficiaries. According to the international standards of national accounts, these social transfers in physical terms constitute the actual disposable income of households. Therefore, the share of the actual disposable income of households in these countries is significantly higher than the share of the nominal disposable income of households. China is not a country with a high level of welfare. Although the government has provided a certain amount of social transfers in physical terms to households, the amount is not as much as that in countries with high level of welfare. Therefore, the share of actual disposable income of households in China is significantly lower than that in developed countries.

As mentioned earlier, from 2010 to 2014, the relative income gap between urban and rural households gradually narrowed, and the income ratio of urban and rural households shrunk from 3.33 in 2009 to 2.97 in 2014. However, as the absolute income of urban and rural households increased, the relative income gap shrunk, and the absolute income gap still expanded significantly. In 2009, the per capita net income of rural households was

Table 7.3. Share of disposable income of households, enterprises, and government in national disposable income

(Unit: %)

Country	Year	Households	Enterprises	Governments	Error item
Australia	2012	68.5	12.1	19.4	0.0
	2011	68.2	13.4	18.5	−0.1
Canada	2012	62.5	14.1	23.2	0.2
	2011	62.3	14.7	22.9	0.2
France	2011	64.8	8.5	21.7	5.0
	2010	65.3	9.5	20.4	4.8
Germany	2012	64.0	11.2	20.3	4.5
	2011	63.7	12.1	19.5	4.7
Italy	2012	66.3	9.5	19.1	5.0
	2011	67.1	9.5	18.5	4.9
Japan	2012	64.3	20.6	15.1	0.0
	2011	64.7	20.6	14.6	0.1
United Kingdom	2012	65.0	12.4	15.5	7.2
	2011	62.8	15.5	15.7	6.0
United States	2012	75.4	13.2	10.0	1.4
	2011	76.2	13.5	9.7	0.7
Brazil	2009	64.5	10.8	20.0	4.7
	2008	62.1	12.1	20.5	5.3
China	2011	61.0	16.9	19.3	2.9
	2010	60.8	18.0	18.5	2.6
India	2011	89.0	—	10.7	0.3
	2010	81.0	—	11.3	7.8
Russia	2011	58.4	11.1	27.9	2.5
	2010	62.6	11.2	23.6	2.6
South Africa	2012	59.8	11.7	19.3	9.1
	2011	58.5	13.1	20.1	8.3

Source: United Nations National Accounts Database, OECD Database.

5,153 yuan, while the per capita disposable income of urban households was 17,175 yuan. In 2014, the per capita net income of rural households was 9,892 yuan, and that of urban households was 29,381 yuan.[4] The difference between the per capita disposable income of urban households and that of rural households was 12,022 yuan in 2009 and 19,489 yuan in 2014, and the latter was 1.6 times that of the former.

---

[4]In order to maintain comparability with the indicators in 2009, the per capita disposable income of urban households here uses the indicators with old coverage of urban household survey before the reform of urban and rural household survey. After the reform of integration, the per capita disposable income of urban households was 28,844 yuan in 2014.

As mentioned earlier, from 2009 to 2014, the Gini coefficient of Chinese household income kept shrinking from 0.491 in 2008 to 0.469 in 2014. There is no international organization or literature which give the most suitable Gini coefficient standard, but many scholars believe that a Gini coefficient less than 0.2 means a too even distribution of household income, a Gini coefficient between 0.2 and 0.3 means a relatively even income distribution, between 0.3 and 0.4 means a relatively reasonable income distribution, between 0.4 and 0.5 means a big income gap, and greater than 0.5 means a huge income gap. The current Gini coefficient of household income indicates that the income gap of Chinese households is still large.

7.2.5. *Challenges facing the structure of foreign trade*

7.2.5.1. *Development of trade in services is seriously lagging behind*

The development of China's export of trade in services lags behind its export of trade in goods. As shown in Figures 7.11 and 7.12, from 1995 to 2014, the proportion of China's export of trade in services to the export of trade in goods and services demonstrated a trend of decline, and it was always lower than the proportion of China's import of trade in services to the import of trade in goods and services. Therefore, China's trade in

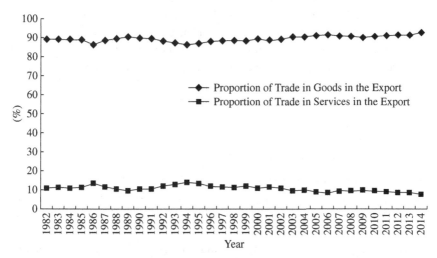

Figure 7.11. Proportions of China's export of goods and export of services in total export of goods and services, 1982–2014

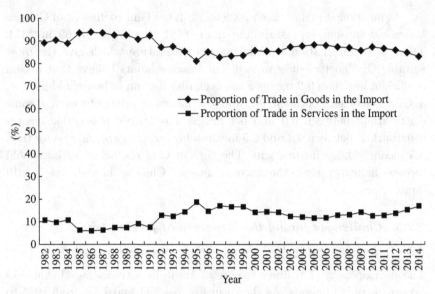

Figure 7.12. Proportions of China's import of goods and import of services in total import of goods and services, 1982–2014

services continued to be in deficit and it was expanding. China is a country with a large surplus of trade in goods, and also a country with a big deficit of trade in services, fully indicating China's unbalanced trade in goods and services and sharp contradictions in the foreign trade structure.

As shown in Table 7.4, the proportion of China's export of services in the total export of goods and services is not only far lower than that of developed countries, but even far lower than other BRICS countries, which fully demonstrates the gap of export of services between China and developed countries and other BRICS countries.

7.2.5.2. *Export of goods is under pressure by both developed countries and developing countries*

After the reform and opening-up, especially after China's accession into the WTO, the advantages of China's export-oriented economic growth lie mainly in three aspects: import of technology, population dividend, and cost advantage. The import of technology from developed countries, the transfer of labor force from agriculture to manufacturing and service industries, and the participation in international competition with low-cost advantages are

Table 7.4. Proportion of goods and services trade in major countries of the world to their imports and exports

(Unit: %)

Country	2012				2013			
	Import		Export		Import		Export	
	Goods	**Services**	**Goods**	**Services**	**Goods**	**Services**	**Goods**	**Services**
Developed countries								
United States	84.9	15.1	71.0	29.0	84.5	15.5	70.5	29.5
Japan	83.5	16.5	84.9	15.1	83.8	16.2	83.2	16.8
United Kingdom	79.8	20.2	62.1	37.9	79.1	20.9	65.1	34.9
France	79.5	20.5	72.5	27.5	78.4	21.6	71.3	28.7
Germany	79.8	20.2	84.1	15.9	79.1	20.9	83.5	16.5
Italy	82.4	17.6	82.8	17.2	81.7	18.3	82.5	17.5
Canada	81.9	18.1	85.4	14.6	81.9	18.1	85.5	14.5
Australia	80.5	19.5	83.1	16.9	79.6	20.4	82.9	17.1
BRICS countries								
China	86.6	13.4	91.5	8.5	85.6	14.4	91.4	8.6
India	79.2	20.8	67.1	32.9	78.6	21.4	67.2	32.8
Brazil	75.0	25.0	86.4	13.6	75.0	25.0	86.6	13.4
Russia	76.3	23.7	90.1	9.9	73.5	26.5	88.9	11.1
South Africa	88.1	11.9	87.2	12.8	88.6	11.4	87.6	12.4

Source: World Trade Organization database.

the main drivers of China's export of goods. After the outbreak of the international financial crisis, the re-industrialization of developed countries such as the United States and European countries led to the return of high-end manufacturing to developed countries; and the rising labor costs in China led to the relocation of low-end manufacturing to Southeast Asian countries with low labor costs. This is another outstanding structural contradiction faced by China's foreign trade.

7.3. Some Thoughts and Recommendations on China's Economic Restructuring

In response to the severe challenges facing China's economic structure, the following considerations and recommendations are proposed.

7.3.1. *On industrial restructuring*

7.3.1.1. *We should continue to promote the development of the tertiary industry and solve the problems hindering the development of the tertiary industry*

As the development of China's tertiary industry is still lagging behind, we should continue to promote the development of the tertiary industry, especially those service industries with short-term and severe supply shortages, such as high-tech services, medical services, aged care services, healthcare services, and environmental governance services (including water pollution control, land pollution control, and air pollution control). Development in these areas will not only help promote the adjustment of economic structure and the transformation of economic development mode but also help improve people's livelihood. At the same time, the development of the tertiary industry is also an important measure to stabilize economic growth in the context of current economic downturn when overcapacity and insufficient demand have led to a slowdown in industrial growth.

7.3.1.2. *We should strive to maintain the coordinated development of the three industries*

It is somewhat inevitable for China's secondary industry to have a higher proportion. China's manufacturing industry has produced a large volume of products for export, making the country a big manufacturer and a world factory. This has made important contributions to ensuring the rapid growth of China's economy over the past 30 years since the reform and opening-up, and has played an important role to solve China's employment problems, increase national wealth, and improve the people's living standards, and laid the foundation for the development of China's tertiary industry. While accelerating the development of the tertiary industry, we must not neglect the development of the manufacturing industry and ignore the development of the secondary industry. Otherwise, the tertiary industry will lose the foundation for stable development. Only by achieving the coordinated development of the three industries can the sustainable development of the tertiary industry be realized.

7.3.1.3. *All the three industries need to be developed through innovation*

After more than 30 years of rapid development, China's economic environment has undergone tremendous changes. China's three industries can no longer rely on the traditional development model by relying on resources and low-cost labor. We should transform the economic development mode, and all three industries need to gain new development momentum through innovation.

7.3.2. On adjusting demand structure

(1) We should strive to expand consumption demand and further increase the contribution rate of consumption demand to economic growth.

In view of China's low consumption rate, high investment rate, insufficient consumption demand to stimulate economic growth, and the excessive dependence on investment demand and export demand, we must strive to expand consumption demand and further increase the contribution rate of consumption demand to the economic growth.

(2) We should give full play to the important role of investment in promoting coordinated regional development, coordinated urban and rural development, optimization of industrial structure, and improvement of people's livelihood.

To build a moderately prosperous society in all respects and achieve sustainable development, we need to ease the imbalance between regions and between urban and rural areas in China's economic development. We need to improve the unreasonable industrial structure and need to promote the continuous improvement of people's livelihood. Investment will play a key role in solving these problems. Therefore, while striving to expand consumption demand and further increase the contribution rate of consumption demand to economic growth, we must not neglect investment but should give full play to the important role of investment in promoting coordinated regional development, coordinated urban and rural development, optimization of industrial structure, and improvement of people's livelihood.

(3) We should consolidate the international market share gained through China's long-term efforts so as to ensure that export continues to play an important role in stabilizing economic growth and solving employment problems.

In face of increasing pressure of economic downturn, the impacts of re-industrialization of developed countries in Europe and the United States as well as the low-cost competition of developing countries in Southeast Asia on export, and trade protectionism in various forms, we must consolidate our international market share gained through China's long-term efforts and ensure that export continues to play an important role in stabilizing economic growth and solving employment problems.

7.3.3. *On adjusting regional structure*

We should promote the development of the central and western regions and the coordinated development of the eastern, central, and western regions by continuing to implement the development strategy for the western region, the revitalization of northeast China, and the rise of the central region, and earnestly implement the Belt and Road Initiative, coordinated development of Beijing, Tianjin, and Hebei, and the development strategy of Yangtze river economic belt. We should attach great importance to the constraints of the shortage of talents, the lack of innovativeness, and the slow progress of technology that hinder the economic and social development in the central and western regions. We should attach great importance to the competition from developing countries with lower labor costs, such as Southeast Asia, during the industrial transfers from the eastern region to the central and western regions.

7.3.4. *On adjusting income distribution structure*

We should maintain a basic balance between household income growth and economic growth. We should maintain the simultaneous growth of household income growth with the economic growth, the simultaneous improvement of labor remuneration with that of the labor productivity, and continue to increase the income of urban and rural households, as was required by the *Recommendations of the CPC Central Committee on the Formulation of the 13th Five-Year Plan for Economic and Social Development*. We should adjust the pattern of national income distribution, standardize initial distribution, and enhance the intensity of redistribution adjustment. We should prevent a lower income growth of households than economic growth and a lower growth of labor remuneration than that of the labor productivity. At the same time, we should also prevent a significantly higher increase of household income than economic growth and a significantly higher growth of labor remuneration than that of the labor productivity. Otherwise, it will affect the sustained and healthy development of the economy, which in turn will affect the continued growth of household income. According to the questionnaire survey conducted by the National Bureau of Statistics, in recent years, when small and micro enterprises were asked to pick up the "three prominent problems currently faced," more than 60% enterprises chose "faster increase in labor costs," which was much higher than the proportion of those who identified other problems, indicating that the production and operation of small and micro enterprises was obviously under the pressure of rising labor costs. If a considerable number of small and micro enterprises are unable to withstand the pressure of rising labor costs, which might even affect their survival, it will affect the sustained and healthy development of the economy, which in turn will affect the sustained growth of household income.

We should continue to narrow the income gap of households, including the income gap of households between urban and rural areas, between regions, and between high-income groups and low-income groups. This is an inevitable requirement for building a moderately prosperous society in all respects and a necessity for the stable economic and social development.

7.3.5. *On adjusting foreign trade structure*

We should unswervingly promote the opening-up of the service industry, the development of China's trade in services, and the coordinated development of China's trade in goods and services, so as to promote the transformation of economic development mode, the improvement of employment and people's livelihood, and China's transformation from a trader with large volume into a trader of quality.

https://doi.org/10.1142/9789811229077_0008

Chapter 8

Evolution of China's Balance of Payments Structure

Wang Chunying, Zhao Yuchao, Chang Guodong, and Guan Enjie[*]

Abstract

This report expounds the evolution of China's balance of payments structure from 2003 to 2015, reviews the changes of the operating environment of the balance of payments, analyzes the characteristics of the overall balance of payments situation in different stages, and reveals the specific changes of major issues of the balance of payments from the aspects of trade in goods, trade in services, primary and secondary income, direct investment, portfolio investment, and other investments.

With the end of the Asian financial crisis in 1998 and China's accession into the WTO in 2001, the operating environment of China's balance of payments entered into a new phase, and the net inflow of cross-border capital started to climb, especially prominent after 2003. The 13 years (2003–2015) can be broadly divided into two major cycles based on the fluctuations in the domestic and foreign economies, complex and changeable financial markets, and significant changes in the operation of the balance of payments. In the first cycle of 2003–2013, both the current account and the capital and financial account were in the surplus, and foreign exchange reserves saw rapid growth. In the second cycle since 2014, the current account had been in surplus while the capital and financial account had been in deficit (especially the second half of 2014), and the foreign exchange reserves declined.

---

[*]Wang Chunying, Zhao Yuchao, Chang Guodong, and Guan Enjie are employees of the State Administration of Foreign Exchange.

8.1. Operating Environment of Balance of Payments

Since 2003, the international economic and financial environment has mainly experienced three stages, namely, the global economic boom from 2003 to 2007, the outbreak of and response to the international financial crisis from 2008 to 2013, and the slow recovery and the division of the global economy since 2014, which have had a great impact on China's balance of payments.

8.1.1. *Global economic boom (2003–2007)*

This period was featured with the smooth performance of developed economies, robust growth of emerging economies, and outstanding performance of the Chinese economy. Internationally, the developed economies just went out of the shadow of the bursting of "Internet bubble," and had an economic growth rate hovering at around 3%, failing to return to 4% level at the end of the 1990s. The emerging economies entered their most prolonged and strongest sustained growth period in history, with an average annual economic growth rate of nearly 5 percentage points higher than that of the developed economies, becoming the main force to boost world economic growth (see Figure 8.1). Domestically, China's accession into the WTO and the population dividend became powerful weapons for "Made in China." China has undertaken the industrial transfer of the manufacturing

Figure 8.1. Economic growth of the world's major economies

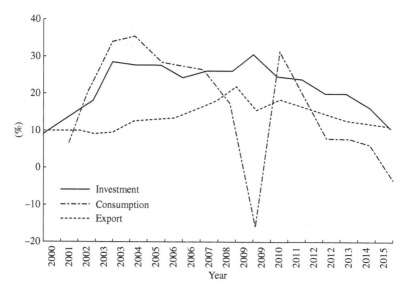

Figure 8.2. Growth of the "Troika" for the Chinese economy
Source: International Monetary Fund, National Bureau of Statistics.

industry from developed countries. Investment and export become the dual drives, and consumption demand increased steadily (see Figure 8.2), leading to a double-digit, high-speed economic growth.

There was no basis for spread trading, and the periods of dollar depreciation and RMB appreciation overlapped. From the perspective of the interest rate market, the spread of domestic and foreign interest rates (i.e. "domestic interest rate — US interest rate") turned from positive to negative, and the negative growth was expanding. From the second half of 2004 to the beginning of 2007, the Federal Reserve kept hiking interest rates; as a result, the interest rate of the federal funds grew from as low as 1% to more than 5%. China only slightly raised interest rates twice in a row during this period, and frequently raised interest rates six times in 2007 alone to curb overheating and asset price bubbles (see Figure 8.3). In the exchange rate market, the US dollar entered a long-term depreciation cycle since mid-2001, with a cumulative depreciation of over 30% by the end of 2007. Only the interest rate hikes by the Federal Reserve led to a short rebound. The sustained surplus of imports and exports in China brought pressure for RMB to appreciate. From the start of exchange rate reform in 2005 to the end of 2007, the accumulative RMB-US dollar exchange rate increased by 13% (see Figure 8.4).

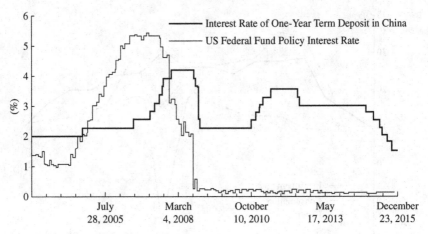

Figure 8.3. A comparison of interest rate markets between China and the United States

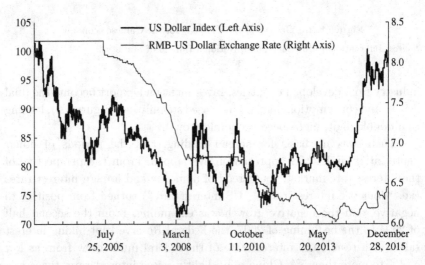

Figure 8.4. US dollar index and trend of RMB exchange rate

Source: People's Bank of China, CEIC.

8.1.2. *Outbreak and response period of the international financial crisis (2008–2013)*

The developed economies recovered slowly after a V-shaped reversal, and the emerging economies recovered slowly after a W-shaped bottoming, and

China's economic growth rate dipped after sharp rises to a high level. Internationally, the sub-prime mortgage crisis that first broke out in the United States swept across the world. Countries invested heavily to rescue the market and stimulate the economy. Among the developed economies, the United States witnessed the most eye-catching recovery, coupled with a steadily declining unemployment rate. The aftershocks of the debt crisis in the Euro Zone continued, with a high unemployment rate. Japan's economy tossed and turned between recovery and recession. The emerging economies first rose and then declined, and some countries gradually exposed their economic fragility by showing increasingly serious economic downturns and capital outflows. In China, the economy recovered strongly thanks to massive economic stimuli, and the mode of economic growth turned to domestic demand-driven growth, which had made outstanding contributions to the rebalancing of the global economy. However, with the deepening of China's economic transformation after 2012, the country's economic growth began to slow down.

The easy monetary policy in the developed economies increased positive spreads both at home and abroad, the US Dollar Index broadly consolidated itself, and the RMB exchange rate appreciated again. In the interest rate market, after 2009, the Federal Reserve introduced three rounds of quantitative easing monetary policy (QE), lowering the federal funds rate to a historical low of 0–0.25%, which stayed at this level for seven years. Excessive external liquidity made China's monetary policy regulation more difficult. In 2008, the interest rate of the domestic one-year term deposit was lowered several times to a historical low of 2.25%. The subsequent interest rate hikes to cool the housing market, and a slight interest rate reduction in response to the European debt crisis led the interest rate to 3% at the end of 2013. In the exchange rate market, the US Dollar Index consolidated in the range of 70–90 for a long time under QE pressure. It did not fall below the lowest point set in the first half of 2008, mainly because the US dollar assumed certain risk-aversion functions during the crisis. Most emerging economies' currencies experienced a sudden change from appreciation to depreciation around 2013. After 2008, under the combined influence of internal and external factors, the RMB continued to appreciate. The RMB-US dollar exchange rate had appreciated 20% again before the end of 2013, in which it remained relatively stable from the second half of 2008 to mid-2010.

8.1.3. *Slow recovery and division of global economy (2014–2015)*

Economic performance within developed economies and between emerging economies began to divide. Abroad, the economic growth of developed economies rebounded for two consecutive years, among which the United States and the United Kingdom recovered well, while Europe and Japan recovered slowly. Economic growth in emerging economies declined for five consecutive years since 2011, and some countries fell into recession. Domestically, China's economy changed from high-speed growth to medium-high-speed growth, faced growing downward pressure, and saw slower growth rates of investment and consumption. The decline in bulk commodity prices and other factors resulted in an expanding trade surplus.

The spread between domestic and foreign currencies gradually narrowed, the diversified monetary policies in developed economies led to the emergence of a strong US dollar, and the RMB exchange rate faced a growing pressure of depression. At the interest rate market, the Federal Reserve continued to maintain ultra-low interest rates, and the Euro Zone began to implement negative interest rates. To maintain reasonable domestic liquidity, China repeatedly lowered interest rates and deposit reserve rates, dragging the interest rate of the one-year term deposit down to 1.5% at the end of 2015. At the exchange rate market, the expectations on the rise of interest rate by the Federal Reserve and the QE expansion in Europe and Japan stimulated the rapid appreciation of the US dollar, leading to a cumulative appreciation of more than 20%. Under the influence of the appreciation of the US dollar, weak domestic macroeconomy and narrowing interest spread, the RMB exchange rate showed two-way fluctuations and faced higher depreciation pressure. The cumulative depreciation of RMB against the US dollar exceeded 6% in 2014–2015.

8.2. Overall Situation in the Balance of Payments

8.2.1. *Main characteristics in 2003–2013*

8.2.1.1. *There was a large-scale surplus in the balance of payments, and the contribution of capital surplus increased after 2009*

The balance of payments continued to see twin surpluses (except in 2012), and foreign exchange reserves accumulated rapidly. From 2003 to 2013, China's current account surplus totaled US$ 2.23 trillion, and the surplus of the capital and financial account (excluding reserve assets, the same below) totaled US$ 1.51 trillion, with a total balance of payments surplus reaching US$ 3.74 trillion, and a total of minus US$ 0.18 trillion in absolute net error and omission. In this case, the foreign exchange reserve assets in reserve assets (balance of payments data, excluding the impact of non-transaction value changes such as exchange rates and prices, the same below) increased by US$ 3.54 trillion. At the end of 2013, China's foreign exchange reserve balance was US$ 3.8213 trillion, which was significantly higher than the balance at the end of 2002 (US$ 286.4 billion).

Before 2008, the current account was the primary source of the balance of payments surplus, while the net capital inflows accounted for more than half of the surplus after 2009. From 2003 to 2008, the current account surplus and the capital and financial account surplus totaled US$ 1.25 trillion and US$ 0.44 trillion, respectively, accounting for 74% and 26% of the total balance of payments surplus. From 2009 to 2013, the current account surplus and the capital and financial account surplus totaled US$ 0.98 trillion and US$ 1.07 trillion, respectively, accounting for 48% and 52% of the total balance of payments surplus. On the one hand, this was partly due to the fact that China's current account balance had further improved since 2009, and the size of the surplus had generally declined, with the ratio of surplus to GDP falling to about 2% since 2011. On the other hand, it was because the QE policies of major developed economies increased global liquidity, and China's capital inflows under the capital account increased significantly (see Figure 8.5).

8.2.1.2. *Most of China's external assets accumulated are official reserves, and after 2009, the proportion of external assets accumulated by market players rose as a whole*

Within the 11 years, 70% of the US$ 5 trillion external assets accumulated were all reserve assets. From 2003 to 2013, China's external assets increased by US$ 5.09 trillion. Of this total, the proportion of reserve assets increased by 70%, while other investment assets abroad (external loans, overseas deposits, receivables from export, etc.) by domestic market players increased by US$ 1.01 trillion, accounting for 20%, and the outbound direct investments and portfolio investment made by domestic market players accounted for 8% and 2%, respectively.

In terms of the trend of change, the proportion of external assets accumulated by domestic banks, enterprises, individuals, and other market players rose as a whole, while the proportion of official reserve assets

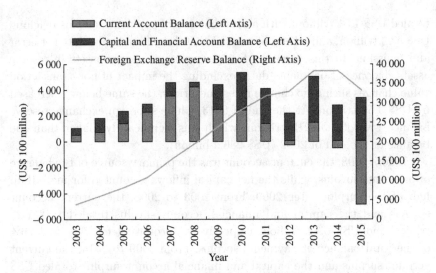

Figure 8.5. Balances of the current account and the capital and financial account and foreign exchange reserve balance

Source: State Administration of Foreign Exchange, People's Bank of China.

declined. From 2003 to 2008, China's external assets increased by US\$ 2.35 trillion, of which the increase of reserve assets accounted for 76%. From 2009 to 2013, China's external assets increased by US\$ 2.75 trillion, and the proportion increase in reserve assets decreased to 65%. The proportion of assets in other investment and outbound direct investment made by domestic market players increased significantly, accounting for 24% and 10%, respectively, which was 9 percentage points and 6 percentage points higher than that in 2003–2008 (see Figure 8.6).

8.2.1.3. *Most of China's external assets come from high-stability channels like current account and direct investment, and short-term capital inflows increased after 2009*

Of the 11-year accumulation of external assets, 80% came from high-stability channels such as the current account surplus and the net inflow of foreign direct investment (FDI) into China. China's accumulation of external assets mainly comes from two sources: the current account surplus and the inflow of foreign liabilities, i.e. inflow of foreign capital (see Figure 8.7). From 2003 to 2013, China's current account surplus totaled US\$ 2.23 trillion, equivalent to 44% of China's external assets capitalization

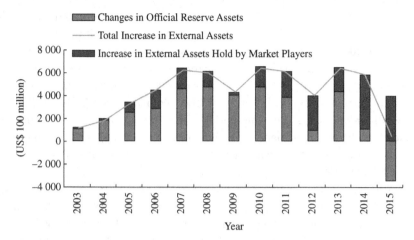

Figure 8.6. Accumulation of China's external assets by official reserves and outbound investments by market players

Source: State Administration of Foreign Exchange.

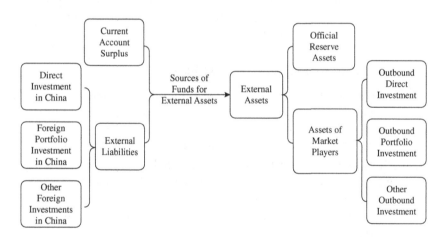

Figure 8.7. The main types and sources of external assets in China

during the same period (US\$ 5.09 trillion); net inflow of foreign direct investment to China totaled US\$ 1.85 trillion, equivalent to 36% of China's external assets capitalization. That is to say, the current account surplus and the net inflow of foreign direct investment to China (with high stability) totaled about 80% of China's external assets capitalization. On the other hand, the volatile foreign short-term capital inflows to China (portfolio investment, overseas borrowings, and other investments) totaled US$ 1.15 trillion, accounting for 23% of China's external assets capitalization.[1]

After 2009, the stability of China's external assets accumulation weakened, and the contribution of the current account surplus declined while that of net capital inflow increased. From 2003 to 2008, China's current account surplus totaled US$ 1.25 trillion, equivalent to 53% of China's external assets during the same period (US$ 2.35 trillion). The net inflows of foreign direct investment to China totaled US$ 0.67 trillion, and the net inflows of short-term capital to China amounted to US$ 0.33 trillion, contributing 28% and 14%, respectively, to the external assets. From 2009 to 2013, the current account surplus totaled US$ 0.98 trillion, with an average annual surplus decreasing by 6% compared with 2003–2008, and its share in the contribution to the external assets dropped to 36%. The net inflow of FDI to China reached US$ 119 million, with an average annual growth of 1.1 times, and its contribution rate rising to 43%. The net inflow of foreign short-term capital to China reached US$ 0.82 trillion, with an average annual sharp increase of 1.9 times and its contribution rising to 30%, reflecting the impact of QE in developed economies on the flooding of overseas liquidity (see Figure 8.8).

8.2.2. *Main characteristics in 2014–2015*

In 2014, especially after the second half of 2014, the basic pattern of China's balance of payments took shape, featuring a surplus in the current account and a deficit in the capital and financial accounts. From the second half of 2014 to 2015, China had a current account surplus of US$ 504.5 billion and a deficit in the capital and financial account of US$ 583.5 billion, with a net error and omission of minus US$ 294 billion, and a cumulative decrease of US$ 373.1 billion in reserve assets.

Deleveraging of external debt was initiated for a period of time, which gradually released the risks of short-term capital inflows accumulated earlier. From the second half of 2014 to 2015, the cumulative net outflow of non-direct investment from China amounted to US$ 346.8 billion, equivalent to 30% of the sustained net inflow from 2003 to 2013, and 43% of the net inflow from the major developed economies during the QE period from

---

[1]Due to net errors and omissions, the sum of current account surplus and external liabilities is not precisely equal to the amount of external assets capitalization.

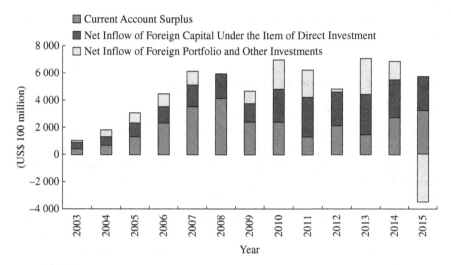

Figure 8.8. Main sources of funds of China's external assets

Source: State Administration of Foreign Exchange.

2009 to 2013. In other words, 30%–40% of the net inflows of non-direct investment in the past decade or so have flowed out of China. However, with the overall improvement of external trade of Chinese enterprises and the widening of investment and financing channels, such overseas financing is expected to maintain a reasonable and normal size after the reduction.

China's total external assets continued to increase, and the official reserve assets fell while the external assets of market players rose. From the second half of 2014 to 2015, China's total external assets increased by US$ 267.2 billion. Of this total, direct investment assets of enterprises and other market players increased by US$ 263.3 billion, equivalent to 66% of the increase over the 11 years from 2003 to 2013; portfolio investment assets increased by US$ 86.5 billion, equivalent to 70% of the increase over the previous 11 years; loans and other investment assets increased by US$ 287 billion, also accounting for 28% of the increase over the previous 11 years. Under the expectation of RMB appreciation in earlier years, Chinese market players were unwilling to hold external assets. However, under the circumstance of two-way fluctuation of the RMB exchange rate, market players were much more enthusiastic about increasing their external assets, which became the main reason for the decline of reserve assets. It is also an inevitable process of "letting the private sector keep more foreign exchange."

8.3. Major Components of the Balance of Payments

8.3.1. *Trade in goods*

Total import and export of goods increased steadily and maintained a large surplus. Thanks to China's accession into the WTO and the continuous liberalization of various external policies, the import and export of trade in goods maintained an overall growth, leading to the rapid growth of China's export-related economy. The sustained large surplus of import and export is an important contributor to China's rapid accumulation of foreign exchange reserves. According to the statistics of the balance of payments, China's export, import, and the surplus of trade in goods increased by 15%, 13%, and 25%, respectively, annually on average during 2003–2015 (see Figure 8.9). Due to the 2008 international financial crisis, China's imports and exports declined to a certain extent in 2009, and then resumed the growth momentum, but with a significantly slower growth rate. In 2014, China's exports and imports of trade in goods reached a historical peak of US\$ 2.2438 trillion and US\$ 1.8087 trillion, respectively. Imports and exports both declined in 2015 due to the sluggish external demand, the decline of prices of bulk commodity, and the slowdown of the domestic economy. Moreover, imports declined more than exports, resulting in a recessionary growth of net exports, in which exports and imports fell by

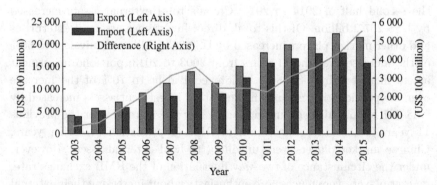

Figure 8.9. China's import and export, 2003–2015 (balance of payments coverage)

Source: General Administration of Customs, National Bureau of Statistics.

5% and 13%, respectively, and net exports increased by 30%, to US$ 2.1428 trillion, US$ 1.5785 billion, and US$ 567 billion, respectively.

8.3.2. *Trade in services*

The size of trade in services grew steadily, with a fast-expanding deficit. With the accelerating pace of China's opening-up, China's trade in services maintained a relatively rapid growth momentum in recent years. Especially, the deficit of trade in services kept a sustained growth driven by the deficit in tourism and transportation and has become the main source of balancing the surplus of trade in goods in the current account. From 2003 to 2015, the size of trade in services increased by 18% annually, which was 3.5 percentage points higher than the average annual growth rate of trade in goods. The deficit in trade in services increased by 37% annually on the average, or 13 percentage points higher than that of the surplus of trade in goods (see Figure 8.10). In 2015, the balance of trade in services reached US$ 755.4 billion, and the deficit reached US$ 182.4 billion.

The rapid growth of travel expenditure was the main reason for the expansion of the deficit of trade in services. Due to the increase in disposable income of households, relaxation of visa policies in some countries, warming up of studying abroad, more attractive shopping abroad, and other factors, the number of outbound tourists and students continued to grow, and the expenditure on travel increased rapidly. From 2003 to 2015, the number of

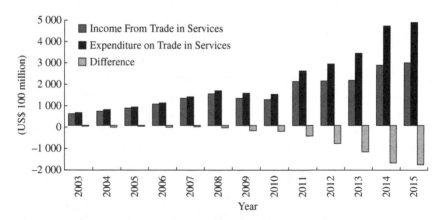

Figure 8.10. Status of trade in services, 2003–2015
Source: State Administration of Foreign Exchange.

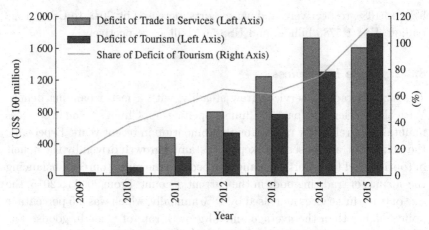

Figure 8.11. Contribution of deficit of travel to deficit of trade in services, 2009–2015
Source: State Administration of Foreign Exchange.

China's outbound travelers increased nearly five times, reaching 120 million person-times in 2015. Travel expenditure increased by 28% annually from 2003 to 2015, while income increased by 17% annually, much lower than the growth rate of expenditure. In 2003, there was a surplus of US$ 2.2 billion under travel items, and the surplus changed to deficit in 2009, and the deficit grew rapidly at 88% annually on the average. In 2015, travel expenditure reached US$ 292.2 billion, and income from travel was US$ 114.1 billion, with a deficit of US$ 178.1 billion (see Figure 8.11).

8.3.3. *Primary income and secondary income*

Primary income items generally showed a deficit, with a surplus in selected years. The deficit of primary income (formerly known as earnings) was US$ 10.2 billion in 2003 and US$ 45.4 billion in 2015, with an average annual growth of 13% (see Figure 8.12). On the one hand, the overall investment income gap in deficit and the expanding deficit explained the changes in the primary income gap. Especially after 2009, the investment income expenditure showed a rapid expansion. In 2013, the investment income deficit reached US$ 94.5 billion, and then slightly fell back to US$ 73.4 billion in 2015. The culprit of the investment income deficit was the unbalanced structure of China's external financial assets and liabilities. Foreign exchange reserves accounted for more than 50% of external assets, and FDI in China accounted for about 60% of external liabilities. Over the

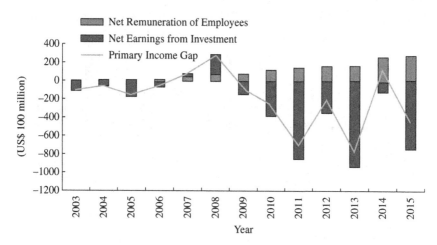

Figure 8.12. Status of primary income, 2003–2015

Source: State Administration of Foreign Exchange.

past decade, with the rapid growth of China's economy, FDI in China, which paid attention to long-term return on investment, played a role in creating employment and taxation, upgrading technology, and other comprehensive economic benefits in China, and at the same time, benefited from China's economic growth. Foreign exchange reserves, in contrast, focused more on preserving and increasing value and ensuring liquidity, with relatively low returns. On the other hand, the surplus in remuneration of employee kept growing steadily, which hedged the trend of growth of the primary income deficit to certain extent. With the increasing number of outbound workers from China, the remittance income earned by Chinese households also increased rapidly. The remuneration surplus of employee increased by 53% annually from 2003 to 2015 on the average, reaching US$ 27.4 billion in 2015.

The gap in secondary income turned from positive to negative. From 2003 to 2012, China's secondary income (formerly known as current transfer) maintained a surplus. The income from overseas donations and other current transfers to China was larger than China's external expenditure. Especially in 2008, the primary income surplus reached US$ 43.2 billion, the highest level in recent years. After 2013, with the increase of overseas donations from Chinese residents, there was a deficit of US$ 8.7 billion in secondary income in 2013 and 2015 (see Figure 8.13).

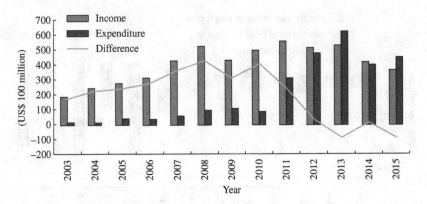

Figure 8.13.   Secondary income status from 2003 to 2015

Source: State Administration of Foreign Exchange.

8.3.4. *Direct investment*

Direct investment showed a relatively large net inflow for a long time. Generally speaking, both FDI in China and China's outbound investment maintained a relatively rapid growth due to the rapid economic growth, the expansion of relevant policies on reform and opening-up, the active promotion of the "going global" strategy, the growing strength of domestic enterprises, and the increasing awareness of investing abroad. However, due to the good momentum of domestic economic development, the stock of FDI in China was relatively large, while the strategy of "going global" by domestic enterprises was in its infancy, and it took time for these enterprises to adapt to the overseas market environment, resulting in a net inflow of direct investment. From 2003 to 2015, the FDI in China registered an average annual growth of 14%, with a total FDI of US\$ 2.8423 trillion by the end of 2015, accounting for about 60% of the external liabilities. In 2003, outbound investment from China was only US\$ 10 million (the total outbound investment was a few billions of US\$ in several years before 2003). After 2008, the outbound investment grew rapidly, reaching US\$ 1.1293 trillion by the end of 2015 (see Figure 8.14).

8.3.5. *Portfolio investment*

As a whole, there were more years with a net inflow of portfolio investment than those with a net outflow. From 2003 to 2015, China's cross-border portfolio investment gradually became active in the context of opening

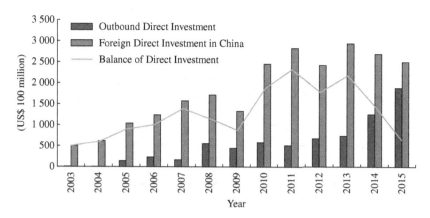

Figure 8.14. Status of direct investment, 2003–2015

Source: State Administration of Foreign Exchange.

capital market and expanding financing channels in the overseas capital markets by domestic enterprises. On the one hand, China's portfolio investment abroad is mainly debt investment abroad made by domestic enterprises through financial institutions such as qualified domestic institutional investors (QDII) and banks, with only a few investment channels. On the other hand, domestic enterprises, mainly domestic financial institutions, absorb a large amount of foreign portfolio investment by listing or issuing bonds abroad, so the scale of investment made by qualified foreign institutional investors (QFII) and RMB qualified foreign institutional investors (RQFII) is expanding. As a result, the overall net inflow of portfolio investment increased from US$ 11.4 billion in 2003 to a peak of US$ 82.4 billion in 2014. However, in 2005, 2006, and 2015, due to fluctuations in the domestic capital market and other factors, there was a net outflow of some funds after profit-taking (see Figure 8.15).

8.3.6. *Other investments*

The scale of the balance sheet of other investment expanded rapidly. With the deepening of China's foreign-related economic exchanges, continued expansion of current account, more relaxed policies concerning cross-border trade and financing, and more dynamic investment and financing activities, the scale of assets and liabilities of other investments maintained a growth momentum on the whole from 2003 to 2015. During this period, assets from other investment maintained a general growth momentum, with an average

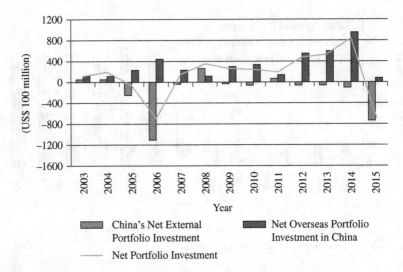

Figure 8.15.   Cross-border portfolio investment, 2003–2015

Note: The positive value of China's external portfolio investment indicates reducing the holding of foreign equity or bonds, while the negative value indicates increasing the holding of foreign equity or bonds. The positive value of overseas portfolio investment in China means increasing the holding of investment in domestic equity or creditor's rights, and the negative value means reducing the holding of investment in domestic equity or creditor's rights.

Source: State Administration of Foreign Exchange.

annual growth of 18%, except for a slight decline in 2009, reaching US$ 127.6 billion in 2015. The overall scale of liabilities of other investment was also expanding, yet with big volatility, especially with three declines during 2003–2015. In 2008, 2012, and 2015, they fell by US$ 15 billion, US$ 28.4 billion, and US$ 351.5 billion, respectively (see Figure 8.16).

There was both inflow and outflow of other investments. Other investments include deposits, loans, and credits (including those between enterprises). On the one hand, influenced by the macroeconomic and financial situation, such as the rapid growth of the domestic economy, positive interest margin at home and abroad, and expectation on the appreciation of RMB exchange rate, other investments in selected years showed a net inflow during 2003–2015. On the other hand, due to the persistent impact of the 2008 international financial crisis on cross-border capital flows in China, other investments showed a net outflow in selected years, and the size of net outflow exceeded that of net inflow. In 2008, in particular, due to the outbreak of the international financial crisis, the

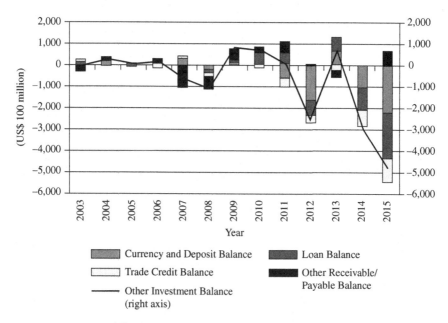

Figure 8.16. Other investments, 2003–2015

Source: State Administration of Foreign Exchange.

sentiment of risk aversion at the international market was high. Domestic commercial banks reduced investment in risky securities and increased overseas assets with sound liquidity such as deposits and inter-bank lending. Domestic enterprises' newly borrowed foreign loans substantially reduced, and export advance receipts declined. In 2012, with the deepening of the sovereign debt crisis in Europe and the intensification of turbulence in the international financial market, foreign institutions recovered deposits in China or reduced short-term financing business funds, and domestic enterprises sharply increased their foreign exchange deposits and other assets and then deposited them in overseas sister banks or lent overseas through banks. In 2014 and 2015, in the context of the domestic and foreign economic and financial environment, such as the stabilization and recovery of the US economy, the expectation of hikes in US dollar interest rate, and the slowdown of China's economic growth, Chinese enterprises took the initiative to increase their external assets and accelerate the repayment of foreign debts, resulting in a net outflow of other investments.

Chapter 9

Characteristics, Challenges and Development Trends of China's Financial Operation

Yan Xiandong and Hu Xinjie*

Abstract

This report reviews the major reforms in China's financial sector in 2015, analyzes the characteristics of major financial indicators such as money supply, social financing scale, loans and market rates from both overall and structural aspects, reveals the outstanding problems in financial operation, and forecasts the trend of development of financial performance in the future.

With the slowdown of economic growth in 2015, the CPC Central Committee proposed that we should attach great importance to coping with the downward pressure of the economy and preventing and resolving systemic risks. To this end, the People's Bank of China repeatedly lowered the required deposit reserve ratio and the benchmark deposit and loan interest rate of deposit-related financial institutions during the year, and guided the market rate to gradually decline through policy instruments such as pledged supplementary lending (PSL), medium-term lending facility (MLF), and standing lending facility (SLF) and through reducing repo rate. In 2015, the money and credit operation was generally stable, and the credit structure was further optimized. However, the financial operation still faced many challenges, and it was more difficult to stay immune from systemic and regional financial risks.

---

*Yan Xiandong and Hu Xinjie are employees of the Statistics and Analysis Department, People's Bank of China. This report does not represent the views and opinions of the institution they work for.

9.1. Active Promotion of Financial Reform

9.1.1. *Speeding up the market-oriented reform of interest rates*

In March and May 2015, the upper limit of floating range of deposit interest rate was expanded from 1.2 times of the base interest rate to 1.3 times and 1.5 times, respectively. In August, the upper limit of floating range of deposit interest rate for time deposits over one year (excluding one-year period) was liberalized, and in October, the upper limit of floating range of deposit interest rate was completely liberalized. In addition, the *Interim Measures for the Administration of Large-Denomination Certificates of Deposit* was issued in June 2015, which allowed financial institutions to issue large-denomination certificates of deposits with market-oriented pricing for enterprises and individuals, and further improved the market-oriented formation mechanism of interest rates.

9.1.2. *Improving the RMB central parity rate quotation mechanism*

On August 11, 2015, the People's Bank of China adjusted the central parity rate quotation mechanism of RMB-US dollar exchange rate. It stipulated that market makers should provide central parity rate quotation to the China Foreign Exchange Trading System before the opening of the daily inter-bank foreign exchange market, by taking into account the situation of foreign exchange supply and demand and the changes of the exchange rate of the major international currencies and referring to the closing exchange rate of the inter-bank foreign exchange market on the previous day.

9.1.3. *Introducing deposit insurance system*

The *Deposit Insurance Regulation* was promulgated on March 31, 2015, and came into effect on May 1, 2015. On April 1, 2015, the State Council issued its approval of the *Implementation Plan of the Deposit Insurance System*, clarifying that the management of the deposit insurance fund shall be undertaken by the People's Bank of China, which shall perform its functions of deposit insurance.

9.1.4. *Accelerating the opening of capital accounts*

On July 14, 2015, the People's Bank of China issued the *Circular on the Use of Renminbi by Overseas Central Banks, International Financial*

Organizations and Sovereign Wealth Funds to Invest in the Inter-bank Market. It greatly liberalized the quota restrictions and investment scope of overseas central banks, international financial organizations, and sovereign wealth funds in the inter-bank market, and changed the auditing system to the filing system.

On September 23, the People's Bank of China issued a circular to further facilitate multinational enterprise groups to carry out cross-border, two-way RMB fund pool business and adjust the macroprudential policy coefficient to 0.5 and further lowered the threshold for enterprises to participate in cross-border two-way RMB fund pool business.

In October, the executive meeting of the State Council decided to deepen the pilot project of financial reform in China (Shanghai) Pilot Free Trade Zone (Shanghai FTZ), gradually improve the convertibility of RMB under capital account within the scope of Shanghai FTZ and, on the basis of existing experience, study and launch a pilot project for qualified domestic individual investors (QDII2), and broaden the channels of foreign RMB investment return.

9.1.5. *New progress in the reform of policy-oriented and development-oriented financial institutions*

In March 2015, the State Council approved and agreed on the deepening of the reform plan on the China Development Bank and the overall reform plan of the Export-Import Bank of China. The Agricultural Development Bank and the Export-Import Bank will further strengthen the orientation of policy functions, adhere to the policy-oriented business as the main body, rationally define the scope of business, and establish a capital adequacy constraint mechanism. The China Development Bank will adhere to the positioning of development-oriented financial institutions, further improve the operational mode of development-oriented finance, and clarify the policy of supporting the sources of funds.

9.1.6. *Expanding the scope of PSLs issuance*

Since October 2015, the People's Bank of China has expanded the targets of PSLs from the China Development Bank to the Agricultural Development Bank of China and the Export-Import Bank of China, mainly to support the three banks in granting loans for renovation of shanty towns, major water projects, and RMB "going global" projects.

9.1.7. *Reforming the deposit reserve assessment system and expanding the credit asset pledge pilot*

Since September 15, 2015, the deposit reserve assessment system has been changed from the current time-point method to the average method, which not only provides a buffer mechanism for financial institutions to manage liquidity but also helps smooth the currency market fluctuations.

In October 2015, on the basis of pilot projects in Shandong and Guangdong, the People's Bank of China decided to promote mortgage and refinancing of credit assets in nine provinces (municipalities) including Shanghai and Tianjin. Credit assets with standard rating results were included in the acceptable range of qualified collateral for refinancing issued by the People's Bank of China.

9.1.8. *Improving the macroprudential policy framework*

First, the dynamic adjustment mechanism of differential reserve was "upgraded" to a macroprudential evaluation system. On the basis of maintaining the core concern for macroprudential capital adequacy ratio, the single index was expanded to more than ten indicators in seven aspects by factoring in both quantity and price, indirect financing and direct financing, and changing from ex ante guidance to interim monitoring and post evaluation.

Second, foreign exchange liquidity and cross-border capital flows were included in the scope of macroprudential management, risk reserve was levied on forward foreign exchange sales, macroprudential management of full-scale cross-border financing with domestic and foreign currency integration was expanded, and normal deposit reserve ratio was implemented for foreign financial institutions deposited in domestic financial institutions.

9.2. Stable Overall Financial Operation and Optimized Structure

9.2.1. *Slight decline in the growth rate of money supply*

At the end of December 2015, the broad currency M2 balance was 139.23 trillion yuan, showing a year-on-year growth rate of 13.3%, or 0.4 percentage point lower than that in the previous month, but still 1.1 percentage points higher than that at the end of the previous year. The M2 balance increased by 1.83 trillion yuan that month, or 144.7 billion yuan less than the increase in the same period of the previous year. The total M2 balance increased by 16.38 trillion yuan in 2015.

From the perspective of allocation of assets of financial institutions, the negative factors affecting M2 growth were as follows: First, the foreign exchange trading was greatly reduced. In that month, the balance of foreign exchange transactions of financial institutions decreased by 629 billion yuan, a decline of 510.6 billion yuan more than the decline in the same period of the previous year. Among them, funds outstanding for foreign exchange in the People's Bank of China declined by 708.2 billion yuan, a decline of 579.3 billion yuan more than that in the same period of the previous year, mainly due to the expansion of the devaluation of the RMB against the US dollar and the intensification of capital outflow. The foreign exchange reserve fell by US$ 107.9 billion that month. Second, the incremental of loans was less than the same period of the previous year. In the same month, loans increased by 597.8 billion yuan, or 345.3 billion yuan less than the increase in the same period of the previous year, mainly due to the reason that, in the context of the slowdown of the economic growth, banks' real non-performing loans ratio increased significantly and banks tended to lend cautiously. Third, the purchase of assets held under resale agreements decreased. In that month, financial institutions' purchase of assets held under resale agreements dropped by 208.4 billion yuan, a decline of 152.7 billion yuan more than the decline in the same month of the previous year, mainly because of more purchase of assets held under resale agreements from financial institutions in the securities industry and special purpose vehicles.

The main positive factor affecting M2 growth was the sharp increase of equity and other investments. In that month, the equity and other investments of financial institutions increased by 1.52 trillion yuan, an increase of 870.8 billion yuan more than the increase in the same period of the previous year. On the one hand, the China Development Bank and the Agricultural Development Bank of China injected into the CDB Development Fund and the China Agriculture Development Key Construction Fund in the form of equity investment. On the other hand, commercial banks invested 686.5 billion yuan more in non-standardized creditor's rights such as securities funds, financial management, and fund trust, and 458.1 billion yuan more in equity investments of special purpose vehicles in China.

9.2.2. *Less increase of social financing than that of the previous year*

In 2015, the increment of social financing was 15.41 trillion yuan, or 467.5 billion yuan less than the increase of the previous year. Analyzed by quarter, the size of social financing was 4.65 trillion yuan, 4.13 trillion yuan, 3.18 trillion yuan, and 3.44 trillion yuan, respectively, in the first, second, third, and fourth quarters.

In terms of structure of social financing, in 2015, RMB loans to the real sectors of the economy increased by 11.27 trillion yuan, or 1.52 trillion yuan more than the increase in the previous year. Loans in foreign currency to the real sectors of the economy decreased by 642.7 billion yuan, or 766.2 billion yuan less than the increase in the previous year. Entrusted loans increased by 1.59 trillion yuan, or 582.9 billion yuan less than the increase in the previous year. Trust loans increased by 43.4 billion yuan, or 474 billion yuan less than the increase in the previous year. Non-discounted banker's acceptance bills decreased by 1.06 trillion yuan, or 937.1 billion yuan more than the decrease in the previous year. Net financing of enterprise bonds was 2.94 trillion yuan, an increase of 507 billion yuan compared with that in the previous year. Equity financing on the domestic stock market by non-financial enterprises was 760.4 billion yuan, an increase of 325.4 billion yuan compared with that in the previous year. In December 2015, the scale of social financing increased by 1.82 trillion yuan, an increase of 792.7 billion yuan and 247.7 billion yuan when compared that in the previous month and in the previous year, respectively.

9.2.3. *Significantly higher increase in loans and more optimized structure*

In 2015, the size of loans from financial institutions increased substantially, which strongly supported the development of the real economy. The credit structure was further optimized. The loans to the central and western regions grew faster than those to the eastern region, with a faster growth of medium- and long-term loans and a higher balance of loans to small and micro enterprises. At the end of December, the balance of RMB loans was 93.95 trillion yuan, up by 14.3% compared with the end of previous year, or 0.6 percentage points lower than that at the end of November, and 0.6 percentage points higher than that at the end of 2014. The accumulated increment for the whole year was 11.73 trillion yuan, an increase of 1.81 trillion yuan over that in 2014. Following is an analysis by the structure of loans.

First, the loans to the central and western regions grew faster than those to the eastern region. At the end of December, the balances of loans to the eastern, central, and western regions increased by 10.9%, 16.5%, and 14.6% respectively, and the growth rates of loans to the central and western regions were 5.6 and 3.7 percentage points higher, respectively, than that to the eastern region.

Second, medium- and long-term loans grew rapidly. At the end of December, the balance of medium- and long-term loans grew by 15.4% year-on-year, or 0.9 percentage points higher than that in the same period of the previous year. Among them, the balance of medium- and long-term loans to the industrial sector increased by 5% year-on-year, or 3 percentage points lower than the growth rate of the same period in the previous year; the balance of medium- and long-term loans to the services sector increased by 14.4% year-on-year, or 1.3 percentage points lower than the growth rate of the same period in the previous year.

Third, the balance of loans to small and micro enterprises increased. At the end of 2015, the balance of RMB loans to small and micro enterprises was 17.39 trillion yuan, up 13.9% year-on-year, or 1.6 percentage points lower than the growth rate at the end of the previous year, and 2.7 and 5.3 percentage points higher, respectively, than the growth of loans to large- and medium-sized enterprises in the same period.

At the end of 2015, the balance of loans to small and micro enterprises accounted for 31.2% of the balance of loans to enterprises, which was 0.8 percentage point higher than that at the end of the previous year. In the whole year, loans to small and micro enterprises increased by 2.11 trillion yuan, or 14.6 billion yuan less than the increase in the previous year. The increase in the loans to small and micro enterprises accounted for 38.1% of increased loans to enterprises in the same period, which was 3.7 percentage points higher than the increase of loans to large-sized enterprises and 10.6 percentage points higher than the increase of loans to medium-sized enterprises in the same period.

Fourth, the growth of loans to rural households was higher than that of all other categories of loans. At the end of 2015, the balance of loans in domestic and foreign currencies to rural areas (county-level and below) was 21.61 trillion yuan, up by 11.2% year-on-year, or 1.2 percentage points lower than the growth rate at the end of 2014. The increment of loans for the whole year was 2.23 trillion yuan, or 225.1 billion yuan less than the increase in the previous year. The balance of loans to rural households was 6.15 trillion yuan, up by 14.8%, or 4.2 percentage points lower than the growth at the end of 2014. The increment of loans to rural households for the whole year was 782.3 billion yuan, or 73.3 billion yuan less than the increase in 2014. The balance of loans to agriculture was 3.51 trillion yuan, up by 5.2%, or 4.5 percentage points lower than the growth at the end of 2014. The increment of loans to agriculture for the whole year was 189.7 billion yuan, or 116.7 billion yuan less than the increase in 2014.

Fifth, the growth of loans to individual housing purchase continued to accelerate. At the end of 2015, the balance of loans for real estate development was 21.01 trillion yuan, up 21% year-on-year, or 2.1 percentage points higher than the growth at the end of 2014. The increment was 3.59 trillion yuan for the whole year, or 843.4 billion yuan more than the increase in 2014. The increment of loans for the real estate development accounted for 30.6% of the increment of all categories of loans for the whole year, or 2.5 percentage points higher than that in 2014.

At the end of 2015, the balance of loans for housing development was 5.04 trillion yuan, up by 17.9% year-on-year, or 3.8 percentage points lower than the growth at the end of the previous year. The balance of loans for land purchase and development for housing was 1.52 trillion yuan, up by 12.8% year-on-year, or 12.9 percentage points lower than the growth at the end of the previous year. The balance of loans for individual housing purchase was 14.18 trillion yuan, up by 23.2% year-on-year, or 5.7 percentage points higher than the growth at the end of the previous year, and 8.9 percentage points higher than that of all categories of loans. The increment of loans for individual housing purchase for the whole year was 2.66 trillion yuan, an increase of 936.8 billion yuan more than that in 2014.

9.2.4. *Lower overall market interest rate than previous year*

Market interest rates fell in the first five months, rebounded after June, and gradually fell in the fourth quarter, with the overall level lower than that in the same period of 2014. The market interest rate rose slightly in December, with the average interbank lending rate of 1.97% and the weighted average mortgage repurchase rate of 1.95% in that month, or 0.07 percentage points and 0.1 percentage points higher than that in the previous month, and 1.51 and 1.55 percentage points higher than that in the same period of the previous year, respectively. The average overnight Shibor rate was 1.84%,

0.05 percentage points higher than that of the previous month and 1.18 percentage points lower than that of the same period in the previous year.

The main reason for the slight increase in market interest rates in December was the tightening of capitals at the market. Despite the increase in the fiscal expenditure at the end of the year and the decrease of treasury deposits by 1.24 trillion yuan in that month, which provided large liquidity for the market, funds outstanding for foreign exchange of the People's Bank of China fell by 708.2 billion yuan in that month, and the base currency created by funds outstanding for foreign exchange was insufficient. In the same month, the People's Bank of China's refinancing to financial institutions dropped by 368.9 billion yuan, the balance of reverse repurchase operation on the open market dropped by 20 billion yuan, and the overall liquidity on the market became tighter (the overstock rate of most large Chinese banks declined), which led to a slight rise of market rates.

The yield to maturity on the bond market declined significantly. At the end of December, the yield to maturity of one-year Treasury bonds was 2.3%, or 28 basis points lower than that at the end of November; the yield to maturity of 10-year Treasury bonds was 2.82%, 22 basis points lower than that at the end of November. The yield to maturity of 10-year China Development Bank financial bonds was 3.13%, 30 basis points lower than that at the end November; the yield to maturity of 10-year corporate bonds (AAA) was 3.82%, 27 basis points lower than that at the end of November. The following reasons mainly explained the decline of bond yield: (1) Amid the slowdown of economic growth, due to the sharp rise in the real non-performing loans ratio of banks and the greater pressure on asset quality, credit investment tended to be prudent, leading to a corresponding increase in the allocation of bond assets; (2) The stock market shrank, and institutional funds flowed from the stock market to the bond market, and the clearing funds of security companies' clients dropped by 1.01 trillion yuan in that month; (3) The scale of bond issuance was greatly reduced, and there was less pressure of market supply. The issuance of bonds in that month was 701 billion yuan, or 1.14 trillion yuan less compared with the previous month, which was much lower than the average monthly issuance of bonds in the whole year (1.16 trillion yuan), mainly because the issuance of local government bonds fell sharply in that month, from more than the monthly average of 500 billion yuan since May to 136.1 billion yuan.

The interest rate of loans of non-financial enterprises declined as a whole. In December 2015, the weighted average interest rate for new loans was 5.22%. Since May, the rate has been falling with a cumulative decline of 1.32 percentage points, down by 1.66 percentage points from the same period in the previous year. The bill discount rate recorded decline since February, and the average monthly interest rate of bill direct discount in Yangtze River Delta and Pearl River Delta in December were 2.50% and 2.55%, respectively, 0.09 percentage points lower than the previous month and 1.96 percentage points lower than that in February. The loan prime rate (LPR) gradually fell back to 4.30% at the end of December, 1.21 percentage points lower than that at end of 2014.

The gradual decline of interest rate of loans for enterprises was mainly due to the following reason. On the one hand, the policy effect from the People's Bank of China by lowering the benchmark interest rate of deposits and loans of financial institutions several times during the year gradually emerged. On the other hand, from the perspective of the debts cost of commercial banks, with the further reduction of the deposit benchmark interest rate, the deposit interest rate fell; the expected rate of return of financial products had dropped for five consecutive months, and the average expected rate of return of financial products for one year in December was 4.51%, or 0.09 percentage points lower than that of the previous month, with a cumulative decline of 1.02 percentage points during eight months. In addition, due to the sharp decline in foreign exchange share in 2015, the People's Bank of China has limited its channels to create base currency through funds outstanding for foreign exchange, so it had repeatedly reduced the required deposit reserve ratio of commercial banks (part of the required reserve of commercial banks was converted to excess reserve), and provided low-cost liquidity for commercial banks through PSLs, MLFs, and other refinancing vehicles, to help reduce the cost of commercial banks' liabilities, thus creating conditions for commercial banks to reduce credit interest rates.

9.3. Outstanding Problems in Financial Operation

9.3.1. *Rapidly rising financial risks*

At the end of December 2015, the ratio of non-performing loans in the banking sector was 1.99%, up by 0.35 percentage points over the end of 2014; and the balance of non-performing loans of the whole year increased by 524.8 billion yuan, an increase of 268.4 billion yuan more than that in 2014. Although the nominal ratio of non-performing loans of commercial banks remained below 2%, the real ratio of non-performing loans of commercial banks rose rapidly due to the slowdown of economic growth and the decline in the quality of loans to industries with overcapacity and to small and micro enterprises and individuals. In order to meet the regulatory requirements and maintain the market image, some local governments put forward requirements for the non-performing loans ratio of commercial banks without loosening the regulatory indicators on commercial banks. The disposal of non-performing assets was facing many difficulties and great loss of profits. Commercial banks had limited space to reduce the non-performing loans ratio by disposing of non-performing assets. Generally, they make the non-performing loans ratio look lower by means of extension, bridge loans, borrowing new loans to repay old, relaxing the standard of non-performing loans recognition, false statement, capitalization of interest, and so on. Commercial banks mainly have three ways to cover up non-performing assets. First, they may relax the five-category classification criteria of loans in the actual implementation, and the more deviated from the loan classification, the higher the risk of hidden non-performing assets. Second, some banks exclude their non-performing assets by means of non-real transfer. Third, some banks temporarily mitigate risks through renewal or bridge loans.

Due to the slowdown of economic growth, there will be limited room for commercial banks to deal with the book non-performing loans ratio in the future, and both the book and the real non-performing loans ratios will continue to rise, and the pressure of "trading time for space" will continue to increase.

Therefore, at present, we should objectively evaluate the real level of non-performing loans of banks, strengthen the disposal of non-performing assets, properly handle the relationship between economic development and non-performing loans of banks, properly improve the risk tolerance of banking institutions, innovate and enrich the disposal methods of non-performing assets, severely crack down on debt evasion, so as to achieve the common development of financial enterprises and local economy.

9.3.2. *Non-negligible local debt risks*

The base of local government debt limit is underestimated. The first is the underestimation of the aggregates. In the debt screening at the end of 2014, the debts borrowed for some public welfare projects and quasi-public welfare projects were not included in the local government debt. The second is underestimation in the structure. The classification of debts was unreasonable. Some of the debts (i.e. debts in the first category) which the government is actually responsible for repaying were included in the second and third categories.

Under the quota management, the nominal growth rate of local government debt declined sharply. From the end of June 2013 to the end of December 2014, the cumulative increase of debts in the first category was 4.5 trillion yuan, with an annual growth rate of 26.0%, and the cumulative increase of contingent debts was 1.6 trillion yuan, with an annual growth rate of 14.7%. In 2015, room for the net growth of the first-class debt was only 600 billion yuan, with a growth rate of only 3.9%. This means that the nominal growth and growth rate of local government debt in 2015 were declining sharply compared with the previous years. If the debt limit was strictly enforced, the broad fiscal deficit of local governments would be substantially tightened.

Financing platforms fall into a debt spiral, and the cost of maintaining debt security is getting higher and higher. Platform companies are enterprises in name, but play the role of "the second treasury" in essence. Their main function is to implement the government's investment plan and complete the government's investment task through financing. Most of the projects invested by platform companies are public welfare and quasi-public welfare projects lacking cash flow or having insufficient cash flow, which are generally repurchased from platform companies by the government according to agreements. The main source of funds for repurchase is the income from land transfer. Even in years with active land transaction, land transfer income could not cover the demand for repurchase funds. The depression of the land market in 2015 intensified the pressure of local government expenditure.

In order to protect the financing ability of platform companies, local governments cannot indefinitely default on the repurchase payments and usually pay the repurchase payments in the form of land injection. The cash flow of the platform companies essentially depends on the expansion of financing, i.e. to pay the principal of the debt due through financing, with the receivables or land assets as collateral. In an economic downturn, platform companies also have to undertake new investment tasks, i.e. to borrow new loans to repay old ones, to repay interest and to invest, so they shoulder a heavy financing task. Because of the increasing debt, after the maturity of these debts in the future, it can be expected that the local government finance will still be unable to substantially pay the repurchase, and the platform companies will still have to rely on expanding financing to maintain their operations. Therefore, platform debt will inevitably spiral upward.

Under the high pressure of fiscal revenue and expenditure and the tightening of local debts management, the contradiction between economic growth and debt growth has gradually emerged. In the short term, stable growth mainly depends on stable investment, stable investment mainly depends on government investment, and there are contradictions between government-backed investment and debt constraint. Therefore, local governments are in a dilemma of "stabilizing growth" and "deleveraging." With the accumulation of pressure on platform companies to borrow new loans to repay old ones, to repay interest and to invest, the cost of maintaining debt security will continue to increase.

9.3.3. *Weakening of credit demand and difficulties in adjusting credit structure*

Amid an economic downturn and industrial restructuring, some enterprises, especially small and medium-sized enterprises, are affected by multiple factors, such as the decline of market demand, the rise of labor costs, and the weakening of profitability. Their willingness to expand reproduction is not strong, their willingness to invest in medium and long term is low, and their credit demand is insufficient. At present, enterprises can be divided into three categories. In the first category, enterprises with a sharp decline in product sales, a decline in profits, and a reduction in profit-making and cost-bearing capacity would passively reduce the scale of operation and financing. In the second category, high-quality enterprises with relatively stable operation in the industry generally have a cautious attitude of preparing for an economic downturn, and they reduce investment in operation, take the initiative to reduce the financing scale, and even repay loans in advance. In the third category, enterprises that conform to the national green energy-saving and environmental protection policy and produce marketable products with good quality see a rising market share, show a prosperous production and marketing situation, and have a higher demand for credit financing to expand production capacity and improve production, but the number of such enterprises is relatively small.

In addition, commercial banks still have "size preference" and "ownership preference" in credit strategy. "Size preference" means that banks tend to lend to large enterprises and are more cautious about small and medium-sized enterprises. "Ownership preference" means that banks tend to allocate more credit funds to state-owned enterprises, while being more cautious with private enterprises. Commercial banks believe that even if a state-owned enterprise falls into a financial crisis, the government will give assistance, so loans to a state-owned enterprise are equivalent to a "safe card" of funds issued by the government.

In the economic downturn stage, the industries with excess capacity are facing more serious cyclical shocks than other industries. The sharp decline in the prices of steel, coal, and other commodities has led to a sharp deterioration of the financial situation of enterprises in related industries, while it is not easy for commercial banks to deleverage in the industries with excess capacity. On the one hand, depressing corporate loans increases liquidity pressure of enterprises whose financial situation has worsened. The industries with excess capacity are all asset-heavy industries, where fixed assets account for a large proportion of investment, and initial investment mainly depends on bank credit. In order to ensure the normal operation of such enterprises, banks are forced to maintain credit lines to support the enterprises to tide over difficulties. On the other hand, the government's pressure to stabilize growth and ensure employment restricts the credit reduction. As enterprises in industries with excess capacity take a big share in local economy and employ a larger volume of labor force, some local governments explicitly require that financial institutions should not reduce the scale of credit granted to these enterprises, and even hope that banks will further increase the credit lines.

9.3.4. *Growing pressure of capital outflow with non-negligible risks in exchange rate*

In 2015, funds outstanding for foreign exchange of the People's Bank of China dropped by 2.21 trillion yuan, while the figure in 2014 was an increase of 641.1 billion yuan. The cumulative foreign exchange transactions of all financial institutions dropped by 2.84 trillion yuan, while the figure in 2014 was an increase of 766.2 billion yuan.

Due to the strong expectation of RMB devaluation against the US dollar, residents increased the operation of "foreign currency as assets and local currency as liabilities," resulting in a big deficit of purchase and sale of foreign exchange. In 2015, the purchase of foreign exchange was US\$ 1.72 trillion, down by 9.11%; the sale of foreign exchange was US\$ 2.19 trillion, up by 23.7%; and the deficit of purchase and sale of foreign exchange was US\$ 465.9 billion, while the year 2014 recorded a surplus of US\$ 125.8 billion.

From the perspective of supply and demand of foreign exchange, the difference between the sale and purchase of spot foreign currencies against RMB and the sale and purchase of forward foreign currencies against RMB reflects the supply-demand relationship in the foreign exchange market. The difference between the sale and purchase of spot foreign currencies against RMB and the sale and purchase of forward foreign currencies against RMB excludes the effect of repeated calculation of the performance in the sale and purchase of spot foreign currencies against RMB, that is, "the difference between the sale and purchase of spot foreign currencies against RMB and the sale and purchase of forward foreign currencies against RMB = difference between the sale and purchase of spot foreign currencies against RMB + the change of the difference between the sale and purchase of forward foreign currencies against RMB before maturity." In 2015, the difference between the sale and purchase of spot foreign currencies against RMB and the sale and purchase of forward foreign currencies against RMB was in a deficit of US\$ 571.1 billion, while in 2014, it was a surplus of US\$ 85.6 billion, indicating a strong market demand and insufficient supply in 2015.

On August 11, the People's Bank of China improved the mechanism of RMB-US dollar central parity rate quotation, and the RMB-US dollar exchange rate depreciated. At the end of December, the central parity rate of RMB against US dollar was 6.4936 yuan/US dollar, which was 5.77% lower than that at the end of the previous year; the spot exchange rate of RMB against US dollar (CNY) in the onshore market was 6.4936 yuan/US dollar, which was 4.46% lower than that at the end of the previous year; and the spot exchange rate of RMB against US dollar (CNH) in the offshore market was 6.5687 yuan/US dollar, which was 5.42% lower than that at the end of the previous month. The difference of exchange rate between the RMB offshore market (CNH) and the onshore market (CNY) widened, reaching 751 points at the end of December, an increase of 663 points over the end of the previous year. At the end of December, the one-year Non-Deliverable Forwards (NDF) of RMB depreciated by 4.45% against the dollar, an increase of 2.3 percentage points over the end of the previous year.

In terms of balance of payments, in 2015, the current account surplus was US\$ 293.2 billion, of which US\$ 578.1 billion was surplus in trade in goods and US\$ 209.4 billion was deficit in trade in services. The capital and financial account (including net errors and omissions) had a deficit of US\$ 161.1 billion, of which the deficit of the non-reserve financial account (including net errors and omissions) was US\$ 504.4 billion and the reserve assets decreased by US\$ 342.9 billion.

Customs statistics showed that in 2015, the value of exports was US\$ 2,276.6 billion and that of import was US\$ 1,682.1 billion, with a trade surplus of US\$ 594.5 billion. In 2015, the settlement of foreign exchange for trade in goods was US\$ 1,182.4 billion and the sale of foreign exchange for trade in goods was US\$ 1,220.3 billion, with a deficit of US\$ 37.9 billion between the settlement and sale of foreign exchange. The difference between the trade surplus and the deficit between the settlement and sale of foreign exchange of trade in goods was US\$ 632.4 billion. Customs statistics showed that in 2014, the trade surplus was US\$ 382.5 billion, and the surplus of the settlement and sale of foreign exchange for trade in goods was US\$ 317.6 billion. The difference between the two was only US\$ 64.9 billion. The disparity between the two in 2015 can be explained by two factors: (1) the difference between the trade surplus of import and export and the surplus of foreign exchange receipts and payments, and (2) the difference between the surplus of foreign exchange receipts and payments and the deficit of foreign exchange settlement and sale.

In terms of trade surplus of import and export and surplus of foreign exchange receipt and payment, customs statistics showed that the trade surplus in 2015 amounted to US\$ 594.5 billion, while the net cross-border capital inflow of trade in goods (foreign exchange receipt by bank agents − foreign exchange payment) was US\$ 214.3 billion, with a difference of US\$ 380.2 billion between the two. The main reasons are the following: First, the repayment of cross-border financing funds to banks increased, as the balance of cross-border financing for imports by enterprises decreased by about US\$ 110 billion in 2015. Second, the value of export-related deferred receipts and import-related advance payments between foreign trade enterprises and foreign traders increased to about US\$ 100 billion a year. Third, the receipts rate of foreign exchange declined and the payments rate of foreign exchange rose. The receipts rate of foreign exchange (current receipt of foreign exchange/current earnings of foreign exchange) is used to measure the receipt of foreign exchange by enterprises and individuals, with the export value in customs statistics as the current earnings of foreign exchange. The receipts rate of foreign exchange of trade in goods in 2015 was 90.4%, which was 1.8 percentage points lower than that in 2014. The payments rate of foreign exchange (current payments of foreign exchange/current expenditure on foreign exchange) is used to measure the payment of foreign exchange by enterprises and individuals, with the import value in customs statistics as the current expenditure on foreign exchange. The rate of payments of trade in goods was 109.6% in 2015, which was 3.5 percentage points higher than in 2014. Fourth, there were other factors, such as export earnings of enterprises staying abroad, false increase in export performance, cooking up export figures, and so on under the pressure of meeting the target of stabilizing growth.

In terms of the surplus of foreign exchange receipts and payments and the deficit of foreign exchange settlement and sale, the net cross-border capital inflows of trade in goods in 2015 amounted to US$ 214.3 billion, while the deficit of foreign exchange settlement and sale in trade in goods was US$ 37.9 billion, with a difference of US$ 252.2 billion. The main reason was as follows. First, RMB-denominated cross-border settlement of trade changed from deficit to surplus. The RMB-denominated trade surplus will lead to the reduction of China's reserve assets, that is, the deficit of foreign exchange settlement and sale. The balance of RMB-denominated receipt and payment of trade in goods turned from a deficit of US$ 140.1 billion in 2014 to a surplus of US$ 128.8 billion, resulting in a deficit of foreign exchange settlement and sale of US$ 128.8 billion. Second, the settlement rate of foreign exchange declined and the sale rate of foreign exchange increased. The settlement rate of foreign exchange (current settlement of foreign exchange/current sale of foreign exchange, and the current sale of foreign exchange should exclude the RMB-denominated settlement) measures the willingness of enterprises and individuals to sell foreign exchange. In 2015, the settlement rate of foreign exchange for trade in goods was 79.9%, which was 3.8 percentage points lower than that in 2014. The sale rate of foreign exchange (current sale of foreign exchange/current payment of foreign exchange, and the current payment of foreign exchange should exclude RMB-denominated settlement) measures the willingness of enterprises and individuals to purchase foreign exchange. In 2015, the sale rate of foreign exchange for trade in goods was 87.5%, up by 12.5 percentage points from 2014. Third, the foreign exchange loans of domestic enterprises and individuals decreased, deposits increased, and the balance of foreign debts declined. In 2015, the balance of foreign exchange loans to enterprises and individuals in China dropped by US$ 100.6 billion, while the foreign exchange deposits of enterprises and individuals increased by US$ 36.4 billion.

9.4. Outlook of Financial Operation in 2016

9.4.1. *Creating a sound financial environment for stable economic operation*

Global economic recovery was weak. The world economic growth slowed down in 2015. Except for the steady growth of the US economy, the Japanese economy continued to see ups and downs, the Euro Zone economy slowly recovered, the emerging market economies declined, and the international financial market fluctuated significantly. The momentum of economic recovery in the United States was weakening. In 2016, the global economy will continue to stay in a period of deep adjustment. The interest rate hikes of the US Federal Reserve will further polarize monetary policies in major developed economies and increase the volatility of the global economy and financial markets in the future. Some emerging market economies may face severe downward economic pressures. The prices of bulk commodities are expected to fluctuate at a low level and the pressures of economic downturn and debt risks of bulk commodity exporting countries will increase. The slowdown of global trade growth is expected, which will drag down the global economic growth.

In 2016, the Chinese economy still faced the heavy pressure of downward economic trend. First, the demand for investment is weak. Due to the continuous decline in profits of industrial enterprises, excessive capacity of some industries, and low demand at home and abroad, the growth rate of investment in the manufacturing industry continued to slow down. The financing channels of local governments were limited, the income of land transfer was greatly reduced, the capital for investment in construction was tight, and the growth rate of investment in infrastructure did not show significant recovery. The floor space of newly completed housing projects in China still declined significantly year-on-year. Although the real estate market in the first-tier cities rebounded significantly, the real estate prices in the second- and third-tier cities continued to decline year-on-year, resulting in a relatively high inventory pressure. Therefore, on the whole, real estate investment in the whole country continued to maintain a low growth rate. Second, the growth of consumption slowed down along with the slowdown of income growth. In 2016, the wage income of employees generally slowed down, and some industries even experienced a negative growth. Third, external demand continued to be sluggish. International market demand is insufficient, with a decline in export orders. Labor costs were rising, and some foreign investors relocated production lines to other emerging economies, which aggravated the reduction of orders. The prices of bulk commodities in the international market continued to fall, depressing the prices of exports and dragging down the growth of export value.

Employment pressure of labor force increased, and hidden unemployment became a prominent problem. First, the increase in hidden unemployment covers up the severity of the current employment market. Because of the defective employment statistics system, part of the unemployment has not been included in the monitoring results. Enterprises still paid social insurance after some employees were laid off and diverted, who are not included in the unemployed population, but the impact and risk they have to bear are not substantially different from the unemployed. Second, the structural contradiction of employment was still outstanding. University graduates, mid-aged laid-off workers, and low-skill migrant workers faced a greater employment pressure. Short-term flexible employment, temporary public welfare employment, and minimal security employment accounted for a large proportion, and new employment was vulnerable.

In the long run, the efforts to stabilize growth and prevent risks complement each other. Stabilizing economic growth is an effective means to resolve financial risks, while preventing and controlling financial risks is a necessary condition for sustained economic growth. There is a dilemma between stabilizing growth and preventing risks under the current mode of development, mainly because of the weak consumption and external demand, therefore stabilizing growth mainly depends on stabilizing investment. When the prospects of investment in manufacturing and real estate are not good, stabilizing investment mainly depends on infrastructure investment; and investment in infrastructure by social capital is insufficient, so investment in infrastructure mainly depends on the government. Government-backed investment and debt constraints are contradictory and regulating local government borrowing will lead to fiscal tightening, which will further aggravate the pressure of economic downturn. If economic growth continues to decline, it will lead to massive unemployment and disorderly spread of financial risks.

In order to keep a good balance between stabilizing growth and preventing risks, first of all, we should gradually transform the current mode of development into one that fosters the endogenous power of economic growth by stimulating market vitality. In order to get rid of the macro-regulation mode of "government investment-driven" and let the market play a decisive role in the allocation of resources, the government should stimulate market vitality by creating a good institutional environment.

Second, in the process of transformation, attention should be paid to maintaining the coordination of regular macro-policies, and the balance between economic growth and debt growth. We should properly lower the target of economic growth in 2016 and alleviate financial and financial pressures. We should implement active fiscal policies, get a clear picture of the size of local government debt, expand the scale of debt replacement and the scale of new deficit. We should continue to implement the monetary policies with proper force, make flexible use of a variety of monetary policy tools, maintain appropriate liquidity, and guide commercial banks to increase credit. Finally, we should give full play to the underpinning role of social policies. We should implement proactive employment policies, strengthen vocational skills education, actively support entrepreneurship, improve unemployment assistance and social security systems, maintain basic stability in employment, and strive to reduce the impact of structural adjustment on people's lives.

9.4.2. *Increasing market liquidity with multiple monetary policy tools*

In 2016, the loan increment will not exceed that in 2015. The main reasons are as follows: First, in 2015, bill financing increased substantially, and it is difficult to continue to increase in 2016. Second, in 2015, financial institutions issued more than 1 trillion yuan of loans to securities financial companies, and this factor will not be easily be reproduced in 2016. Third, a lot of local government bonds were issued to replace stock of loans, and the balance of bank loans decreased accordingly. Due to the continued slowdown of economic growth in 2016, the insufficient demand for credit in the real economy and the rising risks, commercial banks are not willing to lend, and the increased credit lines through replacement is unlikely to be fully used.

Because of the sharp decline in funds outstanding for foreign exchange, the gap in base currency is large. According to our estimation of the changing trend of funds outstanding for foreign exchange and financial deposits, if the deposit reserve ratio is not adjusted, in order to achieve a M2 growth of 12% in 2016, China needs to add 3.30 trillion yuan of base currency, and the base currency gap will be 4.94 trillion yuan; in order to achieve a M2 growth of 12.5%, China needs to add 3.44 trillion yuan of base currency, and the gap will be 5.08 trillion yuan; and in order to achieve a M2 growth of 13%, China needs to add 3.56 trillion yuan of base currency, and the gap will be 5.22 trillion yuan. From this we can see that, the base currency gap in 2016 will be large.[1]

Analyzed by quarter, the first three quarters of 2016 will see a large gap of base currency. The gap of base currency will narrow in the fourth quarter as fiscal deposits decline. The central bank should use a variety of monetary policy tools to actively supply base currency to ease the liquidity pressure of the money market. First, efforts are required to reduce the deposit reserve ratio. Because of the reversal of the growth trend of funds outstanding for foreign exchange, the base money supplied by funds outstanding for foreign exchange will be converted into recovery of base money. This is inherently contradictory to the growth of money supply and base currency required by economic development. Therefore, it is necessary to reduce the deposit reserve ratio to make up for it. Second, we need to actively make use of instruments such as refinancing, SLF, MLF, and PSL to supplement market liquidity and enhance policy transparency to effectively guide market expectations. Third, open market operations should be carried out flexibly to regulate short-term liquidity through reverse repurchase and short-term liquidity operations (SLO). Considering the gap of long-term liquidity and the advantages and disadvantages of various monetary policy tools, the main operation mode of monetary policy in 2016 is to reduce the deposit reserve ratio, supplemented by SLF and MLF to balance the supply and demand, and open market operations and SLO to regulate the short-term liquidity and seasonal liquidity of the market, in order to meet the liquidity needed for economic development and ensure the basic stability of interest rate in the money market.

---

[1] On March 1, 2016, the People's Bank of China cut the deposit reserve ratio of deposit-related financial institutions by 0.5 percentage points, releasing 622.6 billion yuan of liquidity, thus narrowing the base currency gap by 622.6 billion yuan after March.

Bibliography

China Tourism Academy (2016). China's Tourism Performance: Review & Forecast (2015–2016), January.

China Association of Automotive Manufacturers (2014). *Research on China Automobile Development Strategy* (China Machine Press, Beijing).

China Automobile Finance Laboratory of the 21st Century News Groups (2015). *2015 China Auto Finance Almanac*, November 22.

China Automotive Technology and Research Center, and China Association of Automotive Manufacturers (2003). *China Automotive Industry Yearbook 2003*.

ChinaDaily.com.cn (2015). Six Chinese automobile companies entering the world top 500, with the number ranking first with Japan, July 27.

Department of Industrial Statistics, National Bureau of Statistics (2015). *China Industrial Statistics Yearbook 2015* (China Statistics Press, Beijing).

Department of National Accounts Statistics, National Bureau of Statistics (2011). *China Input-Output Table 2007* (China Statistics Press, Beijing).

Department of National Accounts Statistics, National Bureau of Statistics (2015). *China Input-Output Table 2012* (China Statistics Press, Beijing).

Department of National Accounts Statistics, National Bureau of Statistics (2008). *Method on Compiling Gross Domestic Product of China in the Non-census Years* (China Statistics Press, Beijing).

General Administration of Quality Supervision, Inspection and Quarantine of the People's Republic of China and the China Standardization Administration (2011). *Industrial Classification of National Economic Activities (2011)* (Standards Press of China, Beijing).

Insurance Association of China (2015). China Motor Insurance Market Development Report (2014), December 16.

Lu, F. and Feng, K. (2005). *Policy Options for Developing China's Auto Industry with Independent Intellectual Property Rights* (Peking University Press, Beijing).

National Bureau of Statistics (2013). *National Statistical Survey Programs (2013)*.

National Bureau of Statistics, National Statistical Database.

National Bureau of Statistics (2012, 2014). *China Statistical Yearbooks 2012 & 2014* (China Statistics Press).

National Bureau of Statistics (2015). *China Statistical Yearbook 2015* (China Statistics Press, Beijing).

National Bureau of Statistics (2016). *China Statistical Abstracts 2016* (China Statistics Press, Beijing).

National Bureau of Statistics (2016). *Statistical Communiqué of the People's Republic of China on the 2015 National Economic and Social Development* (China Statistics Press, Beijing).

State Taxation Administration (2015). *China Taxation Yearbook 2015* (China Taxation Publishing, House, Beijing).

State Council (2010). Decision on Accelerating the Cultivation and Development of Strategic Emerging Industries (Guo Fa, No. 32), October 10.

State Council (2012). Notice on Printing and Distributing the "Development Plan for Energy-Saving and New Energy Automotive Industry (2012-2020)" (Guo Fa, No. 22), July 9.

State Council (2013). Opinions on Accelerating the Development of Energy Conservation and Environmental Protection Industry (Guo Fa, No. 30), August 1.

State Council (2015). Notice on Printing and Distributing the "Made in China 2025" (Guo Fa, No. 28), May 8.

Wang, L., Zhang, P., and Lu, J. (2003). Development and Application of Automobile Steel Sheet Produced at Baoshan Iron and Steel. Available at: https://wenku.baidu.com/view/a73e4ad53186bceb19e8bbfa.html.

Wu, J. (2011). Reference and enlightenment of high-speed railway Model to the development of strategic emerging industries. *Fortune World*, Issue 15.

Xu, X. (2013a). Accurate understanding of China's income, consumption and investment. *Social Sciences in China*, Issue2, 2013.

Xu, X. (2013b). The reform in current key statistical areas in China. *Economic Research Journal*, Issue 10, 2013.

Xu, X., Jia, H., Li, J. *et al.* (2015). Research on the role of real estate economy in China's national economic growth. *Social Sciences in China*, Issue 1.

Zhang, Y. (2007). Comparative analysis of the automotive industry policies in the Republic of Korea and Mainland of China. *Forum of World Economics & Politics*, Issue 6.

Index